The Ultimate Guide to Using ICT Across the Curriculum

Web, widgets, whiteboards and beyond!

Jon Audain

B L O O M S B U R Y
LONDON • NEW DELHI • NEW YORK • SYDNEY

Bloomsbury Education

An imprint of Bloomsbury Publishing Plc

50 Bedford Square
London
WC1B 3DP
UK

1385 Broadway
New York
NY 10018
USA

www.bloomsbury.com

Bloomsbury is a registered trade mark of Bloomsbury Publishing Plc

First published 2014

British Library Cataloguing-in-Publication Data
A catalogue record for this book is available from the British Library.

ISBN: PB: 9781441144003
ePub: 9781441199003
ePDF: 9781441195852

Library of Congress Cataloging-in-Publication Data
A catalog record for this book is available from the Library of Congress.

10 9 8 7 6 5 4 3 2 1

Typeset by Fakenham Prepress Solutions, Fakenham, Norfolk NR21 8NN
Printed and bound by CPI Group (UK) Ltd, Croydon, CR0 4YY

This book is produced using paper that is made from wood grown in managed, sustainable forests. It is natural, renewable and recyclable. The logging and manufacturing processes conform to the environmental regulations of the country of origin.

To view more of our titles please visit www.bloomsbury.com

Online resources accompany this book at:
www.bloomsbury.com/ict-across-curriculum

Please type the URL into your web browser and follow the instructions to access the resources. If you experience any problems please contact Bloomsbury at: companionwebsite@bloosmbury.com

Contents

Acknowledgements

A friend and academic colleague, Lisa, recently introduced me to the delights of Mary Berry and 'The Great British Bake Off!' It struck me how baking a cake is a similar process to writing a book: the preparation, the ingredients, the time, the care, the helpers and the final testers. In the production of this book, no friends, colleagues or editors were harmed in the process and the shredded gratitude of a working author continues to live on. So take one author, two publishers, four editors, endless refreshments, friends, people, conversations, discussions and agreements and Hey Presto… *The Ultimate Guide to Using ICT Across the Curriculum*! Throughout the development of this book there have been many changes and a whole raft of people who have supported me through all these times, so if you will forgive me, here are a few thank yous for my band of merry men and women:

To my reading group Jo Rhys-Jones, Classteacher, Ex-Inspector/AST/MFL expert (for some of the title, her tenaciousness, enthusiasm, straight-talking and endless supply of sticky notes; you now have a final version!); Anthony Evans, Classteacher, Ex-LEA Advisor and 2Simple guru; Samantha 'Spoo' Philips, Classteacher and DT AST; Fiona Aubrey-Smith, Head of Primary SSAT (*The Schools Network*) and Katy Thompson, Deputy Headteacher for their frank and honest advice and humility at ensuring that the teacher's voice came through loud and clear throughout the entire book.

To my amazing ex-AST colleagues Phil Bagge and Emma Goto and current and past inspectors and advisors Martyn Wilson, Stella Kenny, Sue Savory and Janet Roberts for providing great feedback and opportunities to talk endlessly about ICT and their experiences. Their encouragement, ability to develop people and the role of ICT in the primary school really nurtured the ethos from the ICT Lead Teacher days. As David Warlick said, 'We need technology in every classroom and in every student and teacher's hand, because it is the pen and paper of our time, and it is the lens through which we experience much of our world' – an ethos the colleagues above always helped to foster in Hampshire schools.

To all the staff I have taught and worked with for the common experiences that have built the foundations of this book as well as my University of Winchester-based newbies (Lisa-Marie Martin, Maria Vinney, Victoria Randall and Jane Jones) for their enthusiasm and friendship as well as academic colleagues Sharon Witt and Sue Anderson-Faithfull for their support with the geography and history areas of this book.

Writers always need the talents and patience of their editors. I was lucky enough to have four over the creation of this book. Firstly, thank you to the editorial team at Continuum Melanie Wilson and Rosie Pattinson for their constant 'newbie' support at the start of this project. The largest thanks must go to my two exceptional editors – Holly Gardner and Jane Morgan. Thank you both for your patience, good humour, encouragement, mindmapping, negotiating, talking, hard-work and belief. The tremendous amount of work you gave is reflected throughout. There would be no book without the two of you and I truly thank you!

To my parents and family (Janet, Andrew, Rob and Chrissie) and friends especially Louise for always being my champion, Omega for the support and great goal-setting as well as Ewa, Mel, Katrina, Jane, Anne, Tracey, Sid, Nicky, Sarah and Emily G who are now able to have a drink (for the time being) in peace without book chat. Without of you in different ways this project would never have succeeded. Also thank you to Dawn Hallybone for her support on games-based learning, and a big thank you to Professor Stephen Heppell for writing an excellent foreword for the book.

Finally the hundreds of children I have worked with who will continue to inspire me, challenge me, develop my practice and push me to aim for excellence all the time.

Two of my all time favourite quotes about technology drive the reasons for this book. The first Nancy Kassebaum remarks that 'There can be infinite uses of the computer and of new age technology, but if teachers themselves are not able to bring it into the classroom and make it work, then it fails' – an ethos I always share. Creativity is at the heart of exciting, interesting teaching and learning, none more so with the use of technology. The teacher is fundamental as great technology use is driven from the heart, mind and soul of an engaged practitioner.

The second muted by friends Sarah Younie and Marilyn Leask in their book *Teaching with Technologies: The essential guide*. They explain that, 'Digital technology is not static and is a constantly developing and rapidly changing field. It will be many decades before practice in the poorest schools equals that of the best. At issue is the patchiness of technology provision and practices in schools.' This book aims to support all teachers in their development of using technology so we can level the playing field in the use of technology in schools and so all children, in the modern world, are provided with the opportunity to demonstrate ICT excellence.

Foreword

It seems like just the other day that our primary school children were marvelling at the exotic cyan and magenta of their BBC B computer monitors. They were captivated. Even in the 80s the nation could see how important all this would be for education. However, very few anticipated the extraordinary, seductive, delightful, playful, creative, connected world that technology has brought into our classrooms and into our lives, in this exciting century of learning.

Back then, of course, things were nice and simple: was there something that was really hard to teach? Telling the time, or bearings perhaps? Technology could join the team, take up the baton from tired hands and inject new pace, renewed interest. Primary school writing had never been so finessed, maths had never been so playful. We challenged technology to do what we found tricky and it delivered. But today, technology challenges us right back. It can do just about anything we want, so what would we actually like to do? Need a global audience for your 8 year olds' writing? Just blog it. Need to see the exotic flora and fauna from far away schools? Just Skype them. Need to engage your community in your school news, and share theirs? There's Facebook.

Now this sounds as wonderful as it is, but the pace of change lays down some significant challenges to traditional systems, and to our wonderful golden generation of teachers. New technologies emerge so rapidly that to wait for a government edict, or for a five year controlled trial (!), or for a shared insight from a national institution, would be to wait for far too long. Our children only get one chance at their childhoods, one chance for the joy of learning to take root firmly enough to last them a lifetime. We can't afford to wait to be told what to do, we need to help each other. We need to help each other now.

And that is why this book is just exactly what is needed. It is filled with sensible pragmatic advice, from the way it helps teachers to self-rate themselves, through its wonderfully grounded 'here is a technology, why might you use it, what can you do' approach, to its recession-aware reference back to the costs of each technology. The advice is rooted in the classroom and in the best effective practice found there. The book was necessarily written quickly; it is full of today's advice, today's technology and really helps today's teachers build a properly digital school, right away. It embraces phones and Twitter and Skype – it doesn't lock and block, it embraces them and puts them to work, today.

It is a measure of the pace of this wired world, and this book, that I'm writing these words aboard a plane bound for China, beaming it back mid-flight to the publishers. The TV channels on the plane are full of learning, as entertainment. Folk learning to dance, to sing, to cook. Learning has never been so cool. This book has never been so needed.

Professor Stephen Heppell, March 2014
Bournemouth University, England and Universidad Camilo José Cela, Madrid, Spain.

Introduction

As the use of technology in schools grows, teachers are having to acquire a variety of new skills and knowledge to keep up! With software becoming easier for children (and adults) to use, the challenge is to find opportunities and creative ways of making use of ICT to enrich, challenge or support the topics you are teaching. With the implementation of the new Computing curriculum looming (September 2014), there has not been a better time to get your knowledge of ICT and the best way to use it in the classroom up to scratch!

If technology hasn't always worked for you or if you're the one to break the digital camera (they rarely ever survive after bouncing off the ground!) then this book aims to give you the confidence to take that first step to integrating technology into your teaching. If on the other hand you are a confident tweeter and iPad whizz, but you are looking for some creative ways to integrate all this into your teaching across the curriculum, then there are activities and ideas for you too. ICT is like spider glue, attaching itself to different subjects throughout the curriculum; it can and should be integrated whether you are teaching maths, English or PE, and this book will provide you with the tools to do so!

Take one book, a dash of ideas, hints and useful activities and hey presto, you're an ICT pro and will be able to get your class (and possibly even other teachers) excited about the potential of using technology across the curriculum!

About the author

I was a class teacher who came late to the technology party. There was a time when technology was not a big part of my teaching. With stronger interests in music and drama, there were different priorities and interests for me in school. However, more and more pieces of equipment found their way into my classroom which meant that I had to spend time learning how to use them and working out how they could be used in my lessons. I bought myself my first computer, threw away the manual and set about having a go with this technology 'stuff'. Many people were far ahead of me in the game and were prepared to show me, except they all went incredibly fast and often ended up exclaiming 'It's easy don't you see?' followed by 'Move out the way and I'll do it quicker myself!'

During my teaching career, I was fortunate enough to be appointed as an Advanced Skills Teacher (AST) in Primary ICT. This was a role I simply adored until the government sadly ceased its existence. It involved teachers supporting other teachers in a subject they were passionate about while still doing the day job and remaining in the classroom.

Through this work I met many teachers, headteachers, classroom assistants and, of course, children. Over that time, I met hundreds of ICT coordinators and teachers who had recently been made an ICT coordinator. I had worked as a subject coordinator since qualifying, however, it always struck me how immense the task of an ICT coordinator was when I was finally made one. It is a feeling still felt by many new to and in the role. The combination of encouraging teachers to use technology across their practice; working with the leadership team to make at times huge financial decisions concerning whole-school technology as well as trying to embed its use across the whole curriculum is a mammoth task for one person.

After many meetings with teachers who asked the same kinds of questions, I decided that I wanted to be able to leave a tiny part of me to help guide and assist them. So I set about writing a book with hints, tips, answers to the common questions as well as advice from my own personal practice as a teacher, head of year, subject leader and finally a county-based Primary ICT AST. I now work as a university academic, researcher, teacher-trainer, keynote speaker, consultant/adviser and ICT trainer. All this allows me to constantly support and engage with teachers as I develop my own personal crusade to see teachers inspire others in their use of ICT so they continue to push the boundaries of technology, ICT and learning for all young people.

How to use this book

Use this book as a dip in and out of guide or read it chronologically. There are tips for planning and preperation as well as step by step activities to use in your lessons. Look out for the boxes with icons in them throughout the book with include levelled content depending for different abilities (see the ICT personality test that follows), really creative activities and mobile device activities and information. There are also online resources that accompany this book. Visit the website at: www.bloomsbury.com/ict-across-curriculum for extra resources including ICT advice sheets for a range of people including trainee teachers and teaching assistants, information for using ICT in the early years, planning documents, templates for writing a whole school ICT policy, an acceptable use policy, a health and safety policy, ICT induction policy, clickable links and much more.

Who is the book aimed at?

Many different people will use ICT across the primary school. This book offers advice to everyone working in a primary school, including teachers at all levels, higher level teaching assistants, ICT coordinators and senior leaders. The hope is that at whichever level you work there will be something in each chapter for you to try and adapt into your practice. But before you get started let's find out what type of ICT teacher you are.

As you grab a refreshing cup of tea after that challenging English lesson or PE with the apparatus, take a break and fill in the ICT personality test on the next page.

ICT personality test

1   Which statement best describes your ICT confidence?
   a My OHP still works fine so why do I need all this modern stuff?
   b Up and down depending on whether it's working or not.
   c Love it! I really enjoy using technology in my teaching.

2   How often do you use some form of technology, excluding your whiteboard, in your lessons?
   a Do whiteboard pens count as technology since I upgraded from chalk?
   b Roughly about once a week or on special trips; I try to remember to use the digital camera to keep my lovely ICT coordinator happy.
   c I try to use different types of technology every day… it's my life… my passion… and the reason why my bank balance is always so low!

3   What are the meanings of these commonly used ICT words? Twitter, Web 2.0, Voki?
   a Twit-who… something to do with birds; Web… spiders; Voki… something from Star Wars. Am I close?
   b They are all modern technology words. Twitter's something I use but I'm not sure how it works.
   c Twitter is a form of social networking whereby users share information in under 140 characters; Web 2.0 refers to using the web to collaborate, create and then share with others that creation. Vokis are talking animated avatars that can be used to provide instructions to children.

4   Do you think technology enhances learning?
   a No.
   b When it works, yes.
   c Definitely.

5   How much time do you spend on using ICT throughout the week?
   a No more than I have to.
   b I try to use it as often as I can.
   c Many, many hours… I just love technology.

6   When new technology hits the market, do you:
   a Groan and say, not another piece of technology! Bring me back my OHP!
   b Show that you are interested but will wait for others to have a go first (well, I wouldn't want to spoil their fun).
   c Line up, love it, play with it and work out all the different curriculum topics I can use my new gadget for.

7 If you were asked to become ICT coordinator in your school, would you:

    a Laugh uncontrollably and say that's a great joke. Hilarious and witty and it's not even the end of the school day yet!

    b Smile and say that is an interesting suggestion but that you are going to need some support.

    c Buy wine and a takeaway and celebrate. It's a goooooodddd day!

8 If equipment doesn't work in your class, do you:

    a Give up, it never works for me. Now hand me the chocolate.

    b Write it in the book for the charming technical team to sort on one of their maintenance days.

    c Persevere; there's got to be a way!

9 How would you feel if the budget in your primary school was bigger for ICT than for other curriculum subjects?

    a Outraged! We should be spending more on books and pencils instead of objects which do not work half the time.

    b Needs must. If it benefits the children then I'm for it.

    c Absolutely fine. ICT is expensive because it affects the whole school and it needs to be right and spending has to continue every three years so equipment doesn't get slow.

10 Do you have a teaching and learning blog?

    a No: I have a life.

    b I've set one up but need to remember to write on it more frequently.

    c Yes. I really enjoy receiving the comments.

So which type of digital teacher are you?

Mostly As – Nervous beginner

Some still live in the good ol' days, looking into the dust of the people who have left. The pace is too fast for them. Is that you? Teacher training was about traditional teaching and the majority of learning happens from the board. GOOD NEWS though – although you may think that you're a tough nut to crack, there's still hope for you at the end of the technology tunnel. The technology will work for you and is getting much easier to use in the classroom so why not give it a shot? The children might know more, so let them teach you and I guarantee you will have fun along the way. Remember to just take it one step at a time.

You sound like a nervous beginner. Look out for the 'nervous beginner' boxes throughout the book – they all have the 'nervous' icon in them. These activities, applications (apps) and suggestions are really easy to have a go at. Once you are confident with these, then why not go back and try out the other boxes and ideas from the 'Ready to get going' boxes.

Mostly Bs – Enthusiastic learner

Some people are open to change but need or like to move at a slower pace so they understand what's going on. You are such a person and often need a little support. This is great as it means that you are willing to learn which means that your children will look forward to trying out some new technology in their classroom. Don't worry about the speed of colleagues. Try to select one area of ICT to work on and then try a different area every few weeks. Remember to try a new skill every few weeks so it keeps you on your toes.

You sound like you are ready to get going with using technology. Look out for these 'enthusiastic learner' boxes throughout the book which have the 'enthusiastic' icon in them. These activities, apps and suggestions require a little more confidence, from someone like yourself. You've read the idea and you're raring to give it a try. Once you are confident with these, then why not go back and try out the 'expert user' or 'ICT coordinator' boxes if you fancy having a go!

Mostly Cs – Expert user

Some technology enthusiasts left some time ago, excited and looking for that new world and the promise of a future which is moving forward to a land where technology is used to enhance learning and to change the way lessons are delivered. They are the very people who will drive the agenda and inspire many teachers. Your work is never complete, but you feel a real sense of achievement and pride to see the children using technology. You use the latest kit and software to test and explore the educational gains. Keep up the exceptional and progressive work you are doing and remember to share and support the work of others in your bid to become a truly digital school.

You sound like you are already a pro at using technology. Look out for these 'expert user' boxes throughout the book. These activities, apps and suggestions require confidence to deliver them, which you possess and will take you to the next stage.

Throughout the rest of the book there are three other icons you will come across:

Creative projects

Creative projects are activities which are linked to areas of the curriculum, drawing together the children's different skills. They may take a longer amount of time in class, but will encourage many different aspects for the children (for example, team work, incorporating many different subjects to produce a finished result).

Mobile technology

The use of mobile technology is set to grow exponentially in the classroom by the year 2020. Many schools are beginning to adopt mobile devices in some form. Chapter 3 is dedicated to thinking about this issue. However, spread throughout the book is also a collection of ideas and apps for using mobile technology in the classroom which I hope you will find useful.

The ICT coordinator

If you are the ICT coordinator in charge of your whole-school ICT provision you will find extra tips in these boxes.

If we can find ways to open up the world of ICT into every classroom, then we as a profession have the potential to radically change and challenge the ways children learn as well as forge new ways for the next generation of learners. If as teachers we cannot identify and exploit the learning potential of technology, then we develop weaker learners with reduced access to a global world. Technology is embedded throughout all of society. Teaching all aspects of ICT to children will set them up to function highly in the connected world.

The Ultimate Guide to Using ICT Across the Curriculum is written to get you started. With ideas and activities to get you thinking and creating, I hope you will find the book both useful and inspiring.

1 Planning your provision

The ever-changing world of the internet, interactive whiteboards, computers and mobile technology (so small the connected world can fit in your pocket), impacts the way we think, interpret and express ourselves, as well as impacting our learning and that of our students'.

While you are reading this chapter, cast your mind back to the technology that was available to you in your childhood. Perhaps the video recorder, the Walkman with tapes, or the vinyl record which you bought from the shop before eagerly walking home and lifting the delicate arm and needle of the record player to hear the music.

Technology evokes strong memories for many people who use it. It is a BIG deal. It can be compared to the ideals of the fashion industry, the glitz, glamour and anticipation of what is going to be the next 'big' thing to get our hands on. These things will enter our homes, the family environment and will be used by our children. Ultimately, they will also change the way we educate ourselves and learn.

The changing face of technology

I both struggle with, and am excited by the rate of change technology can deliver. As a teacher I was acclimatised to the speed of new initiatives and was then left to discover how these could change the culture of my classroom (sometimes not for the positive). I was talking to some students once about what it is like to 'grow up' using Facebook. By growing up, I am referring to the way young people use social media to post photographs and comments about their daily lives online. I asked them why they made the choice to be on there. Here are some of their answers:

"It's a photographic record of fun times and events. Just as people used to print off their photos and put them in an album, this is our way of doing that… "

"It's my main way of communicating with friends."

"My friends use it to help me get organised. We use it to collaborate and keep ourselves on-task."

At another time I was teaching a young person and we were working on performing a piece of music together. I asked her to listen to another performer playing the piece. I explained that it was on YouTube and why it was a great example to listen to. She responded by explaining that she couldn't go on YouTube at home because her dad had blocked it but it was OK because she would have a look on her phone! My point is that technology is all around young people and there are a variety of different ways of accessing it. The barrier the parent had placed did not faze this girl at all. She is growing up with technology and it is forming part of her culture, it is her background.

Background is important as it helps to shape our experiences in each phase of our life. And early experiences matter. In April 2012, The National Trust launched a campaign entitled, '50 things to do before you're 11¾' (www.50things.org.uk). The campaign sets out 50 challenges for children and families to complete together which enable children to have outdoor experiences creating exciting childhood memories. Bravo! If children were to complete these tasks, then they would indeed add many fond memories to their childhood, and rightly so.

Technology also adds to the background of a person. Think about the technology introduced over the decades. In the online resources that accompany this book there is a table detailing new technology over the decades, from the tv and the walkie-talkie to the Raspberry Pi and the iPad Air. How much of this technology shaped your childhood experiences?

Young people have a different background created from the legacy foundations of old technology. Just as we draw on our own history, so will young people when they are born. We must stop trying to get children to understand the background we grew up in and start getting children to make sense of theirs. This includes how to use technology safely, sensibly and responsibly so they are able to survive in their environment.

How ICT motivates children

Technology has always had an effect on its user. Whether it buzzes, flashes, emits a sound or illuminates, it inherently beckons its user to do something. It is important to remember that all technology has an ON/OFF switch and throughout children's development they need adults to be their filter and help them to moderate their use.

Regardless of the time they spend on the computer, ICT has the potential to motivate children in a number of different ways:

- *Trial, error and review* – by far one of the best processes to come out of using technology, is the fact that computers allow us to change our work and minds in unlimited ways. What is interesting about this is that it changes the way we complete a task, read our work and continue try to improve it until it is finished.

- *Reward with goals* – computers can make a large task achievable. They can be programmed to reward progress at different stages and can keep a user achieving. This is particularly useful for mental maths and other activities which require repetitive stages and rewards.

  A practical example is the introduction of digital badges. Think back to a time when you were a Boy Scout or a Girl Guide, when you used to carry out jobs for the elderly and worked tirelessly for different activity badges. Digital badges take the idea of carrying out different learning activities and transform this process into the 21st century. Imagine trying to combine the web, video and text tools available so that you can learn a new skill or demonstrate your knowledge. Digital badges provide users with a way of learning a new skill. At the end of their learning they are awarded a badge.

  Using the modern methods of social media (Facebook and Twitter) users can share completed badges and let others know about the new learning they have achieved. To learn more about these exciting developments, explore Mozilla Open Badges website (http://www.openbadges.org/) and download the BackPack (http://backpack.openbadges.org/backpack/) to get started.

- *Problem solving* – ICT can be used to present problems in different ways to children. The combination of adding video, text and websites can open up new potential for presenting investigation work. For example, use your interactive whiteboard software to present a maths investigation. The children can then move objects around the screen. The ability to be able to use the 'undo' command in this situation makes it easier for children to explore different answers on a trial and error basis.

  From a teaching point of view, using digital tools and drama can add an interesting twist to the beginning of a lesson or at certain points to progress the learning. For example, when teaching the children to write a newspaper report, use an introductory film clip you have created to introduce the topic. Put yourself in the role of a newspaper editor. Don't worry about it being polished, your children won't mind. I would always tell the children that it was my super-clever brother, which always raised a chuckle! You could also make shorter 'helpful hint' clips to embed throughout the lesson to remind the children to include certain features or editor challenges to stretch your most able children.

- *Creative freedom* – children can use ICT to create anything they wish to communicate. Art tools, web tool and different platforms all allow children to use the medium of technology to express their ideas. Software is making it easier for children to create things. The ability to redo, undo, resize and replace anything and everything on the page helps the user to tailor an idea until they are truly happy with the look as well as the content.

Challenge

Technology can have a poor press from time to time as people take its use to extremes. Anything digital used in excess can risk compressing other areas of life. Part of our nurturing adult role is to encourage children to grow up in a broad and balanced way while encouraging the interests of the individual. All of this is still possible with the introduction of technology. If fact, technology helps individuals to develop awe and wonder, and to try out concepts in a virtual world before committing to real-life situations as well as capturing moments and preserving their memory.

Children will overtake the majority of adults with the speed in which they are able to work out and use technology. However, we as adults have the experience to educate children in the responsible use of the technology and to set boundaries for how they use it. It does not have to be 'the Big Bad Wolf' if it is used as a tool to strengthen and enrich learning. We also need to be able to show children how technology is not just about digital developments, game playing and the internet, but that technology has enriched other areas of the world from travel to medicine.

To that extent I am proposing a challenge to widen this perception. Earlier in this chapter, I referred to the National Trust's '50 Things to do before you're 11¾ '. The same could be applied to digital and technological activities. Have a look at the table below. What other digital activities do you think children could benefit from before they are 11¾?

Awe and wonder	Software related
Experience a planetarium space display. Use a digital video recorder to record a family member or friend's event. Take a digital photograph of the most amazing sight you can see. Learn a skill using YouTube. Watch a 3D movie. Read/experience an interactive book. Interact with a talking robot. Go on a digital scavenger hunt.	Create your own computer game using basic programming. Create a short movie. Create a word cloud using Wordle. Use a different computer operating system. Create a piece of artwork using Tagxedo. Create an animated movie using Lego characters. Learn how to use social media responsibly within a learning context and for connecting with other learners.
Practical with adult help	**Object related**
Change a light bulb. Cook a cake using a microwave. Learn how to re-wire a plug safely. Use the internet.	Play with a remote-controlled toy. Use a touch-screen tablet. Use an interactive whiteboard. Experience using a green screen (this effect is used in the Superman films and you too can become just like Superman flying through the air).

Planning your ICT provision

In any school, the curriculum is integrated and adapted as each successive government changes their view about what education should look like. Among all the curriculum developments, ICT has seen the greatest amount of change. ICT is constantly changing because of the evolution of new gadgets, computers and devices. The next 'new thing' to hit the shelves inevitably transfers in some form into schools. So the skills and activities we use to teach children quickly become out of date. The ICT curriculum will change and must grow to meet the needs of the modern child, not only in terms of the skills which they bring into schools, but also their capacity to demonstrate what they are truly capable of.

From September 2014 primary teachers will be expected to follow the new Computing curriculum. The new guidelines include three main elements: computer science, information technology and digital literacy. Although the new title 'Computing' sounds daunting it does not mean that everything you knew about teaching ICT has gone out the window! The new curriculum covers the ICT students should be using and understanding as well as a new focus on computer programming. There have been overviews and curriculum tweaks since the 1990s and no doubt more changes will be announced during and after this book has been published and read. So how, as a teacher, do you navigate this information and plan a teaching strategy in your school that utilises and integrates up to date ICT as well as government guidelines? As well as this you want to ensure the children in your primary school leave with a rich and wide experience of using technology in a variety if contexts (think back to your 'before 11¾' table!). A plan including the following areas provides a rich ICT provision for your school:

- Creating and presenting ideas
- Key computer skills
- Technical knowledge
- Mobile working
- Evaluating information

- Using data
- Verbal and written communication
- Computer programming
- Digital citizenship/e-safety
- Working together across the web.

On the following pages I explore the aims for each strand. By addressing all these areas you will enable your students to become skilled in using technology and provide them with a solid foundation and skills for life.

Creating and presenting ideas

Provide children with the opportunity to present their work in different ways. Being able to present your ideas clearly is a key skill. Teach children how to set out their work and not crowd the screen, how to use fonts correctly and how a full-screen photograph can enhance a presentation rather than reading endless paragraphs of words. Encourage children to explore different pieces of software to present their work. PowerPoint and Prezi are two examples but also use the interactive whiteboard software.

This area is more than just about presenting using software. It is about encouraging children to have an awareness of the best software to use for the task. Ask them the following questions: Which is the best way to share the story you have written? Is it on a blog so other people can comment? Is it using a word processor or would a desktop publisher be more appropriate so that you can create a story poster? The range of mobile apps available also makes it easier to create content, as I will explore later in Chapter 3. In order to present to peers, children should be able to:

- choose appropriate software for the task
- adapt the look of a piece of work they are working on (font, size, position, wrapping of images, ordering of objects, orientation of the work)
- present different formats of information (leaflet, newsletter, newspaper, story with a picture)
- have experience of a range of different programs so work can be adapted from one medium to another.

Key computer skills

Mobile tablets have been designed to make using technology easier, but the children will learn vital skills by using a desktop computer. To begin with, children should be able to:

- learn how to type quickly with two hands acquired from regular practice either on a keyboard or typing out weekly
- spell on a paper copy of a keyboard
- set a simple password and remember the details
- understand what make a strong password
- log into a network
- navigate confidently around a computer screen
- create folders and organise files into folders
- use a mouse, printer and memory stick and transfer information between devices
- know what to do if the computer crashes
- know where to store work on a school network.

Technical knowledge

Computers provide a fascinating perspective for children to understand how technology works. Allowing children to take apart an old school computer provides a memorable insight into the inner workings of a computer. Knowing the different parts and the different jobs they perform can be useful so children are aware of how computers are upgraded and built. This key knowledge is important for children to learn so they can make the most of the technology they use. To begin with, children should be able to:

- name the various external parts of a computer (USB, thunderbolt, ethernet, wireless switch, CD/DVD/Blue Ray Drive)
- know the correct socket to plug headphones into
- turn wireless on a device
- pair a device with Bluetooth
- know when a network cable needs to be plugged into a computer to make it quicker
- connect using a wireless connection
- know how simple networks work and what a server and client are
- know how software is downloaded from the internet
- understand basic HTML and computer-coding language
- navigate around different operating systems.

Mobile working

Later on in Chapter 3 I will explore different ways in which mobile technology can work across a primary school. It is a good idea for children to find out about the benefits but also the limitations of working in a mobile way. Exposing children to more mobile forms of technology encourages them to look at how it can flow into the work they are completing. Typically smaller and lighter than a laptop, it can be shared more easily during collaborative tasks. To begin with, children should be able to:

- know how to use the multitouch 'gestures' of devices
- know how apps are bought and searched for using a store
- connect an email account to the device
- send an email using the device
- save and access work from a cloud-based storage app
- know how to open attachments in other apps
- upload video work to a private or personal YouTube account

- work on a document, spreadsheet or presentation and be able to export it off the device to continue the working process in a different location
- create digital artwork and compare it to the process of physically drawing or painting a picture
- know how to print work from a device.

Evaluating information

The internet has a wealth of resources children can use to support them in their learning. Children have access to large amounts of digital information in the form of plain text, documents, images, video and audio. As mobile devices play a larger part in their lives, constant information overload is always an issue. Classrooms are shifting from CD-ROMs and encyclopaedias to the entering of key words into Google.

The challenge children now face is that there may be too much information to process as well needing to filter, distinguish and judge different sources of information. You need to teach children to be able to look at information and decided if it's any good, if it's from a reputable source and whether the information will help them to achieve their goal. These are certainly essential skills in the age of information overload. To begin with, children should be able to:

- know which websites will provide factually correct information (e.g. BBC, Woodlands Junior School)
- speed read a webpage to assess if the information is of benefit
- use a search engine
- refine an internet search (e.g. using the word AND to search, using speech marks)
- know the strengths and weaknesses of collaborative websites such as Wikipedia.

Using data

ICT should speed up the way we perform certain tasks using the computer. The ability to crunch data is one such example. Data helps children to present findings in a visual way. There are a number of pieces of software children can use to help develop their understanding of mathematics. The Infant Video Toolkit produced by 2Simple allows children to use basic tools to produce graphs, tables and charts quickly. The Mathsfactor with Carol Vorderman (www.themathsfactor.com) provides examples of exercises the children can use to support their revision as does Interactive Resources (www.interactive-resources. co.uk). To begin with, children should be able to:

- create spreadsheets for real-life purposes
- enter data into a spreadsheet
- total up amounts using the autosum in a spreadsheet
- enter a formula into a spreadsheet cell
- create a simple bar chart, pie chart, line graph and pictogram using software
- use paper methods and software to learn times-table facts and improve speed and accuracy scores
- use software to manipulate 3D shapes and explore other mathematical concepts which would be difficult to understand in other ways.

Verbal and written communication

The power of the written word has not yet disappeared leaving other digital forms to take over. Our ability as humans to communicate to one another using the written word or through the use of our voice is still inherently strong. Children need to gain experience of how they communicate with others through these forms. To begin with, children should be able to:

- record video feedback on a topic
- create a short film with titles and/or narration
- produce a podcast
- use social media to share and communicate well with other learners
- know the features of a blog and how to write a post
- understand the etiquette attached to writing online
- create a document using a word processor
- understand the different styles of online writing from blogs and wikis to Twitter and websites.

Computer programming

There has been a huge focus on making technology easier to use as well as being able to create and consume content. As well as consuming technology, learning how to program and control computers by writing instructions is a great skill and a key focus in the new curriculum. From the early 1980s when the BBC and Acorn Electron were released, they provided the general public with a way of using a computer for everyday tasks but also opened up a way of allowing people to enter in lines of programming code and create a program which worked (or not, depending on your typing skills!).

It is important for children to also experience this side of technology and to understand that technology can be programmed to carry out different tasks and that through our instructions we can control how a computer works. For many years, schools have focused on the control and modelling aspects of the curriculum, mainly using programmable robots. Although this uses aspects of computer science, there is a much wider scope of work for children to explore which also develops, challenges and stretches the children's thinking in different ways. Computer science explores how computers work, how they are programmed, how the computer systems work as well as using a different set of vocabulary to develop the children's thinking.

Computer science is an important strand of ICT because of the different skills and thinking it develops. It encourages children to think in a different way and to try techniques which may or may not work. It encourages them to work logically through their actions to find out what may have gone wrong in a program they have written. A really useful guide which explains this area in plain English is *Computer Science: A Curriculum for Schools* (http://www.computingatschool.org.uk/data/uploads/ComputingCurric.pdf).

To begin with, children should be able to:

- make a remote-control toy move
- write a series of instructions to make a programmable toy move
- understand those instructions and be able to make changes if they do not work
- understand the vocabulary of computer science, for example:
  - **algorithm** (an accurate way of solving a problem)
  - **abstraction** (comprising of the methods of modelling)
  - **modelling** (showing the main parts of information so you can get an overview of what is happening in the same way drawing a story map helps you to understand the whole story without telling you all the details)
  - **decomposition** (breaking a larger problem/task down into smaller sub-steps, e.g. getting ready for school involves getting your bag ready, selecting the books you need for school, packing your PE kit into your PE bag to take with you. All these sub-tasks help you to achieve the overall aim)
  - **generalising and classifying** (making something easier to understand by bringing out the common element or by grouping elements in a certain way)
- write, work out and try a program in order to make something happen
- be resilient and work out what has happened if something does not work in their program
- work out the sequence of everyday programmed events such as the order the traffic lights change in or how a chocolate bar is brought through a vending machine.

Digital citizenship/e-safety

When the internet was introduced into learning in school much was made of web safety and the technical points of using the web. While this was essential at the time, with the developments of the web, mobile technology and social media, the concept has changed and morphed into something different. So children need a broader sense of e-awareness and this needs to be viewed in the same way as PSHE and child protection issues which arise in school.

Teach children how to be responsible and safe online and how to protect their digital footprint. Explain the etiquette of being online, the way passwords work and the notion that the things they write, video, photograph and say are always captured for eternity, more so than when those same elements are produced in the physical world. Ensure that as a school you also have strict online etiquette boundaries and consequences for when pupils cross the line and they also have to take on some sort of education/training before those privileges are renewed again. To begin with, children should be able to:

- be aware of the danger on the internet in the same way as stranger danger
- know how to Google themselves and check their digital footprint
- know how to set a strong password and to develop strategies on how to remember it. Password or 1234 are not the best passwords but are used quite regularly in schools!
- know how to comment on a blog post in a positive and constructive way and know how the comment helps the writer to move on
- know who to tell when they come across situations or web content that makes them feel uneasy
- weigh up and make decisions when faced with an online dilemma
- understand how to build a positive digital image through their online work, blogging, and their Facebook profile if and when they choose to take part.

Working together across the web

Children and teachers now have global access to vast amounts of information and to different people. Being able to work across the internet and use tools to support the process is useful for the world of work. Not only does it widen the skills on offer for a project, but collaborative working also teaches children another way of working and the freedom to work outside the school day if they wish. To begin with, the children should be able to:

- Skype or communicate across the web
- work in a group on collaborative documents

- write a blog post and receive positive feedback and answer the comments in an appropriate way
- send an email and know how to organise, sort, flag and delete messages from an inbox
- produce a learning podcast, convert it for the web and upload it for other people to learn from
- understand how social media works and why it is used
- work on a collaborate online project with another group and preferably another class in a different geographical area.

Planning your provision

Creating and presenting ideas
Begin by setting a goal to use two different pieces of software to encourage children to create and present information – PowerPoint and your interactive whiteboard software. Teach the children how to use the basics of each program (inputing text and images) for presenting information.

Key computer skills
Work on typing skills with the children. Set an aim to encourage as many children as you can to use two hands when they type on the keyboard. Catch the children being good and reward them with a groovy sticker from the Sticker Factory (www.thestickerfactory.co.uk) for excellent typing skills.

Technical knowledge
Know how to locate the various parts of a computer. Learn how to plug the various connections in and how to connect the cable to the Ethernet port. Teach the children how to connect their devices to the school system.

Mobile working
Borrow one of the mobile tablets your school is promoting over a weekend or a half-term. Play with the basic functions of the device. Take pictures, send an email, browse the internet and explore some of the apps that have already been installed. Consider how you would use them in the classroom – the camera, the notes app.

Evaluating information
Discuss with the children how we know if information is accurate on the web. What should we look for? How do we know it is credible?

Using data

Look at ways you can use the autosum spreadsheet function in class. Use a spreadsheet to calculate the number of team points you award each table.

Verbal and written communication

Explore the use of video feedback with children. Provide the children with key question cards. What went well in your work today? Use the video camera to demonstrate areas of your work you think went well and areas your need to develop.

Computer programming

Use the floor robots to write a series of instructions. Begin to look into the definitions and technical terms used in computer science.

Digital citizenship/e-safety

Begin talking to the children about what digital citizenship involves. Explore some of the resources from www.digizen.org to support your teaching of the subject.

Working together across the web

Use email to connect to another teaching friend's school. Compose messages as a class and send these by email. Create a joint sharing project together where you have to swap the finished work or object. For example, swap a class mascot with the school and the class have to take photographs and send updates through email to the other class. Another way is to design a peace quilt, whereby the children share interests or facts about their school. Ask the children to draw on large squares of paper. On one side, the children draw their face so it fills the whole piece of paper. On the back the children could write the first four lines of a poem that someone needs to finish or a set of four philosophical questions for the next person to answer.

Planning your provision

Creating and presenting ideas

Play with different ways of creating presentations. Use a couple of different installed and online pieces of software. PowerPoint and your interactive whiteboard software provide good starts while a program such as Prezi can challenge the children by getting them to think in different ways about how information can be presented.

Key computer skills

Teach the children how to organise their work effectively and about the basic file management. Let them know that it's not a good idea to have endless documents and folders on your desktop screen as it slows down the performance of your computer.

Talk through/remind the children of the procedures for doing certain key tasks on the computer as they arise. 'Remember to always safely remove your memory sticks by ejecting them instead of pulling them straight out so you don't corrupt the disk' or 'What strategies does anyone have for remembering their password? How do you make sure that it is a strong password to use? What does a weak password look like?'

Technical knowledge

Encourage the children to become class technicians – if there are simple jobs which need completing then show them how to do them. For example, how to switch on the wireless on a device they are using and how the Control Panel works on a PC and how the System Preferences work on a Mac if applicable.

Mobile working

Explore some of the apps available to use. Ask yourself how you would use them this week in your lessons. How can you change the method of how you would deliver the lesson?

Evaluating information

Have the phrase 'Is your information from a credible source?' written in your classroom to remind the children when they are searching the internet. Stick a blank poster up in your classroom that has two columns for the children to enter information in. In one column, write 'Title of website' and in the second column write, 'How do I know it is from a trusted source?' As the children find suitable websites then they have to fill in the table. Award team points or stickers for children who complete the table. Share these websites at the end of a lesson or the spare five minutes before playtime so it raises the children's awareness.

Using data

Explore some of the different maths software available to use in lessons. Explore how to make a graph in the quickest way and how to take data and visually turn it into a chart.

Verbal and written communication

Encourage children to use your class blog. Select a team of 'staff writers' to contribute to the class blog even if it is a collection of fun resources or a reflection of four lines or a paragraph or two from your most able writers. Remember to ask the rest of the class and parents to comment on the blog. Send the link out so that parents can comment from work or home.

Computer programming

Explore some of the ITT and school resources developed at https://sites.google.com/site/primaryictitt and by CAS – Computing At School www.computingatschool.org.uk.

Begin to explore how Scratch works.

Digital citizenship/e-safety

Create a digital citizenship display. An acronym that is being used on the internet is THINK (Is it: True – Helpful – Inspiring – Necessary – Kind) Use these terms as a starting point for your display.

Working together across the web

Using your blog, ask colleagues and teaching friends to comment so that children can see that people in the wider world read their work, on the web.

Planning your provision

Creating and presenting ideas

Explore a range of programs for presenting information in different ways so children can build their repertoire of software. Use your interactive whiteboard software, PowerPoint, Prezi, cloud-based software such as Google docs and PrimaryPad. Take a screenshot of the software icon and collect these around your classroom so that children can use them as a reference point when selecting the different pieces of software.

Explore ways in which children can work collaboratively on a presentation using shared documents so they can compare the differences between working with a person side-by-side and working virtually together.

Key computer skills

Encourage the children to tell you the key skills they are using when they work on the computer. Work these questions into your plenary sessions at the end of lessons when the children have used technology.

Technical knowledge

Encourage children to explore the different platforms of Windows and Mac so they can compare the different systems and see their differences. Set up dummy email accounts and teach children how to connect these to a computer. Teach children how to understand simple HTML code and to read it and understand what it means. How does a piece of video or YouTube code you embed in blog or website differ from simple text and tables you write in using code?

Mobile working

Explore how the email function on the mobile devices can facilitate a lesson. Try emailing a list of websites or an activity sheet to each device to support the children during the lesson. As an alternative, you could use the device as the end of a lesson plenary or during group activity. Consider ways that the children will store their work at the end of the lesson when they have finished working.

Evaluating information

Teach the children how to refine searches on the internet using speech marks or the word 'AND' so that children perform more accurate web searches. Discuss with the children why some websites are always displayed first in searches and does this mean that they are credible?

Using data

Collect mental maths or spelling scores using a spreadsheet. Use 'conditional formatting' so the totals will turn into a colour when needed. For example, yellow for children whose progress is not on track or purple for the children who consistently get over a certain score.

Verbal and written communication

Teach the children how to make a podcast or vodcast. Explore the app Explain Everything with the children and encourage them to talk through a presentation they have created or to take on the challenge of making a short tutorial to explain a mathematical strategy.

Computer programming

Teach a programming language such as Python to your children as they create short programs.

Begin a class project to explore the use of the Raspberry Pi from box to screen.

Digital citizenship/e-safety

Provide your class with different digital citizenship scenarios to challenge their thinking. Write them down on cards and use them throughout the term to constantly keep the children thinking about the broad range of online challenges a child may be faced with.

Working together across the web

Make a link with a local, national or international school. Make a commitment to try an online lesson together. Use Skype to hear voices or use Google Hangout to team-teach a joint lesson. Set an aim to find out about the traditions the children have in their schools or the types of playground games they play. Swap these games and play them following the instructions the children provide.

Always keep a strong hold on providing a range of experiences using software and technology as well as whatever it is that makes your school unique as a technology-enabled school. Are you particularly strong in one element? Are you a blogging school? Are you a school using mobile devices to support the creative curriculum? If your children are skilled in their use of technology, then it will show in all aspects of the rest of the curriculum.

Taking the 'whizz' out of ICT

Using ICT in the classroom can be a daunting experience and a little overwhelming. There is a danger of falling into the trap of saying to yourself that you couldn't possibly replicate what someone else is doing in your classroom. The truth is that ICT is like a snowball. The more you keep using it, the bigger the snowball becomes, until you have this massive evidence to draw on and inspire you.

However, there is often a gap in knowledge to begin with and we are left wondering where to start. Some will give up and think that it's for the younger generation of teachers or the ICT specialists and this is where the gap sadly widens between the people who will have a go and those who are frightened to take their first step. The trick is to start small over a term with a small target, identify the possible uses and then build on it throughout the year. See the examples below and on the next page.

Autumn term

What are my objectives for this term?

- Take pictures of the children when they come into the classroom in September and display these on a board showing our class team.
- Use the camera during a drama activity in which the children create a freeze frame about our class rules, showing the dos and don'ts of our classroom. I will then print these off for the children to refer to.
- Use photographs of school events to create a visual timetable to support my children with learning difficulties.
- Use the camera to photograph our school trip, residential trip, Christmas concert, sports day.

Spring term

What are my objectives for this term?

- Use the digital camera to record the children's stories they are retelling orally.
- Give the camera to the children to record how they solve a real-life mathematical problem.
- Use the camera to record our class assembly so that parents can see parts of the assembly if they weren't able to attend.
- Use the camera to make a short movie introduction to a history or English lesson.
- Use the camera to record children making their phonic sounds and then use these to support the children.

Summer term

What are my objectives for this term?

Now I know how to work my digital camera, I will use some presentation software and set up individual presentations for each child. I will then insert the various photographs and video clips I have taken over the year into each child's presentation so it creates a yearbook and shows parents some of their child's achievements.

Just from one piece of technology and small personal targets each term, you've created your own snowball and you can share your journey with other teachers.

Time

Teaching is such a busy job. With the week packed full of teaching the children, planning, lessons, marking, meeting parents, colleagues and the millions of other things which have to be completed, where does ICT fit in? Can it fit into your daily routine? When training teachers, one of the most common excuses that crops up for not using ICT is not having the time to build up the confidence to incorporate it. It's true that using technology does require some input of time at the outset. The more time that you invest in learning how to use it though, the greater the rewards in the classroom as your confidence grows.

Some ideas for making the most of your precious time are:

- Choose one area of classroom ICT that you think you can work on and set aside 15 minutes at the end of the day: five minutes to grab a drink and then ten minutes to play.

- Choose an area to work on with a colleague. Aim to find out something new each week and then join together to share your helpful *did-you-know* ideas.

- Encourage your senior management team to dedicate some time for you to *play* with the technology. It does seem a shame that we encourage many of our youngsters to learn by play and then don't extend the same sentiment to staff developing their ICT awareness.

- Finally, bite the bullet and put it on your performance management. Not only will it encourage you to spend time on your target but it will also give you a great sense of achievement to see your children using it.

A reason for using technology

There must always be a reason for using technology and one very good reason is that it can make learning fun. Take a step back for a minute and remove the technology. Consider the fundamental elements of a good lesson. Now think about the last course you went on, or a staff meeting where you learnt something new, and reflect on how that person got you to learn. So what are some of the key features of a lesson that encourage good learning?

- *The key message is put across in a practical way* – did the presenter get you to carry out a task or activity yourself so that you could see what you were learning and how you were learning?

- *It was made fun* – did they use techniques of presenting which made it sound fun or activities that were fun to do?

- *They used a variety of different techniques* – visual, auditory, active learning and sociable.

- *The presenter was personable* – if we like the people we work with we tend to work harder.

- *The presenter was a leader, guide and challenger all at the same time* – good learning is where we learn small chunks at a time and then we join everything together to form the bigger picture. However, the best learning is where we are also challenged at the same time. Maybe we don't agree with the points or maybe it takes us out of our comfort zone so we have to analyse what we are doing and then reflect on what we have learnt.

What does this have to do with technology? ICT can only be used well if the teaching is good. There is a certain science and artistry to teaching, and the use of technology will not fill a void but will enhance teaching that is already good. For example:

- If you are using technology to affect the **scientific** aspects of teaching and learning, then you are including tools that the children can use to produce an end result to support their learning, such as a graph to demonstrate a science investigation or an online atlas to explore the world and locate places.

- If you are using technology to affect the **art** of teaching and learning, then you are including tools which help children develop the awe and wonder aspects of why they are doing something, such as a video recording to stimulate discussion or the ability to signpost children to different ICT tools in order to further their learning.

Above all, good ICT use is underpinned by good teaching, without it little progress is made.

Adapting planning

It can sometimes be difficult to work out how ICT might be embedded into your lesson plans. The links between the topic you are teaching and the use of ICT can sometimes be tenuous. When planning to use ICT, you need to be aware of the skill levels of the children in your class. You might find these questions useful to reflect on:

- *How well do the children know the piece of software you wish to use?* The more familiar the children are the less instruction you will need to give, leaving more time to push further on with the task.

- *How well do I know the software?* If you know a piece of software well then you know the possibilities of what the children could produce. It can also be useful to say, 'Have you tried this…?' or 'I wonder if you can explore this menu of options?'

- *Are there any special requirements which need to be planned for?* Do the laptops/ICT suite need to be booked in order for the children to carry out the work?

- *How much time do you think the activity will take?* If you are planning creative lessons or lessons where the children will present information then allow three or more lessons so the children have plenty of time to plan and get started before really moving on with the activity.

Use the table which can be found in the online resources that accompany this book as a useful aide-memoire when planning how to use ICT within your lesson.

Introducing the ICT coordinator

So far we have looked at the context of ICT, why to use it, how to plan for it and how to find the time to just have a go. I would now like to extend an introduction to all the ICT coordinators. You have an essential role in developing and managing ICT across your school. Later on in, Chapter 11, we will look specifically at advice for your role and how ICT can be divided into specific areas – hardware, curriculum, training, maintenance and vision.

Teaching Computing as a subject

While the focus of this book is on the embedding of ICT across other curriculum subjects, it is also important to remember that ICT or as it will be called from September 2014, Computing, still needs to be taught and developed as a subject itself. In fact, from 2014, there will be more of a need to introduce lessons devoted to Computing, particularly computer programming into your teaching provision as well as integrating ICT across the curriculum.

Teaching Computing as a subject can appear quite challenging. It relies on not only good teaching skills but knowing and understanding the software; knowing what the general end result will look like and how to teach with the actual equipment. Below are some teaching tips for a successful Computing lesson:

- *Observation* – Computing is a visual subject, we learn through the act of watching what someone else does and then copying it. Children use this technique a lot, copying their teacher, which is one of the reasons why they find it easy to correct your mistakes when you're at the board!

- *Modelling* – this technique involves demonstrating how to do a task or how software works in front of the whole class. Modelling helps children to pick strategies to help them when they do it for themselves. It differs from observation because good ICT modelling involves the use of 'Teacher talk' or thinking aloud, for example, *'A letter has an address that is written on the right-hand side of the page. Now as I write the address I must remember to **justify** the text by pressing these **icons** so all the text will be written on the right-hand side. I know it will type there because the **cursor** is flashing on the right-hand side. When I have finished, then I have to remember to **justify** the text back to the left otherwise I will keep on typing on the right.'* This way of teaching also allows you to highlight the computer vocabulary as well.

- *Breaking learning into small chunks* – when I teach a new song to a class, I have to break up the song into manageable chunks. For example, if a verse has six lines to learn, I will teach the first two lines and sing it through, followed by the next two lines and then go back and sing the first four lines together and then move on to the last two lines. Finally, we sing the whole six lines together as a whole verse. The same technique can be used in terms of teaching Computing by breaking up the input into small chunks and doing a couple of examples at the same time to ensure that everyone has understood.

- *Teaching strategies with equipment* – Computing is a practical subject. There are times in a lesson when I want children to try things out and explore and there are other times when I want all children to listen to me without fiddling with the equipment! Simple classroom management techniques can help you here. You could use 'Right everybody, please turn off your computer screens and make sure you can see my nose' or 'Turn your laptop around to face the middle of the table and look at the board please'. These strategies just remove some of the temptations. If children find this too difficult then use the appropriate classroom sanctions.

- *Teach what ICT use is about* – one of the drawbacks of schools using ICT suites and banks of laptops is that everyone thinks that Computing is just something you do in front of a computer. It would actually be very difficult to accomplish many ICT tasks without a computer but there is more to Computing than just this. Computing involves the following activities and skills:

  - talking about the task with other children
  - planning how work is going to be set out
  - generating ideas for what you are going to do
  - collaborating with others and assigning tasks to be completed
  - evaluating or reflecting on the process or task
  - setting yourself targets or tasks to do next.

  All these are fundamental to excellent Computing work and enable the children to produce work of a higher standard and quality than being left to roam (which can lead to children wasting time).

- *Let children explore the software* – there are many different things that software allows you to do. The only way children find out how it will work is by playing and trying things as well as being taught by you. Hold a mini-lesson 'TeachMeet' so children are encouraged to show the rest of their class things they have found out. If you are not familiar with 'TeachMeets' (http://teachmeet.pbworks.com) as a way of cascading knowledge then do take a look. They are a great way of allowing people to share ideas. Why not promote this technique with the children so they get into the habit of sharing knowledge with others. It will spark ideas and certainly develop discussion.

- *Not every child is a whizz!* – don't assume that all children are competent users of ICT. Some may not have had much exposure to technology at home or are not able to reinforce the skills for one reason or another. This can make Computing difficult to teach at times because children may have varying levels of what they can do.

- *Use branching databases* – branching databases allow you to sort information and generate an easier way of looking at that information by asking questions. Make these practical whenever you can. Bring in objects and sticky notes and physically ask the children to move the objects around. Use the sticky notes to write down the yes/no questions and then group them. Practically showing the branches in front of them is a great way to demonstrate the concept before using the ICT.

- *Teach keyboard skills* – no matter how quick and proficient we want children to be when using the computer, if your children have poor typing skills then half the battle still is not won. Being able to type quickly, with two hands, makes all the difference and is a life-skill children will continue to transfer across all aspects of their work. So the more you can build on these skills the better. Explore teaching programs such as Dance Mat Typing (www.bbc.co.uk/schools/typing/) and typing games (www. typingtest.com/gamesv2a.html, www.learninggamesforkids.com/keyboarding_games. html and www.funtotype.com/typinggames). Embed these across all year groups so the children are practising these skills. Look on Google images for a free illustration of a computer keyboard. Trace the outline of a keyboard on to paper and reduce this down to fit in the back of the children's books. Colour in the 'f' and 'j' keys on the home row and then either laminate or stick a see-through protective cover over the illustration. Use this as a resource to help teach typing. At the beginning of the day when you set some brain-teaser questions for when the children come in also set them five words to type with two hands.

- *Reviewing and assessing Computing work* – at the end of the topic ensure that you do plan in time for the children to produce an evaluation based on their practical work. Try to explore ways which also allow the children to talk about how they created the work. Using screen recording software can be a great way for children to tell the story of their work. It also allows you as the teacher to assess their ICT capability and to determine whether the children created it by way of a series of different ICT 'accidents' or whether they knew how to use the software and each object on the page is there on purpose. There is a big difference between these two scenarios, and often with ICT we assess the end result without looking at the way it is created.

Classroom management and monitoring

Observation is a key way of teaching. It is very easy for children to get distracted when using laptops or computers. This can present several challenges for teachers. If you have a whole class set of laptops running in a suite or classroom at the same time and the projector or board is difficult to see then you are relying on the children's memory skills to remember the different stages you set.

You may consider installing classroom management and monitoring software. Software such as LanSchool (www.lanschool.com), Netop Vision (www.netop. com/classroom-management-software.htm) and NetSupport School (www. netsupportschool.com/) can be a great aid to teaching not just ICT but when computers are used in other lessons. They allow the teacher to remain in control throughout the lesson with controls such as being able to blank everybody's computer screens or allow all the users to see one screen such as the teacher's screen during the instruction phase.

Structuring a lesson

Let's take a look at the structure of a Computing lesson. It is similar to other curriculum lesson structures, but includes a few additions and tweaks to allow for the nuances of teaching the subject. A good, basic Computing lesson should look like this:

- *Setting up the equipment* – whether you are using the ICT suite, laptops or mobile devices they will need to be set up for the children to use so that no time is wasted at the beginning of the lesson.

- *Warm up to get the children's brains going* – this can be with computer vocabulary. 'Can anyone tell me what software I would use for presenting a poster?' 'Here is a numbered image of a web page. There are five things showing: the web address bar, search bar, favourite bookmarks, scroll bars, pop-ups. Can anyone tell me what the number 1 is pointing to?' The question can also be reversed. 'Which number would I use if I wanted to find a website for my favourite television show but I don't know the correct website address?'

- *Introduction of the lesson objectives* – this applies to the content of the lesson but also the ICT skills that the children will be learning as well. If the lesson is combined with another curriculum subject then the specific subject objectives also need to be introduced here as well.

- *Teaching input* – this is the same as any normal curriculum lesson.

- *Show the children 'excellence'* – always show the children what they are aiming for. This could be an example you made or an example of children's work from the past year. I'm a big believer in showing this to the children. By demonstrating excellence in the work, you are showing the children what to aim for when they go off to try the activity on their own.

- *Children going and practising the techniques* – beginning their own or completing additional tasks. This is where your role alters slightly and you take on the role of supporter, troubleshooter, teacher and challenger all at once. For example:

  - *Supporter* – your role here is to fill in the gaps for the children. Children will often say, 'I can remember the first two steps, what do I need to do again?'

  - *Troubleshooter* – your role here is to fix any computer problems. 'I can't connect to the internet!' 'Missss! I can't log in!' or 'Mr Audain, which cable do I need for the digital camera?'

  - *Teacher* – your role (or your classroom assistant's role) here is to revisit the input for the children who need the input again, either because they missed it or because they did not understand.

  - *Challenger* – your role here is to know how to extend the children in the current activity. This requires some thought and a knowledge of how the children will progress. For example, you are teaching the children how to create an interactive storybook using action buttons in PowerPoint. You have taught the children how to begin new slides and type out their work on to the screen.

    The next stage of your input in your lesson is to teach the children how to insert action buttons. You don't want to set the earlier finishers of the typing task onto the next stage because you want to give the input on how to insert action buttons to the whole class. You do want to extend the task though, so you ask these children to collect images to illustrate their story.

    This means that the slower children can catch up while the quicker children have also got a task before you all move on to the next stage together.

- *Sharing of completed work* – it is important for children to gain ideas and to be encouraged to recognise good work. Some children refer to this as 'copying' but really seeing other people's work should inspire the children.

- *Plenary* – the plenary allows the lesson to draw to a close and for you to get the children to explain their learning and to assess whether the learning objective has been achieved. It also allows you to check the key Computing terms and to explain the next step in their learning.

- *Pack away of equipment* – have ICT monitors (children) who help to take the equipment back. This can involve a number of your class which is great when you are allocating jobs to do at the beginning of the year. For example, at the end of the lesson you will need some children to take the computers back to the trolley; some to collect the cables and others to return any other kit while the rest of the class returns the room back to normal. Time this and build it into your lesson plan so you always finish on time and don't overrun.

Creative project: Running a mini-fair

Why not use ICT to promote the children's entrepreneurial skills? Explain to the children that they have to plan, run and evaluate a mini-fair. They will invite members of the school community to attend the fair and raise money for the year group, school or a charitable cause. Below are some ways ICT can be used within the planning process.

- *Data handling* – ask the children to create an online survey to help them to establish the types of games people enjoy playing. The survey can then be embedded into the school website or class blog. Ask the children to collect the data and then examine the results which you can then discuss as a class.
- *Spreadsheets* – as the children set up their stall, provide them with a budget. Put the stock in one cell and teach the children how to create a formula so that every time someone buys something it shows on the spreadsheet. Link this up to your interactive whiteboard so children can see the results in real time.
- *Advertising* – create posters or instructions for how to play each of the games.
- *Go global* – link with other schools from different parts of the country or the world. Ask the children in those classrooms to describe some of the games they like to play at a school fair. There may be local games and the children could then teach these through video conferencing to the children.
- *Blogging* – each group has to keep an online account of what they are doing to create their activity for the fair. Each person in the class must be responsible for blogging their progress. Ask parents to keep an eye on their blog and comment. After the fair the children should evaluate the success of the event on the blog.
- *Discussion forums* – explain to the children that 10% of whatever they take will go towards charity and 15% will go to the school for cost, leaving them with 75% of what is collected for them to decide what to do with. Talk to the children about percentages, how they are created and how they will work out their profit at the end of the day. Discuss with the children the idea of giving to charity. Do they agree with it? Do they not? Should they support national charities or charities local to home?

Ask the children to research and select a charity they would like to support. Ask them to post this in a discussion forum and explain why they believe that their charity of choice is a good one.

App for gathering ideas

MOBILE

Collect ideas and brainstorm for the mini-fair by using the app Mural.ly (https://mural.ly). This allows the class to work independently while enabling the groups to collect ideas. Ask the children to use the mobile app to take pictures of their ideas and work, to make notes, insert useful web links they find or to sketch their ideas. They can upload these on to a mural, which you can then use within your plenary session at the end of the lesson.

Further things to go and explore...

Sometimes just watching a video can be an excellent source of learning and can challenge your thinking. Below are just a few videos worth a watch.

Professor Stephen Heppell

Professor Stephen Heppell is a superb down-to-earth speaker who talks about the use of technology from the ground up and the perspective of the children. Take look at his blog which aims to collate all his speeches in one place (http://heppelltv.blogspot.co.uk/). Enjoy watching the videos especially on learning spaces. For more information, Stephen's website also provides useful information (http://www.heppell.net/).

Professor Sugata Mitra

Professor Sugata Mitra (http://sugatam.wikispaces.com/) conducted an experiment entitled 'Hole in the Wall'. He explored what happened to learning when a computer was embedded in the wall in a similar way to ATM machine and then instead of a teacher's intervention, what happens when children were left to their own devices to learn. The results inspired the movie 'Slumdog Millionaire' and demonstrated the potential and capacity people have to learn.

Three of his talks (http://www.ted.com/talks/sugata_mitra_the_child_driven_education.
html), (http://www.ted.com/talks/sugata_mitra_build_a_school_in_the_cloud.html) and
(http://thinkingdigital.videojuicer.com/sugata-mitra-educational-technologist/index.html)
are well worth watching for inspiration.

Sir Ken Robinson

Sir Ken Robinson (http://sirkenrobinson.com/) is a guru on the use of creativity across
the curriculum. He speaks on the creative potential people have and is engaging in
talking about why we should be looking at changing the education we have at present.
He is a fascinating and witty speaker to watch. Great videos to explore are his: Changing
Education Paradigms (http://youtu.be/zDZFcDGpL4U), his original TED talk Schools Kill
Creativity (http://www.ted.com/talks/ken_robinson_says_schools_kill_creativity.html) and
his follow-up talk Bring on the Revolution (http://www.ted.com/talks/sir_ken_robinson_
bring_on_the_revolution.html).

Learning Without Frontiers

This conference (http://www.learningwithoutfrontiers.com/) always has a fascinating
number of speakers who not only talk about technology in some of their presentations
but who all focus on the challenges to learning. Explore some of the talks and find out more
(http://www.learningwithoutfrontiers.com/talks/).

2 Exploring the digital kit

Picture this… I once visited a small, neat school nestled in the countryside. As soon as I stepped into the school there was a buzz and a tremendous warmth and pride emitting from the children's artwork displayed on the walls. The school twisted and turned down winding corridors and where two corridor walls met, a scene from a *Harry Potter* book of a vast landscape was painted from the floor to the highest point of the ceiling. It lit the rather gloomy, dark corridors and gave them an exciting vibrancy.

Through to the library, which had been turned into a living rainforest, there was a gorilla saying, 'Look after your books'. On to the hall, a magnificent Chinese dragon used during an assembly to re-enact the Chinese New Year had been suspended from the ceiling. I stepped into a classroom, and the same ethos, rhythm and heart of the school radiated from every wall. This was a creative school and one that was out to give the children (and staff) the necessary buzz to be creative.

The digital school

It got me thinking about creativity, music, dance, drama and arts; subjects I absolutely adore. These art forms have to be displayed for people to see, appreciate, think about, talk about and be inspired by. The arts are often as much about process as the product. Is this the same for ICT, I wondered? What would a digital school look like? What are the elements needed to make a school stand out as a cutting-edge digital school that puts equipping its children and staff for the future at its heart?

In this chapter, I will explore how schools can make the most of their ICT in order to build what I call the *digital school* – a school with the technology, solid pedagogic knowledge and a broad and exciting curriculum to enable all children to fulfil their greatest potential and learn the skills they need for the future.

There are three layers in the process of building the digital school: the first is to train all staff and invest time in the school. The second is exploring and using digital tools found on the web to create learning experiences and the third is using hardware actually found across the school. Children (and at times staff) need to be trained how to integrate these tools into their school life and how to look after the equipment they use.

Having a capable and enthusiastic ICT team at the heart of the school is essential if technology is to thrive. Over the years, technology has seen a welcome boost in the amount of money schools have received to fund it. Billions of pounds have been channelled to support the vision of all children having access to and benefiting from ICT.

The next time you're in school, take a look at the ICT equipment you have. There will be 'bits of technology' floating around. Some will:

- be mobile so the children can access and use them for learning
- be there to aid teacher preparation
- form the necessary infrastructure the school needs
- add a little luxury to certain lessons – what I call 'upgrading equipment to First Class' (e.g., swapping the paper-made A, B, C, D voting cards for an all-singing-all-dancing interactive voting system).

Looking at classroom equipment

When looking to improve the level of ICT across the school, the first place to begin is looking at the equipment in the classroom. If we have equipment close to hand then we usually find ways to integrate this more in lessons.

Try this useful exercise with teachers in their classrooms. Go through real-life classroom examples of when they may want to use a piece of technology. For every piece of equipment place a tick or create a list so you are aware of the technology each classroom has. Note that some of these pieces of technology are amalgamated into one when you use mobile technology.

Real-life learning	Equipment required	✔	✘
Is there an opportunity for a child or teacher to capture moments of learning *i.e.: great work produced, art work, work written on whiteboards, curriculum work for the class or school blog.*	digital camera *How many?* *1 per class or 1 per group? (6 cameras for a class of 30 children)*		
Is there an opportunity to record children's music or drama work? Spoken evaluations? Class assemblies? Children retelling stories using a story map?	digital video recorder/flip camera *How many?*		
Can the children record ideas, sentences and thoughts orally?	microphones		
Can the children's work be displayed?	projector/interactive whiteboard		

Luxury pieces of equipment

Can the children display their work instantly or can the teacher demonstrate techniques and methods instantly?	visualiser		
Can minibeasts and materials be viewed close up?	digital microscope		

This forms a baseline of equipment in the classroom. The smaller items would form what I have called the digital toolkit (see below).

The classroom digital toolkit

Having the correct kit in your space is necessary for those times when you need to record achievement, learning or just moments in pupils' lives. Hopefully, gone are the days where ICT has to be signed out from a central place. When equipment is placed in the classroom, it creates more opportunity to use it on the spur of the moment. This is a far more natural way for a teacher to use it and build confidence in doing so. This then promotes a different way of using technology and allows the possibility for children to self-record their work.

Every classroom should have a box of ICT equipment which they are responsible for in the same way as the painting resources, books and the other stuff which resides in your cupboard. First you will need a strong plastic box with a lid which can be stored at child level. It should contain at least:

- *Digital cameras* – aim to have one or two in the box. These are so versatile and children can use them for their work. I really like to hear children saying things such as 'Miss/Sir… I need to take a photo of this; I know how to use it… can I go and do it? Pleeeeeassee!' When using the digital cameras, ensure that the children know:

  1 How to put their hand through the camera strap.
  2 How to know how to switch it on and how to 'wake' it up when it goes into sleep mode.
  3 How to check that the camera is at the correct setting and not set to video.
  4 How to safely delete 1) a single photograph, 2) more than one and 3) wipe the entire memory card.
  5 How to check their photograph to make sure it isn't blurred or not entirely what they thought they were photographing.
  6 When to use the flash and the video settings.

7 How to charge the battery.

8 How to transfer pictures and then use the print wizard to print the pictures.

When using the cameras, ensure that you have also purchased a suitable memory card as, without one, you can only take a limited number of photographs. The amount of pictures you can take on a memory card varies. As a rough guide explore the 'Choosing the right memory card capacity' guide on the digicamhelp page http://www.digicamhelp.com/accessories/memory-cards/capacity/#comments

This can only be a guide for a number of reasons. Firstly, it depends on the mega pixels of the image you are taking. Without getting too technical, the more mega pixels you have, the clearer your photograph will be when you enlarge it. Therefore a school camera set on a high mega pixel setting will produce large photographs because the photo will have more pixels crammed into each section and will take up more memory on your card.

So does this matter I hear you cry? Well, not really in a classroom setting but it depends what you are going to do with the photographs. If you are going to use the photographs in a presentation, then good quality photographs will work well. Be aware that if you use the maximum settings then this can lead to the file size becoming larger. The real difference comes when you want to use your photographs on the web.

The web likes to load photographs quickly. For those of you reading this book who can remember the joys of dial-up internet connection, you will remember the computer taking ages to load a photograph, painfully loading line by line as well as becoming hindered by the speed of the internet. If the photograph was too big then it was 'make-the-coffee-time' until it had loaded. In comparison, with the faster internet speeds of today, photographs can load more quickly but will still take longer if the size is massive. Therefore, it is extremely good practice to keep the file size of a photograph as low as possible.

If you take photographs of a large size, and then want to use them in a blog, you will need to resize them so that they are smaller and can load quickly. This is not as complicated as it may sound and there is plenty of software on the web which can help you with the process (www.picresize.com, www.shrinkpictures.com and www.resizeyourimage.com are a few examples). If the photographs are only going to be used on the web it is a good idea to reduce the pixels on the camera, therefore the file sizes will be smaller.

- *A digital video recorder* – for school trips, or to film fantastic explanations of how to solve real-life mathematical problems and science investigations. Every year I used to set off with my class on a residential trip. Packed in my class plastic box along with an assortment of chocolate was more and more equipment from our digital toolkit: our digital cameras to hand out to children so that they were responsible for photographing throughout the day; an iPad for blogging and a handheld flip digital video recorder. These flip video recorders are great little devices. They are easy to use and they plug into a USB port at the side of your computer so you can move or copy the video over to your school network without the faff of looking for a cable. This allows your class to produce some great digital work alongside the physical work they produce from the residential trip.

- *Scanner* – a scanner can be a real asset for demonstrating the children's work. Scanners take an exact copy of whatever you put underneath them just like a photocopier. You can then save the file and insert it into presentations, documents, the web and virtually anywhere where images can be uploaded. This is a great tool to use to support writing or school work in general. Why not have a piece of work of the day/week, during which you scan a piece of work for all the class to comment on positively. The scanner can also be used as an assessment tool. Be sure to check out your school photocopier as well. Most of the modern photocopiers will have a 'Scan to folder' option allowing you to scan work into a specific network folder.

- *Microphones* – these can be really handy for podcasting or for those times when you would like to add sound to documents or flipcharts. Plug one into your whiteboard/laptop/PC to encourage you to use it. If you are a Promethean user, the sound recorder is a great tool to explore during lessons. Click it and then record a sentence and instruction or the entire flipchart page. If you do this before a lesson then the flipchart can be used as a support for your less able children. You could ask the children to write a story using the text tool and then peer-assess it with a friend who can embed their comments into the flipchart.

Digital toolkits

There are many other digital toolkits you can put together, with different uses, which can be stored more centrally. These can be specific to a subject or curriculum area and they tend to include more equipment. For example you might have:

- a control toolbox where you can store all the programmable toys (BeeBots, Roamers, remote-controlled toys, mimics)
- a science and ICT toolbox where you can place digital thermometers, decibel readers, digital microscopes and the data-logging equipment
- a visualiser and microscope box
- a digital video media box containing a digital video camera, a laptop, a hard drive to store the data, a web camera and material for using the Chroma Key effect (green screening just like in the Superman film)
- a mobile technology box containing a full or half class set of tablet devices.

These boxes can then be checked out to be used for specific topics or projects. Inside each box you may want to put idea cards for staff to use or to support the children in making good choices when selecting equipment.

Using ICT to support your administration workload

ICT can decrease the time we all spend on any given task. Whenever you begin a new job in a different school there are always new templates and documents to create. Once in place, ICT can certainly make the routine administrative tasks you need to perform as a teacher much easier. Below are some different ways you can use ICT to support you.

- *Using spreadsheets to collate test results* – spreadsheets can also be great for collecting your class data, from spelling tests to weekly mental maths results. Using a spreadsheet will allow you to sort the children so you can monitor progress. Look in the different menus for the 'conditional formatting' function. This allows you to set up rules or set the conditions, for example, if the cell contains a certain number then to apply a certain kind of colour formatting. So if you were entering in mental maths scores out of 20, you could set it so that, for any child who scores 18 and above, their spreadsheet cell is instantly coloured in gold – for great progress. Use this to track children's spelling scores and identify who are your strongest/weakest spellers for that week.

- *The autofilter function in a spreadsheet* – there are various filters in a spreadsheet that you can use to sort information. The filter option is under the *data* tab in the menu. When this is applied it will search the column and allow you to select specific groups, list the results in ascending or descending order and also see the top ten results. Your school will probably have a tracking system in place but why not use it to track the children in your own class or work with your teaching assistant to track the results from your SEN intervention programmes so you can also monitor progress?

- *Create templates* – any Microsoft Office document can be saved as a template file. Every time a template file is double-clicked it creates a new document based on the template. These can be incredibly useful for quick classroom tasks. Spend some time over the summer holidays while watching a DVD creating your exceptional quality templates for class newsletters, task-time cards for independent work or reading record templates. When the new term begins, all you have to do is use the templates you have created each time.

- *Create a filing system and spring clean* – schools, in fact a large majority of teachers, are notoriously poor at organising digital files unless they spend time getting rid of files they no longer use. Have a policy that if you haven't accessed it in two years then it is time to delete the file. Create a logical set of folders in your documents to organise your work. Have two main folders – one for school-level work (policies, reports, class newletters) and one for the day-to-day teaching resources you use in school. Within these folders have sub-folders. Try not to have too many and try to set up your system during summer holidays or half-terms so the system is in place.

Resourcing ICT hardware – having the kit!

Schools will have a variety of 'kit' in their building but inevitably, there will be some pieces of equipment that staff will not yet have heard of, let alone used in their lessons. Because the pace of school life moves so quickly, we often stick to using technology that we are comfortable with and confident using in our lessons. However, if we do not find out what this new technology can be used for, then we cannot inject new life into our teaching; and this is so important for keeping lessons creative, for sparking new ideas and different ways of learning. In this next section, I will look at the different types of equipment you might come across in your school. This is not an instruction guide or an exhaustive list of all the technology around by any means, and no doubt by the time you read this there will probably be a host of other new inventions finding their way into education. But the main aim is for you to share information with colleagues when you are planning and be able to make interesting and good suggestions.

Throughout the subject-related chapters which follow, specific ideas of how to use certain pieces of equipment are included. It goes without saying that the more you spend on equipment the higher the quality will be. However, it is not always the case that you need the most expensive equipment for you school's needs. When planning to purchase any ICT equipment, remember to do your research: ask in any ICT forums you belong to, cluster groups or your local authority advisers.

> **Key**
> £ – relatively inexpensive
> ££ – affordable
> £££ – expensive
> ££££ – extremely expensive
> £££££ – Whoa!!! So that's where my ICT budget has disappeared for the next five years!

Curriculum hardware

Digital cameras

Where it could be used in the curriculum: all curriculum subjects
Cost: £ – ££
The digital camera is one of the best pieces of equipment that I use on a daily basis in my classroom. These were once incredibly expensive to buy. But now the cost of a digital camera has reduced dramatically, meaning that more and more classrooms are investing in this tool.

Digital microscope

Where it could be used in the curriculum: Science, outdoor learning

Cost: ££ – £££

Look deep for this one in your school. Back in September 2001 to August 2002, the government launched a focus on science and 'Science Year' was born. As part of that initiative, each maintained primary and secondary school received an Intel Play QX3 Computer Microscope. Somewhere you will find this little blue microscope hanging around. If you haven't yet used it then now is the time! These microscopes were good for basic work and could magnify objects. This is one piece of equipment where you do get what you pay for. The clearer you wish the image to be the more expensive the microscope you will need.

These microscopes are great for bringing science to life and, when plugged into a projector or interactive whiteboard, can provide that moment of awe and wonder and trigger that inquisitive scientific curiosity we want to develop in our children.

The basic functions of these microscopes allow you to:

- *View objects in a clearer way* – for example, seeing minibeasts under a microscope really brings them to life. It also allows children to see how the minibeasts move without scaring or mishandling the creatures.

- *Photograph it* – once your minibeast has been captured, use the software to take a snapshot of it. Print these out for the children to produce sketches or diagrams based on the detail they can observe in the photograph.

- *Take a short video* – why not film your subject and upload it to your Virtual Learning Environment (see page 65) or ask the children to create a multimedia presentation using the clip. The video could also be used to create a branching database or a description for an 'animal-police witness statement' for an English piece of writing.

USB microphones

Where it could be used in the curriculum: All curriculum subjects

Cost: £ – ££

Sound, and by that I mean the ability to record a sound, can be one of the most under-used tools in ICT and across the curriculum. Reading and writing are, of course, fundamental building blocks to all children's development. Some children struggle with writing and translating their thoughts into the written form. These children will often find their 'writing voice' by being able to record their work first vocally.

There are many free applications that enable you to record and manipulate sound with the help of your USB microphone. A good one to begin using is Audacity – http://audacity. sourceforge.net/.

Overhead projectors (OHPs)

Where it could be used in the curriculum: Science, English, drama, art

Cost: ££ – £££

Who would have thought that our folders, once brimming with see-through acetate, would be replaced by the gleaming interactive whiteboard found in many classrooms today? People sometimes say that we should get rid of all the old equipment, but that isn't always the answer, because some of the old ways informed the new teaching pedagogy. This is just one case. Once, the children were all sitting in front of me in the hall, waiting for singing practice, when the projector bulb in the interactive whiteboard blew without warning. The trusty OHP was wheeled out and a demonstration of technology working simply by the flick of a switch was executed!

Just because the technology is not shiny and new doesn't mean it should be dismissed. Some of the techniques we use on the interactive whiteboard are those we have discovered through using older technology. For example, you can look at a paragraph of text and cover all the *said* words and then replace them or read a story and reveal it line by line. Does any of this sound familiar? There are different uses for the OHP that you may not yet have come across.

There are some great ways in which you can use an OHP and develop the theme of shadow theatre with your class. Hungarian based black light shadow theatre group, Attraction, which won the 2013 Britain's Got Talent show on television, produced some stunning work. Here are some useful starting points for inspiration:

- Attraction's first audition on Britain's Got Talent. http://youtu.be/a4Fv98jttYA
- http://www.shadowlight.org/slp/docs/shadowTheatreManual.pdf
- http://fingerandthumbtheatre.com/1.html
- http://www.exeter.ac.uk/bdc/young_bdc/shadows/shadows2.htm

Digital video cameras/digi blue/flip video

Where it could be used in the curriculum: All curriculum subjects

Cost: £ – £££

The use of digital media in the curriculum is an exciting addition to any classroom. Everyone can take on the role and become a film director, an editor or an actor. This can then be used to help your pupils demonstrate different areas of learning and add a visual dimension to any topic they might be studying.

Some video equipment can be incredibly expensive and will capture and deliver footage in crystal clear high-definition (HD) quality, enabling students at A Level to produce exceptional pieces of work. In comparison, your latest HD HDD digital video camera might not survive the morning in Reception. There are some excellent and robust cameras available that can withstand being handled with a little more curiosity and prodding. The disadvantages of using these cameras include the following:

- The footage collected may be of a lower quality than an HD digital video camera will capture.
- They will only record for a short amount of time; usually a couple of minutes.
- They record on to the camera and have to be transferred in some way. Some will need a USB cable or the USB will plug straight into the computer.

However, these little cameras are ideal for the classroom and for capturing improvisations or small-group work. In addition to this, if the children know they only have a limited amount of time, then they will have to prepare their work and be more succinct.

Here are some things to consider when using your digital video camera:

- *Size and cost* – consider the purpose for which you intend to use the camera. Do you want high quality footage to show to parents and other children during assemblies? Do you want the children to handle the technology and use it frequently and confidently in the work they are doing but are prepared for the quality of the end product to be pretty average? There are some cameras that can be operated in the smallest of hands and can be used to train children for when they are ready to use the more expensive pieces of kit.

- *Time* – filming using the camera can be relatively quick. Once set up the children can press the record button, film away and then the capture is complete. When planning to use digital video cameras in class, time must be allowed for the editing process. During this time, the children must collaborate to trim out any of the unnecessary pieces of film they do not require as well as being able to put other effects such as headings and transitions in. All this requires the children to have time to make these decisions.

- *Tape/hard disc drive* – how will you store your work? Most up-to-date cameras will store the footage you record on a hard disc within the camera. This means that as you record, every time you press the record button to begin and end recording the camera will log it, making it easier to locate your work on the disc. With cameras that use tape, the user will often need to search to find their footage so they can import it. Cameras using tapes will also need regular cleaning and the quality can diminish if the tape is re-recorded over numerous times.

- *Other equipment* – in the classroom it is worth investing in a tripod for your camera. 'Shaky hand syndrome', as we used to call it in my class, can set in as trying to hold a camera steady and at the correct height can be challenging for most children! Other equipment like microphones, extra lighting and so on can be purchased, but for curriculum use a well-lit classroom will normally be fine.

- *Transferring data* – the photographs you take with your digital camera will normally be transferred using a USB connection or by putting the SD card into a card reader. However, when shooting live images and transferring them over to the computer the connection needs to be much quicker. Most digital video cameras use an IEEE 1394 connection known as a *firewire*. It is shaped differently to a USB cable and plugs into a special computer port so that you can import the footage into software like iMovie or Movie Maker.

Here are some reasons to use your digital video camera:

- *Active work* – just as drama is about creating a story through action, gesture, dialogue and collaboration, the same is true of using digital video. It encourages all children to become involved. All children can find a role they are confident in carrying out whether that would be acting, or behind the camera as a director, in charge of sound effects or as part of the set. Hold up a pair of old dark curtains and you have your very own tomb for Tutankhamun or cave to hide away in.

- *Critical analysis skills* – the majority of the analysis happens during the editing process. Children have to make decisions about what to cut, where to place titles, whether to include a sound effect for the aliens (if so, which one?), whether to use the shorter close-up shots to move the story on more quickly and so on. Many of these decisions rely on teamwork and discussion with team members.

- *Group work* – show the children the end credits from a film. Ask them to note down all the different jobs that go into producing a film. The roles of director, camera operator, actor, props master and scriptwriter can be shared among the children.

- *Creative possibilities* – using a digital video camera can add a different perspective and really bring some topics to life, especially historical ones. A video diary from the perspectives of Anne Frank, Lord Carnarvon, Howard Carter or Henry VIII can really test the children's understanding and subject knowledge.

- *Incredible excitement* – because you can watch the footage immediately, the children are able to analyse and evaluate their thoughts more quickly. Furthermore, there is often general excitement, hiding behind hands and much laughter when watching the footage back.

- *Self-awareness* – being able to see yourself and hear what you sound like can aid reflection, and, in time, confidence.

Visualisers

Where it could be used in the curriculum: English, Maths, Science, Art, MFL, DT and any other subject with written work or practical work
Cost: £££ – ££££
A visualiser is a piece of equipment used to project live images on to a board. Imagine a smaller version of an OHP projector crossed with a microscope. This is one of the luxury

items you may find in your classroom. The more expensive machines are capable of magnifying objects in amazing, crystal-clear detail. When used well, they can add greater clarity to the concepts you are trying to teach.

Scanners

Where it could be used in the curriculum: All curriculum subjects involving written work
Cost: ££

If you have not got access to a visualiser in the classroom, a scanner is an excellent alternative for displaying written work and finished flat art work. You can also scan in books depending on copyright restrictions. This then allows you to scan in your pages, enabling you to build all your whiteboard resources into the same flipchart.

Programmable toys/Roamers/Bee Bots

Where it could be used in the curriculum: ICT, Mathematics, literacy
Cost: £ – ££

Roamers and Bee Bots are great little devices used to deliver part of the ICT curriculum. Being able to control and plan a sequence of instructions on these toys is an exciting way of getting children to problem-solve in a group and introduces them to computer programming. It is one of the areas teachers feel less confident in but where there is a great deal of fun to be had making things move and work.

Try to think creatively when including control technology. There are different resources available to support the teaching of this area of Computing. For example, there are various mats, traffic lights and robots that can be bought that really engage the children. They can navigate maps, farms, different 2D shapes and treasure islands. Alternatively, you can devise your own version for the children to solve. With some small pieces of apparatus and some quiz question cards at each point of the course you can create your very own interactive treasure hunt. You can even divide your classroom into two and have two teams competing against each other.

Here are some other scenarios for the children to navigate around:

- A navy ship hunting for pirate ships. For each one the children capture successfully, their team earns so many points or house merits.

- In the style of Janet and Allan Ahlberg's book *The Jolly Postman* (Puffin), set up various homes and give the children letters to deliver to each homeowner. When each letter is delivered they receive their next clue or set of instructions to get to their next house.

- Devise a mini town with roads for the children to drive around. You could even use this as an opportunity to teach the children some of the basics of road safety.

- Decorate the Roamers, using paper and art resources, to make each one look like a world traveller. Ask the children to navigate to places around the world. Ask other adults to support this task and then at each country the children visit they could get a fictitious 'passport' stamped by the adult.

DVDs

Where it could be used in the curriculum: All curriculum subjects

Cost: £ – ££

There are many high-quality DVD resources available to use in the classroom. These help children to understand historical events or difficult concepts that are hard to explain. There are many free and reasonably-priced resources for teachers. BFi/Film Education (www.bfi. org.uk) have produced many excellent multimedia DVDs that can be used to stimulate written work in literacy lessons and drama work. There is also a wealth of clips online that can be used within lessons, For example:

- www.literacyshed.com/about.html
- http://antsict.wordpress.com/2012/06/02/9-videos-you-could-use-to-inspire-writing/

Web cameras

Where it could be used in the curriculum: ICT, animation, MFL, science

Cost: £ – ££

Web cams are small cameras that are plugged into a computer and can be used to take still photographs or to film live video. When introducing 3D animation, web cameras are a good resource to use. They are light and can be manipulated flexibly by little hands. They can also be placed on the desk, making them a better alternative to the web camera on laptops. There are also many projects around the world which have webcams so people can see what they are doing – such as a webcam in a French bakery or bird boxes placed around the United Kingdom. The BirdBox Project (http://birdbox.segfl.org.uk) provides one such example.

Whole-school hardware

Digital signage

Cost: £££ – ££££

Communicating information with visitors and parents often takes different forms in a school, from the use of the school website through to electronic copies of newsletters. Developments in flat-screens have seen schools installing digital signage in reception areas and around the school. It provides the ability to create slides and put photographs, text and other forms of media on to a page or a set of slides and have these rotating for visitors and parents to watch.

Some ideas for using digital signage are:

- *School events* – sports day, musical concerts, student council elections… the list goes on. In the pursuit of a balanced and broad curriculum, many schools offer their children a variety of experiences. Why not showcase these for visitors and parents to watch?
- *Messages to parents* – as parents gather to collect their children you could flash up *don't forget* messages or announcements regarding children who have been awarded special certificates during celebration assemblies.
- *Online prospectus* – provide prospective parents with a virtual tour of your school. Include some sound bites from your latest inspection report or a description of what the school uniform should look like.
- *Examples of good practice* – display excellent examples of work from different children around the school. If your school focus is writing, then examples of children's early mark-making through to the opening paragraph of a story can be a great way to display writing for a purpose.

Replacing equipment

As an ICT coordinator, there are occasions when you have to replace large quantities of equipment. Consider the range of equipment out there. Here are some thoughts and different implications:

Desktop PCs
Cost: £££

Whether you have an ICT suite or a hub of computers, the likelihood is that this will comprise desktop PCs. With many pieces of technology becoming more mobile, the numbers of desktops appear to be reducing, but there are many advantages to having them:

- Although bulky, they provide a permanent place of access that doesn't rely on a good wireless connection.
- They are easier to upgrade with more memory when required, therefore increasing the speed and life-expectancy of your machines.
- They share a cabled connection back to the server; therefore, everything should be quicker including running updates and installing new software.

Laptop PCs

Cost: £££

We want to take our technology and information with us as we carry out our daily tasks. Learning tied down to a specific place like an ICT suite is slowly changing. Mobility is becoming key in bringing technology into the hands of children and when trying to integrate it successfully into the classroom. Laptop computers can be a great way of having small groups working on a task together or for accessing software if another class is using the ICT suite.

Here are some ideas for encouraging the use of laptops with the children:

- *Ensure that your wireless system is up to the job* – a strong wireless signal is essential if laptop computers are to work in the classroom. If the signal is not strong enough, children will experience difficulty trying to log on, access programs and save their work, causing much frustration.
- *Consider its use in the curriculum* – there are many areas of the curriculum where the use of laptops can enrich the children's experience of the primary curriculum. When planning, ask yourself if using a laptop will enhance the activity or if it could be used as a tool to support the children's learning. Reading a book and then answering questions using the laptops can be valuable if the children then use this work to refresh their memory a week later.
- *Create cross-curricular links* – if laptops have the portability factor, then utilise this by asking the children to create a spreadsheet when collecting their science results or use simple database software to create records of useful resources at the beginning of a history topic.

Mini-netbooks

Cost: ££

These are smaller formed versions of laptops that can be used to do many of the tasks we use laptops for. So which would be a good addition to your school hardware and why use them? Look at the table below.

Netbooks – Pros	Laptops – Pros
<ul><li>Can sit comfortably in little laps</li><li>Can be loaded with most software</li><li>Cheaper</li><li>Able to access the internet</li><li>Many come with a camera</li><li>Most make use of Wi-Fi access</li><li>Can be popped into a bag and taken on school trips</li></ul>	<ul><li>Can handle different applications that may be power hungry on the memory, space and on the graphics card</li><li>Additional features may be included such as Bluetooth, card readers for digital cameras and more USB and firewire ports</li></ul>

Netbooks – Cons	Laptops – Cons
• Smaller amount of memory • Smaller amount of hard disk space • Some programs will not run as they need more memory or hard disk space • Some keypads can be fiddly to type on	• Can be quite bulky and heavy • The battery life might not be as long

Mobile tablets

Cost: £££

Mobile tablets can provide an alternative solution to laptops, netbooks and desktops. They can provide access to the internet, email and notes as well as different apps that can be used to carry out tasks. You need to think carefully about how they will be implemented across the school and how work can be stored as well as how the apps will be managed. Schools are beginning to look at different ways children can use their own devices in school and there are several different schemes such as Bring your own device and the 1:1 scheme that schools can use as a pedagogical model to support their thinking when implementing mobile devices (more of this is explored in Chapter 3).

The number of mobile devices in schools is steadily rising as educationalists explore how this lightweight, easy to carry piece of technology can be used in lessons and through a child's education. One cautionary note is to try not to make your mobile device work like a PC or a desktop computer as they work in different ways but both are just as good to support learning.

The server/network

Cost: £££ – ££££

If you are a new ICT coordinator, technician or just new to the management of ICT and the network, then this is one big beast of a machine to which you should become acquainted. Most primary schools will have the setup of a main server, which manages the curriculum, where pupils save their work and where the teachers and staff can place resources. The office staff and senior management will usually be on a different server. Some schools will have the setup whereby there is only one server managing the whole school.

The server is the whole engine that manages every computer and user of your network, where profiles of people, software and data are stored. Linking computers together in a network enables each user to have their own personal login username and area to store their documents.

It is useful to have a good knowledge of how your server works as there are time implications for installing new software, adding a new pupil, changing passwords and other tasks. If you feel that this is way above you, then encourage your ICT technical team to help you with an overview. Each server tends to be set up differently depending on the company installing it and how their technicians like to build and maintain servers. So it is worth talking through how long it will take for software to be installed on your system or when are the best times in the day to update the hardware staff use.

Here are some hints and tips for managing the use of your school server:

- *Keep it up to date* – make sure that you keep the software up to date; check for viruses regularly and ensure the different system updates are all current. This will ensure that your server can deal with the majority of things that are thrown at it. Remember that, just like a personal computer, over time servers can become slower.

- *Maintain a network log* – just like your classroom computers can (occasionally) develop problems or do things you were not expecting, so can your server. You might feel confident to diagnose and fix the problem if it is easy to do so. Remember to keep a server-log detailing the date, what you installed or changed and any additional changes you make on the server. That way if something doesn't work it makes it easier to trace the cause. This is especially important if you have an external company maintaining your server as you then have a way of tracking all changes across your network. This may seem like extra paper but these records can be vital and helpful if there is a major problem.

- *Check back-ups* – there are many, many exciting and enjoyable things about being an ICT coordinator; however, one of the downsides is having to tell a member of staff that their data and their life that was stored on the most delicate of memory sticks has sadly passed away into the gates of memory stick heaven. The dreaded question is then asked – was everything backed up? Back-ups are essential, and even more so on a network as all work is saved on to the server. It may be seen as neurotic but it is good practice to make a back-up and then back-up the back-up too. This way you know that if the server goes down you will be able to restore the files for the whole school from the latest back-up you made.

- *Find out how to reset passwords and other routine technical requests* – technical time is incredibly valuable and expensive when you are paying for it so squeeze every minute of technician time you have by learning how to do the routine requests yourself. In a primary school, the largest number of requests will be to do with resetting passwords the children have forgotten. A close second to this is how to set up new accounts. If you know how to do these routine requests then it will mean that you save your technician time for things that only they can do.

- *File structures* – think carefully about where your users will store their documents.

The easier it is to store their work, the more likely it is that files won't go missing. It is a good idea to split the teachers' resources area into two sections – school and teaching. Anything that takes place at a school-wide level (anything from policies, to self-evaluation forms to assemblies) is placed there and anything that affects day-to-day teaching is placed in the teaching section (curriculum planning, timetables through to rotas). Consider having areas for year-group-specific work.

- *Become an excellent digital housekeeper* – electronic 'stuff' can get everywhere if it is not kept in good order. Take a look at where you currently store your work, and where the rest of the school saves theirs. Could the school storing policy do with a spring clean? Set a date in the school diary where everyone has to tidy up any wayward files, especially towards the end of the school year.

Really 'techy' things to learn about your network

Remember that you should only make changes on your server when you are confident that you know what you are doing. If you are confident then here are some areas to explore with your technician:

- *Password reset* – locate and explore Active Directory on your server. If you do not already have simplified software then find out how to reset student and staff passwords for when they forget.
- *Know your network structure* – know the structure of the network around your school. Know where your server is keep and where the network switches and wireless controllers are if you have them. This can be useful when you need to change back-up or in the event of having to shut down the system for various reasons like power failures and during long summer holiday breaks.
- *Check the condition and speed of your switches* – these boxes manage all the data transfers and are called 'switches' and somewhere around your school will be a rectangular box with many flashing and blinking lights looking really pretty encased in a metal cabinet. The higher the gigabyte, the easier it can handle the exchange of information.

Making sure the whole system keeps working

Maintaining your school network will take work. There are a host of local and county-based companies to help you ease this pain. Here are some tips for getting the best out of your maintenance support. Of course, the same advice applies to individual technicians as well as companies:

- *Check their track record* – has the company been working in education for long? Do they understand how schools work and how they are organised in terms of pupils and how this structure changes each year when they move year groups/sets?
- *Try their support for a trial period* – if possible explore whether there is the

opportunity to have the company support you for a trial basis. This will provide you with a suitable idea of what they are like and how they may support your system.

- *Be interested in the technical* – by this I don't mean replace teaching and learning with the integrities of a server system, but ask the company to help you learn how it works in the same way. If you have a little knowledge of how programs such as Active Directory work and how the basics are organised, then you can perform many of the routine tasks such as changing passwords and so on.
- *Shop around* – look for companies who will provide you with value for money and who do not blind you with technical jargon. A good company will make you feel like you're in control of your system. So remember to shop around to find the best company that will do this for you.
- *Train staff* – use a log system whereby staff record any problems with the system in a special log. The more information they can provide the quicker their problem will be sorted out.
- *Use their time carefully* – the average cost of a technician varies between £350–£400 per day. Ensure that you get your money's worth and that you use your technician for the technical things which go wrong in your system.

Using ICT equipment across the curriculum

The rest of this book focuses on subject-specific advice for how to use ICT equiment. Before moving onto that, below are some more general ways for using the equipment across the curriculum. They are also some quick wins – start using them in your teaching today!

Digital cameras

- *Our year in pictures* – get children to use the technology to record class events throughout the year. At the end of the year, invite the children's parents in to school to see their child's year in pictures.
- *Your first display in the classroom* – when you first meet your new class before the beginning of term, consider taking their photograph for a 'Welcome to our class' display. These photographs can then be reused throughout the year.
- *To display work* – take photographs of the children's work as they complete a piece of work or their work 'in-progress'. These photographs of the stages in the work can have a real element your display.
- *Make learning flashcards* – 'catch' the children being good and take a photograph

of their work. Maybe you find a great piece of editing work that you want to show the rest the children or a particularly good example of a technique that you've demonstrated during the lesson. Take a picture of this and create mini-flashcards for the children. On the back of the flashcard write why it was such a good example and then photocopy these to put in the middle of your tables for children to refer to throughout the week.

- *Assessment* – a digital camera is probably one of the easiest ways of recording children's progress. Grab the digital camera after the children have made something and then photograph it. Using the camera to capture different aspects of children's work means in turn that a more holistic picture of the child's achievements can be seen.

USB microphones

- *On your interactive whiteboard* – some interactive whiteboard software programs have the ability to record sound on to a flipchart. This is a great tool as the children can record their story and draw the pictures to accompany the sound. Alternatively, children could make interactive talking diagrams of, for example, the water cycle or insert sound recordings to complete a new version of a worksheet.

- *Assessment **for** and **of** learning* – on a blank flipchart write all the children's names and then place the objective at the top of the page. At the end of the topic, ask the children to record two things they felt went really well in the topic and one thing they would like to work on.

- *Classroom control* – give pairs of children a microphone during a science investigation, a free group discussion or when reading a book. Ask the children to record the 'highlights' from the discussion and to playback to the class what they have discussed. This always focuses paired discussion if the children know that they have to be able to playback their highlights to the rest of the class.

Digital video cameras

- *Assessment* – let the children talk through how they made a resource or how they solved the maths investigation you set them. By collecting these examples, you can use this formative assessment to assess pupil progress.

Visualisers

- *Peer assessment* – at the end of the lesson, use a visualiser to highlight excellent pieces of work that the children have created or to demonstrate to all the class how to peer assess their partner's work.

- *That's a great idea, let's go under the microscope!* – ask a child (or children) to be a volunteer and work underneath the visualiser while the rest of the class are completing their own work. As the board is linked to the interactive whiteboard, the rest of the class can see a person or group thinking in 'real-time'. They can then use this to help with their work too.

Desktop PCs

- *Focus on small-group work* – use your software programs to support children during group work. Install your interactive whiteboard software on the computer for the children to use during their independent tasks. Interactive whiteboard software allows the children to use the tools to support them. As a teacher you can also share the flipchart file with the children so they can refer back to it to support them during the activity.
- *Use it as an incentive* – keep a list of some really enjoyable games, websites, audio books and children's DVDs. Children who have been consistently good within the classroom and in the playground could be rewarded with time on the computer and could select one of the above activities.
- *Set tasks to develop key ICT skills* – consider having a monthly challenge sheet. Create a help sheet for the children or make a video help file using Camtasia (www.techsmith. com) to support them in the challenge. Choose tasks to improve typing; for example, how many of our high-frequency words can you type in four minutes using two hands? Alternatively ask them to watch a video on how to create a folder and move files into it.

Interactive whiteboards

- *In practical work* – use it as an aide-memoire for the children to use during practical activities. Place an image of a tool or safety hazard on the board and then annotate this with the children's ideas on safety and risk management.
- *Use digital images* – at the start of a topic, use digital images to stimulate a debate on a topic. This can be useful during RE, history and PSHE topics and can provide a way of challenging children's thinking or preconceptions.
- Different peripherals – consider using different peripherals such as the digital camera, microscope or a microphone to add extra interest to your flipcharts.

Gaming equipment

Game consoles or entertainment devices like the Playstation or the Xbox are still used as popular forms of entertainment. There are great reasons why these are popular devices used for 'switching off' at the end of a busy day. Many people wonder what the appeal is, but games can not only transfer you from the everyday environment into a fantasy world, but they can also be a motivating force too. Much like their physical playground counterparts, video games can entertain, challenge, motivate and provide social interaction for the people involved. Gaming equipment and its uses have been trialled in some classrooms to explore the potential to support learning in a different way.

The main contenders

There are different consoles available which have evolved as new technology has developed. Here are some of the main contenders the children in your class will be talking about and a little background information:

Playstation

Cost: £££

Manufactured by Sony, the Playstation has developed from the Megadrive era and games like 'Sonic the Hedgehog'. In 2006, the Playstation 3 was released. The majority of the latest games use the capacity of 'Blue Ray' discs. This means that the amount of data a disc can hold has increased, allowing Playstation 3 games to hold around five times more data than its predecessor. As well as the games which can be played, there are ways of connecting to other devices and to the internet so gamers can play with friends and people across the other side of the world. The console can connect through the cabled Ethernet or using Wi-Fi. It is also capable of playing DVDs and Blue Ray Disks.
Games to look out for: 'LittleBigPlanet'.

Xbox

Cost: £££

The competitor to the Playstation and manufactured by Microsoft. The Xbox 360 uses HD (high definition) instead of Blu-Ray discs. HD means that the image will be clearer and crisper providing an improved gaming experience. It connects to Wi-Fi, cabled Ethernet and will also play older games from previous systems. One unique feature is that it has a Media Centre. If you own a PC which has the Windows Media Center installed on it, you can also stream (pass between one system to another) your pictures, movie files and audio files to it. There are different variations of the Xbox including the Xbox Kinect which allows the user to interact and control with content on the screen in the same way the Wii does.

Games to look out for: The Xbox section on on the Educational Gaming Reviews (www.educationalgamingreviews.com/xbox-360) provides some examples of good games children could play.

Nintendo Wii

Cost: £££

Although the Wii does not have the processing power of the Playstation and Xbox, it has been billed as the entertainment system for all the family. It uses a combination of a sensor bar and a unique controller called a Wii Remote. Inside the remote, motion sensors detect movement from the player. These functions allow the player to be more intrinsically involved in the game in a physically active way. Games like tennis, golf, bowling and boxing take on a different outlook. With the ability to connect the device wirelessly as well, mini-games or applications can be downloaded, such as the iPlayer from the BBC.

Games to look out for: Wii Sports, Wii Fit.

Nintendo DSi

Cost: ££

While most game consoles set out to attract serious gamers with the lure of their sleek and realistic graphics, the Nintendo DSi is intended for gamers who require portability and who want to interact with more people. The DSi is smaller than the Nintendo console with two touch screens that are parallel to each other and can fit into the hands of younger children easily. Although it is small, it does host a range of different in-built features. Children can use the in-built camera, microphone and 'Pictochat', and if another person with a DSi is within the wireless range, they can draw pictures and write text messages to each other. The dual screens encourage a different gaming experience. Instructions can be provided on one screen while the user can interact with the bottom screen.

Games to look out for: educational games like Dr Kawashima's Brain Training (http://www.braintraining.com.au/), Dog Trainer, also various recipe books and fiction books are available.

Playstation PSP

Cost: ££

The handheld equivalent of the Playstation console, the Playstation PSP has a different philosophy to the Nintendo DSi. The music and videos you have stored on your Playstation can also be placed on your PSP enabling you to take content with you on the move. It has a microphone; however, many of the other features have to be added on in the form of peripherals. These range from a camera to take pictures of work to in-ear headsets to listen to MP3s of audio books through to GPS receivers. All these can transform these devices into tools which could be useful in the primary classroom.

Games to look out for: Explore the website Common Sense Media (www.common sensemedia.org/game-lists). Not only is there a range of advice concerning technology, but it also provides lists of games appropriate to the primary age range.

Using gaming equipment in the classroom

Here are some ideas for how you might incorporate gaming equipment into school life:

- *Encourage children to share* – invite the class or a group of children to bring in their favourite handheld device or a picture of their console at home. Link this with literacy and ask the children to write a *getting started* instruction guide to their favourite game or to re-design the back cover of a game.

- *Instructional writing* – invite children to bring in the manuals for their games. Scan in sections or use a visualiser in front of the class. Examine together the different features of an instruction manual for a game and the extra information it needs to have, compared to a cookery *how-to* type set of instructions. For this idea and the one above, make sure you include provision for those children who do not have games consoles at home.

- *Cross curricular projects* – as part of the DT curriculum, ask the children to design and make their own container or purse to house their DS/PSP.

There are some excellent websites to help you get started as well. Below are a few resources that begin to explore the use of games-based learning in the classroom.

- *Futurelab* – Futurelab is an organisation that produces research-based reports centred around the key themes of digital technology. The following link is to a report on games-based learning: (www.futurelab.org.uk/resources/ games-based-learning-experiences-testing-principles-teachers-and-students)

- *Learning Without Frontiers* – this is a global platform whose primary aim is to challange the way we look at the future and the role technology plays in supporting this objective. They have some great videos from many different people. Dawn Hallybone leads the dicussion about the use of games consoles in her classroom (www.youtube. com/watch?v=Qx9nbSK8V5w).

- *Education Scotland* – (www.educationscotland.gov.uk/usingglowandict/games basedlearning/about/aboutgamebasedlearning.asp) provides some useful information and links to different reports from Becta and Futurelab on games-based learning.

- *Tim Rylands* (www.timrylands.com) – explored in his classroom how a computer game entitled Myst could support different areas of the curriculum. His blog is worth exploring for classroom ideas.

- *The Redbridge Games Network* (http://redbridgegamesnetwork.blogspot.co.uk) – provide different links to useful resources and ideas to support using games in the classroom.
- *Nicky Newbury* – has a range of ideas on games-based learning on her blog (http://nickynewbury.wordpress.com)

Interactive technologies

One Christmas, there was a real buzz in my classroom – we were the first, in my school, to get this brand new 'board-thingy with the massive box we could make into a castle!' as one of the boys in my class put it. The gleaming new interactive whiteboard sat there for a few days waiting for someone to come and install it. Once done, my class stepped into the interactive age of learning.

Interactive technologies are about exploring the different ways we can engage and involve children in their learning. By interacting with the content, children are able to test out and play with concepts in a more kinaesthetic way. In this section, we will look at various ways that you can use interactive technology in your classroom, beginning with the one which can now be seen in almost every classroom – the interactive whiteboard (IWb).

Interactive whiteboard

Cost: ££££ – £££££

An IWb consists of three main elements: a computer (which controls the software), a projector (so you can see the image) and finally the board itself. The teacher controls the board by either using a finger (touch sensitive) or by using a special pen (pen controlled).

The IWb offers much potential in the classroom. Used properly, it is more than a chalk and talk device. When combined with sharp targeted questioning, maximum visual use of the board's tools and space and well-thought through learning activities, it becomes a powerful learning tool. Unfortunately, when it is used primarily as an electronic chalk and talk device the classroom still remains didactic in nature.

Touch sensitive

The most well-known brand of board in this category is the SMART board. These IWbs have a thin membrane on the surface of the board, so that when the user makes contact with the membrane it sends a signal back to the computer. The user generally controls the board with their fingers but can also use one of the coloured pens located below the board.

Pen-controlled

These IWbs are controlled by using a special pen. Only when this pen connects with the board will it send a signal back to the computer. Most of the pens have a right-click button that works just like a computer mouse would do. The most well-known brand of boards in this category are Promethean boards (the newer boards produced are also touch-sensitive).

Getting started

Here are some tips for using your IWb for the first time

- *Control panel* – explore the settings for your board. Look for the control panel or the *teacher's menu.* Under these options you will find many different settings that allow you to change not only where the toolbar is placed on the screen but everything from the thickness of your pen to the properties of shapes and objects on the screen.

- *Calibration* – there are occasions when you place the pen on the board and the pen and cursor are not aligned to the same point. Calibration enables both to accurately 'sync' together.

- Echalk (www.echalk.co.uk) also has some free classroom-based resources for you to explore.

- *Opening and saving* – before you begin, find out how to open and save an IWb file to your computer so that you can prepare your work from home if needed.

- *Know where the basic tools are* – find out how to select a squared grid for maths and how to draw lines for handwriting for the times when you can't remember how to find the handwriting paper.

- *Find the fill tool* – this tool can be useful in different ways. In some schools the board cannot be seen as clearly as you would like for various reasons – this might be due to natural light, where the board has been positioned in the classroom or a weak projector image. By filling the screen with a different colour, preferably a dark one, you can use a different, lighter colour to write with to make your writing clearer for the class.

- *Find out where the 'special tools' are* – one of the advantages of having an IWb in the classroom is that there are some great 'special tools' you can use. Some maths tools like protractors and rulers will allow you to demonstrate how to measure angles, but when the pen tool is placed against the side of the protractor it will allow you to draw different angles and even a full pie chart. Dice, web browsers, linking files, on-screen calculators and many more tools are available to use with your class.

- *Begin to build units of work into a flipchart* – consider creating flipcharts for topics you teach in advance rather than as you go along on a daily basis. This way you are thinking about the learning as a whole and designing your flipchart to fit the topic.

Think about where you might put blank pages to collect the children's thoughts and ideas; where you might have pages of information or key questions or objects for the children to sort. Then add your next lesson on to that. By doing this you can track the progress of learning throughout a topic.

- *'Use the force, Luke'* – those famous words whispered in the science-fiction blockbuster express the same philosophy that you can apply to using your IWb. There are hundreds of excellent resources which have been built for use on the IWb. One of my favourite types of tools are the website capture tools that can be used for research purposes. iCyte (http://www.icyte.com/) is a great tool to use if you find a good website or information on your topic as it will snapshot the website for you to revisit later. Bit.ly (https://bitly.com) allows you collect websites and organise these into 'bundles' of your choosing.

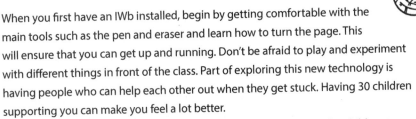

Start small!

When you first have an IWb installed, begin by getting comfortable with the main tools such as the pen and eraser and learn how to turn the page. This will ensure that you can get up and running. Don't be afraid to play and experiment with different things in front of the class. Part of exploring this new technology is having people who can help each other out when they get stuck. Having 30 children supporting you can make you feel a lot better.

From the very start, think of different ways you can encourage the children to *interact* with the board. There are many free educational games available that will help you use your board in a way that you won't have been able to previously. Primary games (http://www.primarygames.co.uk/evalindex.html) provide really fun maths games that the children will enjoy playing. There is also so much learning that can be generated in a mental maths lesson warm-up.

Make sure you install the software on your home computer, make a cup of coffee and spend only ten minutes each day as you drink playing with a part of the software.

Moving your practice on to the next level

So you've had your IWb for a while now. You know where the pens and rubbers are and how to save and load your files. Have you reached the stage where you wonder what different things you can do with your board? Congratulations, you've reached the next stage in your IWb journey! Your next step is to explore how else the board might be used across the curriculum. This is one of the most exciting stages in learning to use your IWb.

It's time to consider how you can replace or extend some of the activities you used to do on your whiteboard. Below are some ideas to get you started.

- *Use the web* – the internet now provides us with a raft of different resources on pretty much every subject imaginable.

- *Don't reinvent the wheel* – use websites and forums to support your planning. Many publishers and individual teachers have already created resources for you to use.

- *Lesson planning* – to make best use of your whiteboard, the way that you build resources into your lessons needs to be adapted. You must plan the lesson so that the ICT supports your teaching and does not interrupt the pace of the lesson. So, you might begin the lesson by stating your learning objective, but how will you introduce the resources throughout the lesson? What about the plenary? If you have voting devices, you may want to check the children's understanding of the lesson through questions you have written on the IWb. Alternatively, you may want to introduce your own assessment for learning (AfL) by creating a *two stars and a wish, show me with your thumbs up* or a *traffic lights* slide created with circles and rectangles using the shape tool.

- *Interactivity* – there are many different forms of media that you can include in your flipcharts. Think about how you might create the lesson so that it is interactive for the children. How will they interact with the whiteboard? Remember the clue is in the name of the board. Here are some suggestions:

  - *Questions* – pose a series of questions for the children. Have some possible answers underneath for the children to match up to the correct question using the arrow lines.

  - *Sorting information* – ask the children to look at the information on the board. Which are the odd statements out? What are the different things children can move around or underline?

  - *Using the tools* – can the children use some of the tools on the board? Demonstrate your workings and then check the answer using the calculator tool.

  - *Group dialogue* – consider how you can structure an activity at the board for one of your groups during a lesson. When you consider the range of tools available for the children to use, what kind of work would you get children to carry out?

Tricks of the trade

Learn some of the tricks of the trade to build in some of the interactivity into your daily flipcharts:

- Hide words or objects behind a shape. Use the transparency slider to reveal them to children.
- Play the old memory exercise 'Kim's game'. Place objects on one flipchart page and then duplicate the page to another one. Take away one object on the second page. Place a shape to cover all the objects on the second page. Show the children the first page and ask them to look at the objects. Explain that you are going to take one object away and they have to spot which one is missing. When you are ready, use the transparency settings for the shape to make it disappear and then reappear.
- Use the 'rub and reveal' technique. Type using the text tool a times-table question and include the answer as well (2 x 5 = 10). Select the largest pen and then the exact same colour as the background. Go over the answer so it appears to be erased. Ask the children to solve the questions in their maths book. When it comes to marking the questions, take a rubber and then remove the pen marks to reveal the answer.

Becoming an IWb whizz

Now that you've been using your board for some time, you will have become confident integrating the different tools into your flipchart. The more advanced users of an IWb will now begin to design flipcharts which promote different kinds of interactivity with the children. They incorporate a range of different media into their flipcharts, exhibit a fluency at the board that does not impede the pace of the lesson and change fluidly been different tools and techniques.

Here are some ideas for using your interactive whiteboard in advanced ways:

- *Sound recorder* – sound can be used in different ways to encourage participation, to support children as well as providing instruction and guidance. Ask the children to record their evaluations of a topic using the recorder.
- *Use different types of digital media* – BBC Learning Zone Class Clips (http://www.bbc.co.uk/learningzone/clips/) are short video clips that you can use to support different areas of the curriculum. Some IWb pieces of software will let you insert a *placeholder* when you go to the *insert* menu. This will embed the video into your flipchart and display the video controls so that you do not need to leave the flipchart environment.
- *Containers* – (For Promethean users only) these are objects which have a certain rule applied to them. When you create an activity you can set the properties of each individual object on the page if you wish so if the children drag a specific word or a

picture on to that object it will accept it and therefore contain that object or reject it. For example, create a piece of text and the children have to drag all the *said* synonyms on to the *said* square or all the proper nouns on to the image of a notebook and so on. For more information see: (http://www.prometheanplanet.com/en/professional-development/activtips/) (No. 68, 69, 81 and 82)

- *Action Buttons* – (For Promethean users only) any object on the flipchart can have an action button applied to it. This means that you can make an object load up another function. For example, if you insert a picture of a calculator, using the action buttons found in the Browser, you can set it so that when the children press the calculator the calculator appears. For more information see: (http://www.prometheanplanet.com/en/professional-development/activtips/) (No. 6 and 7)

- *Explore how your pupils use the software* – IWb software can often be installed on the computers around school. Be sure to install the software everywhere across the school so the children have the same opportunity to use the software. They can use it as an alternative to PowerPoint and they can also view the flipcharts/notebooks you have created. This means that they can interact during group work in a different way.

Getting faster

EXPERT

Focus on developing the pace within lessons. How quickly can you locate and use the tools during teaching? Teachers who are outstanding users of the IWb have a fluency to their teaching using the board. They know how to locate what they want, when they want, so it does not interrupt the learning. They combine several tools, pieces of media and text and manipulate these in a creative way.

As an expert user, explore how quickly you can:

- Insert text and rub out the answer.
- Insert shapes and manipulate them and move them around.
- Remove objects and text from a page.
- Create a flipchart and design it so the lesson is structured with pages built in for discussion and group tasks.
- Link to different objects, websites and tools.
- Group objects together.
- Duplicate/drag and copy/clone different objects.
- Build in other devices into the lesson such as voting devices, slates or interactive tables for group work.

All of the above provide a solid foundation to improvise and develop your IWb practice further.

Interactive whiteboard apps

- There are limited apps connected to the IWb. Some such as Splashtop (www.splashtop.com/whiteboard) will mirror the software and allow you to control the board from a mobile device. Although this is interactive in one sense it only really allows the children to control the board which is useful during whole-class discussions. However, it does depend on your wireless connections and network settings.

- Promethean have a mobile voting app entitled ActivEngage (www.prometheanworld.com/us/english/education/products/assessment-and-student-response/activengage/) which allows you to have virtual voting in your lessons as well as being able to use your other Activote and ActivExpression devices.

- A mobile version of the SMART Noteboard software is available (http://smarttech.com/notebookapp). This is a great tool to encourage children to make their own notebook file. Use a VGA cable to connect the iPad up to the projector to show the children's work to the rest of the class.

Voting devices/learner response systems

Cost: ££££

There are many different types of voting devices around. The basic devices have a small number of buttons numbers (1–6) or letters (A–E). The advanced devices have features resembling those commonly found on mobile phones whereby learners can text their responses, which means that a combination of letters and numbers can be used.

These devices can be used within a lesson to assess the children's understanding. They can be used at the beginning or end of a lesson to find out what the children know. An alternative way is to include them at certain key points within a lesson. When a question is set, the children respond and the data is then collected. This can include the time it took for the children to answer the question. They can be used in a variety of ways:

- *Multiple-choice questions* – ask a question and the children can choose the correct answer. The popular quiz show format works well with this kind of assessment.

- *Two choice question* – here the children choose the preferred course of action. For example, is it right for animals to be kept in cages? Yes/No or press A/B.

- *Thumbs up/thumbs down assessment* – how do you feel about a certain concept in your learning? A) I can do it; B) I need some more help from an adult, or C) I still don't understand, you lost me.

- *Maths assessments* – how about setting your weekly maths test or an end-of-unit test using the voting kit. Break the test into questions around a similar theme which would make it easier to assess how well the children have understood the areas of learning.

- *Self-paced learning* – some voting devices have the option to devise an assessment whereby the children can progress through a test at their own rate. Once they have answered a certain number of questions correctly or obtained a certain score they move on to the next set of questions. Each individual can have the questions randomised so the peer-competitive element is removed. The aim is to see what they can personally achieve without the pressure of being last or friends telling them to hurry up.

If these types of assessments are used in a timely way, they can allow the teacher the opportunity to assess and change the direction of the learning as the lesson progresses, instead of as a summative measure at the end of a lesson.

Video conferencing

Cost: £££££ (Cheaper online versions such as Skype and Google Hangout are available.) Video conferencing works in the same way as a telephone call. Someone who has the same equipment as you dials your number and you can talk in the same way as a telephone call but with the added extra of being able to see the person at the other end.

'Video conferencing is – quite simply – a vehicle for interactive communication. Like all good ideas, it is very straightforward. It enables one set of people to see and hear people in a different location. It brings the world into the classroom, enabling pupils to speak directly to their peers and to experts in other places around the world. When used effectively the technology becomes invisible and provides a powerful learning experience. Through video conferencing, pupils improve their speaking and listening skills and their presentation skills as they work with different audiences in different locations.'

Video Conferencing in the Classroom – Communications technology across the classroom
Tim Arnold, Steve Cayley and Mike Griffith (Devon County Council/Global Leap, 2004)
www.kirklees.go.uk

There are many different types of video conferencing units. These range from cheap web cameras and free software to expensive units costing a few thousand pounds. Don't be put off by the very expensive price tag for the proper kit as there are many great opportunities to connect with people across the world using the free alternatives.

What equipment will you need?

- *A large screen* – you can connect your interactive whiteboard to your video conferencing unit to project the image of the person you are conferencing with. The picture on your whiteboard will only be as good as the projector you also have installed. For clearer results a flat screen LCD television screen can produce excellent definition to see the person you're talking to and look at any documents or presentations you might want to share and discuss.

- *A video conferencing system with an external microphone* – if you opt for a complete system, then it is a good idea to buy two cameras so that they can be placed at either end of the room. A good microphone with a mute button is also a must. It can either be mounted on the wall so all the children can be heard or it can be moved around from table to table.

- *Document transfer unit* – there are additional accessories which can be connected to the video conferencing system. Some units have the facility where slideshow presentations or documents can be displayed so the person on the other end of the conference can share it.

- *Speakers* – a good quality pair of speakers will improve the experience and are worth investing in.

How does video conferencing work?

Each video conferencing unit has a unique name or number. An E.164 number is given to each registered unit. Think of this like your very own unique telephone number so that other systems will recognise who is calling. It also needs a username and a static 'ip' address (this is an unchanged address of the computer connected to your network). When you dial another video conferencing number, all the information is passed through what is called a *gatekeeper*. Think of this like a giant telephone exchange, which connects people to the correct places. The gatekeeper needs your E.164 number, username and password so it knows who is calling. Once it has all this information it allows your connection through and connects you with the person you are trying to call.

The benefits of video conferencing

This is exciting technology. Whenever I have used video conferencing with my class, the children have been really excited about being able to talk to another person from outside the class in real time. There are many benefits to using video conference, such as:

- *Expert engagement* – video conferences can bring a different perspective or an 'expert' to the classroom. Imagine the possibilities of being able to ask an expert from NASA or talk about your maths investigations with a university professor.

- *Improved speaking and listening skills* – because of the exchange in communication, the children have to learn to listen carefully to what the other person is explaining to them without interrupting and then wait their turn to offer their own views.
- *Develop foreign languages and cultural awareness* – why not use video conferencing as an opportunity to link with a school from another country. This is a great way of getting to know another school but also the language from another country.

Some points to consider:

- *Look at the alternatives* – there are alternative low-cost ways to video conference that will allow you to get a taste of how it works: FlashMeeting (http://flashmeeting.e2bn. net) and Skype (http://www.skype.com/en/) are such examples as well as through the Connecting Classrooms section of the Global Gateway (http://schoolsonline. britishcouncil.org).
- *Get the children familiar with using the technology* – this is a different type of technology to get used to and the children will be excited and want to wave at the screen just to check if the other person waves back. This novelty has to happen in order for it to be out of everyone's system so they can focus on the learning that is central to the conference. Try having the cameras and screens on during a lesson so everyone can become familiar with seeing themselves on the screen.
- *Label the port in the switch cabinet* – if you don't want the technology to let you and the pupils down, label the specific cable Do not touch!
- *Time to explore* – when you first set up the equipment, explore video conferencing sites which offer different services for schools like Global-Leap (http://www.global-leap. org/). This not-for-profit organisation, worked with the Department for Education and Skills until 2005, to explore how video conferencing could be of real benefit to learners. Now the project has concluded, but for a subscription they can support you through the whole process from the start. You can book a session called 'My First Video Conference'. They will take your staff through how to video conference, how it works and how teachers can plan for using it.
- *Have you the time?* – remember to check the timings of your video conferencing sessions. They will inevitably run on so allow time at the beginning of the session and at the end so you do not have to hang up in the middle of your sentence. Plan sessions for the afternoon or after breaks so the conference can start during the break when the children are out which means that you can ensure it works and you are ready to go. When you are happy, mute the microphone and turn off the screen but keep the call going and then when the children are settled the screen can be turned on, the microphone un-muted and you're off with your video conference. One final note on time, remember to check the time difference if you are linking up with

someone from another country. Even an hour's difference can have an impact on lunchtimes and the end of the school day.

- *Permission* – do check that parents are happy for their children to participate in the video conference. Most parents are usually quite happy as it is linked to the enrichment of the curriculum and allows children to gain experience; but you should always check.

Here are some ideas for using your video conferencing equipment:

- *Opportunities to promote 'real' communication* – link your class with real people in different places and explore what life is like in another school. The British Council (http://www.britishcouncil.org/schools) is a useful starting point. Even if you just link with another school in your own county, it is really valuable to have a tour around another classroom and talk to children of a similar age. The children can ask questions or talk about special events they hold at their school.
- *Access to experts and other expertise outside the classroom* – museums and other places of interest are beginning to recognise the value of conferencing to schools who cannot visit them geographically. More information can be found through the JANET Videoconferencing Service (JVCS) (https://www.ja.net/products-services/janet-collaborate/janet-videoconferencing-service)
- *Form links with schools* – ask your local authority ICT advisors if they can recommend schools in the area who are on video conferencing. Add them to your address book. Northwood Primary School in Kent (http://www.northwood.org.uk/videoconferencing.htm) provides some superb examples of how video conferencing has benefited their children.
- *Use it for training* – do you have an expert who could share their expertise with other teachers from another school? Why not demonstrate different classroom topics using video conferencing. The same could apply to governor training too.

Digital tools

Web 2.0 technology

Think back to ten years ago. An observation of the type of ICT being used in school would have looked very different then. Acorn computers, one or two PCs and, dare I say it, the BBC Micro computers that were still lurking in the cupboard were the types of hardware you would be likely to see. Learning to use the computer was very much software driven. As well as developments in technology the advent of the internet has enabled schools to share information and teachers to share good practice.

Here are just two examples of available tools for sharing learning and adding interest to presentations:

- *Prezi* (http://prezi.com/) – this is a great way for children to present their work in a completely different way from PowerPoint. The presentation animates and focuses on the key points within the presentation.

- *Voki* (http://www.voki.com/) – this tool can create talking avatars (characters). There are a range of different characters, from religious figures which could be used to introduce RE lessons through to more abstract characters. You can attach spoken text to the character or record your own voice. A different background can also be added, this may be of the school or of your classroom. This is a great tool for teaching a modern foreign language as you can change the accent of the person talking.

This list is certainly not exhaustive, but here are some other good tools to use in the classroom:

- *Animoto* (http://animoto.com/) – collect a few photographs, attach some music and this tool will create a slide show for you.

- *Bubbl.us* (http://bubbl.us/) – a way of creating a brainstorm of ideas online. The mind-map can then be embedded into a project.

- *Classtools* (http://classtools.net/) – on this website you will find templates, countdown timers and other tools that can be used in class. The random name generator enables you to enter the names of your class, click fruit machine and it will randomly scroll through and select a name from the list.

- *Padlet* (http://padlet.com/) – known formally as 'Wallwisher' this tool works like a giant noticeboard and allows the children to write a short message (limited by characters) on the 'wall' for other people to see. Web addresses can also be attached. The messages can then be moved around just like sticky notes.

- *Wordle* (http://www.wordle.net/) – a great way to sum up huge sections of text and to produce art. Enter a section of text or a web page and Wordle will scan all the text and display the key words in a visually stimulating way.

- *Twiddla* (http://www.twiddla.com/) – is a site for holding meetings or lessons online. Great for when the school is closed and you want to continue teaching your students.

- *Sumopaint* (http://www.sumopaint.com) – is a free online art package. Use brushes, paints and other effects to create masterpieces! The finished artwork can then be exported as a jpeg.

- *Voicethread* (http://voicethread.com/#home) – create presentations and allow other users to leave voice comments.

Virtual Learning Environments (VLE)/Learning platforms

Virtual learning is not a new phenomenon, it has been used to support distance learning for a number of years. However, now that the internet has become increasingly prevalent in our lives, more applications using web technology are beginning to appear. An environment used to support learning, which can be accessed virtually anywhere that there is internet access has the foundations of a VLE.

Frog (www.frogteacher.com), UniServity Life (www.uniservity.com) and Moodle (https://moodle.org) are such examples. Open source examples such as Moodle are free to use but require a high level of technical experience to install and implement the solution. Platforms such as Frog and UniServity are product solutions that are bought and implemented along with staff development training. Careful consideration has also been given on how these platforms integrate into a primary school so they are easy to use by the non-specialist teacher as well.

Schools wishing to implement a VLE solution need to think of the type of extended learning they wish to see using the VLE and then select the correct platform/product that fits their requirements. More and more individual schools are selecting a VLE to suit their needs as a school.

VLEs allow the user to store information, collaborate and communicate. Here are some tools you may find on your VLE and some ideas for how you might use them:

Discussion forums

This is great tool for promoting talk amongst your children. When using a discussion forum, encourage the children to write in full sentences and to follow up on the points made by the last person.

When using discussion forums for the first time:

- Teach the children how to post a response. Some of the tools may look self-explanatory but the more training the children have on how to use them the better the results.

- Ensure that you also check the discussion forum and contribute. There have been times when I have seen the discussion needed some help, encouragement and guidance. With a quick post from me, I was able to then refocus the children's writing to promote discussion and to share information.

Galleries/file repositories

Galleries are a very good way of showcasing the children's work. Some galleries allow you to store documents as well as images. Units of work can then be created and housed in one place.

Here are some ideas for how you might use galleries and file depositories:

- *Art work* – galleries usually allow the children to add comments. This is a great way to encourage children to analyse and make positive assessments of their own and classmates' work. A quick comment can be really exciting for children to see.

- *Topic resources* – store film clips, images, worksheets and other resources related to the topic you are currently studying. Once you have finished the topic, the resources can be stored so you can use them again the following year. With many royalty-free resources available on the internet, units of work can be enhanced and kept fresh by using different examples.

- *School improvement* – collect all your policies into a central place that staff can access and download.

- *School awards* – create a gallery of the worker of the week or Magic Moment from the day and then use the comment box to explain why they were awarded that accolade.

- *Music* – have children been composing or maybe you have the next talent-show star in your school community? Upload examples of work that the children have composed themselves so that children can listen to them at home, play to their parents and listen to on their MP3 player.

- *Assessment* – using the comment box, upload a photograph of children's work and then use this to provide evidence towards pupil progress.

- *Phonics* – using a portable digital video camera, record the children making the relevant phonemic sounds with the accompanying action or picture. Children who are learning the sound can then see this and use it to practise.

Calendar events

Calendars are great ways to get children to organise themselves. Have a class calendar in which details about school trips, assemblies and special events are added. You could create calendars that include international events, religious festivals, interesting historical facts or a website of the day.

Message facilities

Electronic communication tools such as email or messaging are important tools for children to learn to use. Files can be attached, web links can be inserted and some messaging tools will allow you to set up distribution lists to all your favourite people as well.

When introducing these tools, talk with the children about how to use them responsibly. Encourage children to see the dangers online as well as teaching them good online manners. I always say to them *'If you wouldn't say it in our school playground then the digital playground is not the place to say it either.'*

Here are some ideas for using messaging:

- *Reminders* – messaging provides a great channel for teachers to send quick reminders about trips, homework and so on to all the children in their class.
- *Topic work* – during a topic, if your system allows, you could set up a messaging account from a fictional character to bring your English/topic work to life. The character could be an angry property developer who wants to build on the school site or a postman who could teach all the children in the class about writing letters.
- *Attachments* – talk about what types of files can be attached to a message and which files might harm a computer or upset someone.

Storage

This is sometimes known as a document storage facility. The children can use it as a travelling memory stick so they can upload PowerPoints or other files at home. Encourage your children to make posters or animations on their computer at home and then upload these to their personal storage area so they can show their work to the rest of the class back at school.

Twitter

With the increasing cost of many Continued Professional Development (CPD) courses, alternative avenues need to be explored. There are many advantages to going on a course: time to reflect on your practice away from the havoc of the classroom and time to talk to teachers from different schools, as well as learning from an expert on a specific subject. Providing that you put what you have learnt into practice, review the impact and share your learning with colleagues, this is an expense worth paying for. Add in the costs of hiring a supply teacher or cover supervisor and allowing staff time out during term time and it can be an expensive investment. Need an alternative? You will have heard of Twitter (http://twitter.com/). Twitter is a micro-blogging website and, as a digital teacher, is well worth getting into.

What's it all about?

The basic principle of Twitter is that you have 140 characters (including the spaces as well) to say anything you like. Has your mind gone blank or are you filled with excitement? However, don't be fooled by the word count as you can become creative. Using URL shortening websites (which, wait for it, shorten website addresses) like Bit.ly (http://bit.ly/) and Tiny URL (http://tiny.cc/) you can take longer website addresses and shorten them into a weblink for other people to access therefore using less of your characters. So imagine the links you could place in a tweet.

Here is the web address for the BBC Schools History site:

http://www.bbc.co.uk/schools/websites/4_11/site/history.shtml (In a tweet this would be 61 characters) but shortened it becomes http://bbc.in/fMmBtk (Only 20 characters).

So imagine the possibilities available for sharing resources, websites and anything on the web by just making everything a little shorter. Some websites like bit.ly will also let you bundle groups of web addresses together so you can provide a collection of weblinks together.

The lingo of Twitter

Well that sounds all well and good, but is it complicated to do? The answer is a resounding 'No' once you get your head around the lingo and the way it works. In ten minutes you can be up and running. Here are the basic terms:

- *Username* – your username is what identifies you on Twitter. Usernames have an @ sign in front of them, making them different from email addresses. For example, my username is (@jonaudain). When you sign up (https://twitter.com/signup) you can make up your own one.

- *Tweet* – these are the collection of words you write. Remember, you only have 140 characters to write your tweet. All tweets are public and can be seen, so make sure that you don't include personal information or anything that could get you into trouble!

- *Follow* – you can follow anyone who is on Twitter. This means that whenever they tweet something it will appear for you to read in your feed.

- *Followers* – other people might decide that they are interested in the tweets that you are writing and will therefore follow you, so your tweets appear in their feed. These people are called your followers.

- *RT* – re-tweet or RT is an easy way to pass a tweet onto your followers so that they can read the information. Someone might have discovered a great resource to use so you re-tweet the message so that other people can benefit.

- *DM* – DM stands for direct message. If a person follows you then you can send direct messages to each other so it does not display in their Twitter feed. Because everyone can see your tweets, you may want to ask that person to message you if you need to have a private conversation.

- *Searches* – there is a search facility so you can search for people or subjects you are interested in. These can be saved for later so you can see the latest updates to your favourite topics.

- *Hashtags (#)* – there may be a subject or event around a common interest that you might want to read. It's very much like pinning your tweet to a subject noticeboard and then everybody can read it. Conferences, general education chat and subject themes will all have hashtags attached to them. For example:
  - *#ukedchat* – is a hashtag for general chat around education
  - *#classblogs* – if you have a class blog and you put this in your tweet then everyone who follows or looks at that search will be able to follow the link to read your blog. This is great for promoting school activities
  - *#edtech* – for discussing technology in education
  - *#p4c* – Philosophy for Children
  - *#mlearning* – mobile learning
  - *#ipad* – anything connected to the iPad
  - *#edapp* – ideas of different apps to use in the classroom.

The list is truly endless when it comes to different searches.

Some words of advice on Twitter

- *Remember it is in the public domain* – everything you tweet can be read. Once it is put out there it cannot be retracted. So remember to remain professional and consider whether you would be happy to say whatever you are tweeting to a colleague's face. If you would – tweet away. Also consider how it looks if you belong to an institution or school. Keep it focused on learning and you will be fine.
- *Connecting with the education world* – Twitter has global users. It is about connecting with different people who share common interests. Want to find out what a school is like in Mozambique? Then just ask. There is a common saying bounced around that Facebook is for the people you went to school with while Twitter is for the people in your own dream school. So many experts are on Twitter for you to glean information from.
- *Who to follow* – follow people that you share common interests with or who have interesting things to say.
- *Dip in and dip out* – a good friend once gave me the advice when I became overloaded with tweets that Twitter is something that you have to dip into and then dip out of now and again. Don't worry about checking it like an email account or you'll become overwhelmed. Dip in – join the conversation – add useful comments and then close the book for another day.
- *Keep on growing* – your own Twitter is your Personal Learning Network (PLN) and has to be grown, nurtured and added to. Communicate with your followers, say thank you

when they offer advice, re-tweet their tweets if you think they might be useful to other people. That way the social networking aspects of Twitter are fostered and mutual professional respect and etiquette are all upheld.

- *Share what you know* – it can be really difficult to get other teachers to share what they know. Everyone has an interesting way of teaching which might help to develop someone else's thinking. Why not share it? It is quicker than a blog post and shared in 140 characters.

- *Ask questions* – stuck for a topic? Need ideas? There will always be someone on Twitter who can help you out. Why not ask for different ways to teach times tables or for great photo history resources. Someone will be able to point you in the right direction. Twitter is especially useful for finding advice on teaching languages, as native teachers can direct you to lessons with correct pronunciations that may be missed when searching in Google.

- *Keep it professional at all times* – there is a lot of rubbish on Twitter if you follow the celebrity rich and famous. Keep your Twitter professional at all times. Tweet about what you do in the classroom and about education and you will find it to be an invaluable source of information. Constantly remind yourself that it is a professional forum for teachers.

There are some interesting resources for exploring Twitter in the classroom:

- http://changinghorizons.net/2010/08/using-twitter-in-the-primary-classroom/
- http://www.teachprimary.com/learning_resources/view/using-twitter-in-the-primary-classroom
- http://classroom-technology.weebly.com/twitter.html
- http://learningandsharingwithmsl.blogspot.co.uk/2013/08/using-twitter-in-primary-classroom.html
- https://blogs.glowscotland.org.uk/fa/ICTFalkirkPrimaries/tag/twitter/

Starting on Twitter

NERVOUS

- Create a Twitter username and begin to explore Twitter.
- Type in 'ukedchat' and read through some of the comments.
- Follow the links you are interested in and use one of the ideas in your classroom.

Following educationalists

- Once signed up, search for common educational words.
- Begin to follow a few teachers or educationalists. Remember to read their first ten or so tweets so you can get a feel for whether you like what they are saying and whether it is of any use to you.
- Find your top ten favourite educational websites for the classroom and tweet these.

Developing a niche

- Share examples of your work in the classroom.
- Use hashtags to your advantage. Remember to tag your posts so they can be across multiple disciplines as well.
- Develop an education niche on Twitter. Be known as the class teacher who's interested in… with their class.
- Retweet and share the word of others.
- Join in the debates, discussions and weekly educational chats.
- Explore the hashtags of education conferences you are interested in as these tweets often have further links for you to explore.
- Introduce people to people. You've grown your own Professional/Personal Learning Network (PLN) through Twitter connections. Why not introduce new people to people with similar interests?

Twitter app

Remember to download the Twitter app for your mobile devices (https://twitter.com/download). With some mobile devices, Twitter has been integrated into the system so you don't need to use the dedicated app when posting a Tweet.

3 Mobile devices

Mobile technology is so cool! Don't get me wrong, a desktop computer is great to work at and there is nothing like being able to sit down and write without the distractions of life interrupting. There is, however, something to be said about being able to take your technology out and about with you! Mobile technology is fast becoming a way of life for all of us. What once resided on your desk is now small enough to fit in your pocket.

Schools in the future

What will schools and flexible working spaces look like in the future? What will children take with them to support them with their learning? Many schools I visit now are exploring a vision in which children use their own technology in lessons or as a school, they provide more mobile forms of technology for pupils to use. In the future, schools will expect children to provide their own browser for their use in their learning. In an Apple Leadership Summit in London, early in 2012, Stephen Heppell described the different observations he had made whilst visiting schools. Explore Stephen's website page on Learning places and spaces – virtual and actual at http://rubble.heppell.net/places/

The concept of what a learning space will look like in the future is interesting. I conducted some research on 'digital leaders', in which children have responsibility and ownership over the ICT in their school. Through talking to the children as a researcher, you gain a sense of their experience, interests and drive for using technology at school and during their leisure time as well. Children bring a wealth of external experience and ideas. Mostly they bring, if they are interested, the unlimited gift of their time. So most children begin their school experience with a level of knowledge and expertise which we can then harness. An eventual school aim must surely be, if we want children ready for the wider world, for them to be allowed to come into school with the key items to support their leaning. So they can bring their own lunchbox, backpack, PE kits and browser.

And why not? The way children use devices in the classroom of the future influences different theoretical and pedagogical views and impacts on the way we teach. Mobile technology will play an integral part in new thinking on working with technology.

Consider the following approaches. All of these encompass elements of the use of mobile devices:

- *1:1 computing* – children have their own personal use of a device for their learning. The school usually requests a specific device. This could be a mobile device or laptop. Parents are encouraged to purchase the device so the children can also use the device at home or the school purchases the devices.

- *Bring Your Own Device (BYOD)* – this approach relates more to children bringing a mobile device into school. This can be connected to the school network but usually involves a pre-registration of some sort so it can be identified on the network. The children are then able to browse the network with the restrictions normally applied by the school internet filters.

- *Bring Your Own Technology (BYOT)* – this approach is similar to the approach above. Children can bring in any mobile device or mobile computer. The difference with the approach above is that children do not need to register the device on the network. They simply turn up and log on! Whatever they have at home they should be able to use. This is quite tricky for a primary school to implement without a considerable amount of technical help.

- *Digital leaders* – digital leaders are selected children who enjoy using technology and share their skills across the school. They support staff, talk about how they use technology in their learning and champion the use of technology throughout the school. Just like children who sit on the school council, digital leaders also form part of the Digital Senate (see page 194) in a similar way.

- *Cloud computing* – the cloud is a mobile's best friend. Instead of installing things on to the actual computer/mobile it accesses the cloud. The cloud can be used to store your work using applications like Dropbox. Apple apps such as Pages and Keynote can save what you make to the cloud so they can be accessed on different devices. Some software applications can be run through the cloud. These are usually cut-down versions with some restrictions compared to the fuller versions you install on your computer.

- *Flipped classrooms* – the Victorian system of teaching is based on a teacher standing at the front of the classroom teaching and sharing knowledge: the didactic method of teaching. During the Industrial Revolution, this method solved one purpose – to educate the person to perform a function or a specific job. This method of delivery has not changed in years. The only problem is that children do not work like machines and the 'technological revolution' has changed the pedagogical and practical ways of teaching.

The flipped classroom concept turns the Victorian view of teaching on its head. Children study the concept they need for the following day at home using the internet and instructional videos. If all children have completed the learning then the teacher sets activities, discussions and tasks to further extend or consolidate the childrens' learning. So the children bring the knowledge with them and the teacher signposts their next steps – a critical role for the teacher.

For more information and to find relevant and related research, go to the EdFutures website, http://edfutures.net

Where to begin?

This chapter is based on workshop training sessions from conferences and schools I have had the pleasure to have worked with. As well as being someone who's involved in technology and education, I also work as a musician and conductor of a community wind orchestra. There are many similarities between the two disciplines. I recently read a book on developing different skills for aspiring conductors entitled: *Teaching Music with Passion: Conducting, Rehearsing and Inspiring* by Peter Loel Boonshaft (Hal Leonard Corporation). He once presented a workshop on the 'The 33Ps of a Wonderful Rehearsal'. There are comparisons between working in music and working with technology, for example:

- planning what to do/play
- rehearsing what to do beforehand
- performing, using the resource in front of a class
- listening to what's around and the things other people have created
- making the most of what you have. Music can develop awe and wonder, technology can have the same effect when enjoying the results of what has been produced
- improvising – when things do not work, make it up, use a structure and go for Plan B!

Although not a 33P Plan, let's use some of these themes and examine how they fit within the agenda of implementing mobile learning.

PLAN – the first things to consider

Mobile devices come in many different forms, from the phones you have in your pocket, to the computer laptop and the flat tablet. They enable you to access the web in an easy 'take-it-where-you-want' way. Make no mistake, before you go out and whack a bunch of tablet devices into a learning environment, they're going to have a huge impact on the way in which you organise your classroom, deliver content and research information. Before quibbling about which platform, device and apps to use, the first questions to explore are: Why have it in your room? What is the purpose of using this technology and are you ready? What are the things that you should consider?

- *Robust Wi-Fi* – mobile technology relies on being able to access the things you want to access wherever you are in the school grounds. This means that that your wireless signal must be strong enough to support the load you put on it. Add your laptops to the number of small devices and if your access points cannot cope then you won't have an adequate service. Contact your network support company and ask them to run a check on your network.

- *Wi-Fi coverage* – if you have no Wi-Fi in your school and you are thinking of installing it then take a look around your school. Where do you want your children to use their devices? Do you want children to be able to use them out and about in the playground or the outside classroom? If you do, then you need to ensure that you have the coverage to reach those places in your school. The signal radiates out from access points. The closer you are to one the stronger the signal and the further away you move the weaker the signal. The more devices you connect to an access point, the more the signal is shared. If you try to connect to a weak signal with multiple devices then the technology will not work for you unless it is boosted further.

- *Invest in Wi-Fi* – the wireless service has to fit the purpose. There is the wireless you use in your home and then there is the wireless you use in a 'business' environment. I choose the word 'business' carefully instead of school. If you are going to invest in Wi-Fi then you have to think in terms of how a small business would run. Businesses invest serious money in ensuring that the technology can function and connect. So don't scrimp on your wireless or you'll end up with a collection of devices that cannot function.

- *Curriculum* – is your curriculum ready for mobile technology? Can you visualise your classrooms with more access to technology? Are you ready? How will it fit into your topics? Do you need to think more about integration of technology into your lessons? Are there specific skills you need to teach to the children?

- *Training* – new technology requires investment in time. To be effective, staff have to be on board and know how to use it. The great thing is that these devices are easy to get used to. The challenge, as with all technology, is for teachers to think about how it can enhance a lesson, subject or concept.

- *Digital champions* – do you have members of your teaching staff who are eager and passionate about using technology with the children in their class? Consider trialling some devices with them. What can they achieve? Some companies, reps, consultants or authorities may even have demonstration kits you can borrow to try out.

- *Scale* – consider from the outset how you see the use of these devices in your school. This obviously depends on the finances but all technology needs a strong scale behind it. Are you looking to equip a class, a key stage set or just a group? Each requires a different way of managing the devices. While a group set of six will enable you to begin small, you still need to think carefully about how you will update them, manage and distribute them in the classroom. That said, a whole class set will enable you to sample what it would feel like to roll out across a whole school.

- *Mobile or mobile phone?* – the word 'mobile' normally conjures up the image of a phone, especially in secondary settings. In a primary setting, however, mobile technology means simply being able to move a device around from one place to another. Although they can access the internet there is usually no need for primary aged children to access a mobile network.

- *Degrees of mobility* – consider how mobile you truly require the devices you purchase to be. Are they going to remain onsite all the time or will there be occasions when you will take them on a school day or residential trip where you will need to access the network? If they are to stay in school only, then the use of wireless-only models may be more appropriate (and sometimes cheaper). If you want the devices to access the internet, email, Twitter or publish to your blog while you are out and about then you need a device with a SIM card allowing you to access these things. For schools which use this approach, a monthly phone network charge is usually required.

- *Vision* – are you looking to roll out a certain scheme, for example:
  - *BYOT (Bring Your Own Technology)* – do you want children to bring their own technology into school and use it for their learning? This includes the use of laptops as well as tablets and other mobile devices.
  - *BYOD (Bring Your Own Device)* – do you want children to bring in their Android or Apple phone or tablet into the classroom?
  - *BYOspecifiedD (Bring Your Own specified Device)* – do you want to specify the mobile device the children bring into school? This way everyone has the same device making training easier for staff. This is also similar to the 1:1 computing scheme.

- *Acceptable use policy* – take a look at yours. Have you thought about appropriate guidelines for protecting children in a mobile environment? See the online resources that accompany this book.

- *Can personal be for everyone?* – take a look at the devices which are around you. If you own your own device, there will be some apps that are the same or similar on each device and some which are completely different. Each device is special to that individual. So how do you use devices defined as personal in a school where everyone needs access? The answer is by taking the personal emphasis out of the device and making it fit for the business. We will explore this more later in this chapter.

Which type of mobile device?

Let's now look at the kind of device you want. There are two main camps – Android devices or Apple devices and is there a difference. So what is this and how do they work?

Android

Android is the operating system created by Google for mobile devices. As it is made by Google it also provides great access to many of its services such as YouTube, Google searching, email and maps. Additional services can be connected by using the app store (Google Play). From here apps can be downloaded to the device. There are many different features that differ slightly from device to device, from note-taking, to internet-browsing and even how you enter text.

Apple

Apple iOS is the operating system of all of Apple's touch screen mobile devices – the iPhone, iPad and iPod Touch. Each device has a core standard of apps: email, internet, voice recording/voice recognition, calendar, notes and reminder apps. The user can begin with a basic standard of apps and then using the App Store can download apps they will find useful providing they have the password. There are also parental controls that allow adults to turn off some features.

iPod Touch

The iPod Touch is a similar to an iPhone with the exception that it is not a cellular phone so uses Wi-Fi to connect to the internet. As it is small in size, it can be used more as a personal device for children to use either individually or within pairs. It is useful as a device of research, individual reading and for using apps.

iPad

The iPad is a larger device that follows the same principle as the iPhone and the iPod Touch. The screen is 9.7 inches which allows the user to use more of the screen for learning. The same range of apps are available as for the iPhone/iPod Touch. Some apps are also just available for the iPad to maximise the screen size. However, some iPod apps can be 'scaled up' to fit the screen of the iPad. The app can then be used, though it may become pixelated. iPads lend themselves more to group work as the screen is larger. There is also an iPad Mini device which is smaller and has a screen size of 7.9 inches.

Apple Distinguished Educators – a slight bias warning…

During my time as a teacher I was made an Apple Distinguished Educator (ADE). ADEs fulfil four roles to Apple: as an advocate, an advisor, an author and an ambassador. Their remit is to promote the teaching and learning opportunities possible on the iPads and other Apple mobile devices. They do this through speaking at conferences, writing for other teachers, advisory work and challenging the normal boundaries. If you use Apple technology and you are interested in becoming an ADE then you should explore https://ade.apple.com/apply/

I am a solid believer in championing the skills of the profession. We have a medical profession which recognises the additional skills practitioners learn above the basic foundation they receive during their initial training. The same should be true for the teaching profession. Schemes such as the one above help you to develop as a practitioner as well as providing networking opportunities with like-minded colleagues.

National and international recognition for practitioners

If you have an interest and use any of the following software, then you might want to explore one or more of the following schemes and pursue some recognition for the work you do in your classroom:

- Apple Distinguished Educators (ADEs) http://www.apple.com/uk/education/apple-distinguished-educator/
- Google Teacher Academy http://www.google.co.uk/edu/programs/google-teacher-academy/
- Adobe Education Leaders http://www.adobe.com/uk/education/k12/adobe-education-leaders.edu.html
- Microsoft Expert Educator http://www.pil-network.com

I am a keen advocate for the right technology for children to use. Most of my experience surrounds the use of iPod Touch devices and iPads in primary schools. The majority of this chapter from now on is therefore based around these two devices. Does this mean that the rest of the chapter does not apply to you? Not at all. All mobile devices have a commonality with some slight differences in the way they work. A tablet is a tablet just as a classroom is a classroom. The pedagogy remains the same.

Laptop or mobile device?

Mobile technology works in a different way from computer technology. I have taught children in many different settings, from ICT suites to using classroom laptops and mobile devices. The way that you deliver a lesson changes because of the instant access you have to the technology. In the middle of a lesson when those 'I wonder questions…' are asked by the children an answer can be found quickly. However, when you decide to use mobile technology in your classroom there are certain questions you need to ask at a class level, a senior management level and a school level. This chapter will explore some of those issues.

Think of your classroom and the type of technology you want it to have. Each behaves in a different way and is managed differently from a teacher perspective. For example, when you use a laptop, consider the stages you need to get going. Laptops need to be set up, powered on, and physically placed around the classroom. If you have laptops which are losing battery life then you also have to consider how you are going to ensure that they have enough power throughout a lesson and that the cables trail safety in your classroom. After the initial set up you then have to consider if you need to plug in computer mice for a faster way of working. With a laptop, CDs can be loaded, the processors are faster and the mechanics of creating work is easier as some functions, such as tables, are easier to create using the power of a computer.

Where mobile technology differs is not just in its ability to take it where you want to go, but with the apps and the ability of *cloud computing* to create a synchronicity between the device you hold in your hand and your computer. Work can be stored and accessed from your mobile device and then you can pick up where you left off from a computer if you need to.

However, this way of working is not without its faults if you expect it to work like a PC would. Working in a mobile way is great for some things like inputting words, numbers and for creating presentations. Let me show you one example:

Laptop/computer

The children have been asked to type up their story about a school trip to a farm using the computer. They have written their story in their English book and now want to type it up. They type out their work using the keyboard. They then decide to change the appearance of the text by justifying it and choosing a funky font which is installed on the school computer. They choose to insert a box around the text and then apply some border art to the box. They then decide to insert some photographs they took while on the trip. They plug in the digital camera and have to navigate to the correct folder to access their photographs and then copy them into their network shared folder. They then go into a word processor and locate the 'insert' task and insert the picture (resizing it as appropriate). Finally they then log on to their own email account, click on new email, compose their email, upload the document and then send it home for their parent to see the work. Additionally, they print their work off to display on the wall.

Now let's explore the same scenario again but this time using an iPad. The extra information in *italics* shows how the 'mobile-ness' changes the way the children are able to work.

iPad device

The children have been asked to type up their story about a school trip to a farm using the computer. They have written their story in their English book and now want to type it up. They *have the choice to either dictate their work or* type out their work using the keyboard. *Previously, the children have had the opportunity to brainstorm their storymap idea using the Toontastic app. The class teacher has also placed a selection of images of settings in the class Dropbox folder for the children to access while generating their ideas. Using these images, the children then collect key words to describe the settings in the Notes app. The children use these key words as a framework to support turning these into sentences. They begin a new document to assimilate their work. Using four fingers, they swipe fluidly from app to app and back again until all the sentences are used or deleted.*

They then decide to change the appearance of the text, justify the text and then choose *a font from the limited but commonly used web and computer fonts.* They then decide to insert some photographs they took while on the trip. *The photographs were taken using an iPad so the children press the camera icon and then choose the photograph they wish to use.* Finally they *click the share button and then the mail icon. They enter the email address and then press send. They copy the class teacher into the email and email the document as a pdf which is one of the options in order not to waste paper.*

How will mobile learning affect the way schools work?

The examples above are not drastically different but provide a different way of working. So how does the use of an iPad change other aspects of the way you can work? Below are some questions frequently asked by coordinators and teachers.

How does mobile learning affect group work?

- *Collaboration* – a tablet screen is a good size to share with others and promote collaborate working. Children can gather around and read or work on a project together.

- *Group talk* – a tablet can promote a focused talking activity. Ask the children to read a section of a book on the iPad and provide them with comprehension questions for which they have to highlight answers or make notes in another app.

- *Pass the iPad* – this is based on the game of pass the parcel and works well with maths apps. Sit the children in a small group. Each child has between three to four turns depending on the size of the group. Place a pot of counters in the middle of the group. Load up a maths app. Every time the iPad arrives at the child they have a choice to answer the question or to pass. When a child answers the question correctly they pass the iPad to another person in the group and pick up a counter. The first child to get to four counters wins the round.

- *Collaborative editing of writing* – it is so easy to take a photograph using a tablet. Children can photograph a piece of writing and then insert it in an app. The Bamboo Paper is a good example of this. You can insert the photograph and then the pens are really easy to use to annotate a piece of work. Group editing and improving work can be made easier using this process.

- *Assessment for Learning* – use the same activity as above, however the children use the iMovie app. The children insert a photograph of their work into the iMovie app and then narrate their two stars and a wish feedback. This strategy could either be used as a personal reflection or for another child to use.

- *Division of roles* – when the children have a large group task to complete they can divide the group into different roles. Out of a group of six children who are preparing a history presentation, two children have the responsibility to write the presentation script in an Office app, two children plan out and prepare the presentation slides using Keynote and two children work together to take and find suitable pictures to illustrate their points. Once each pair has completed their task they then email their work to a designated group leader so they can assemble the work.

How does mobile learning affect individual work?

- *Individual practise* – computers can make rote learning much more exciting for children. They can bring out the competitive side in a subject a child may struggle with. Learning multiplication tables and weekly spellings are two such examples. Bright and colourful apps can motivate children to continue learning and the ability to time how long it takes them to answer a question is a useful feature in some apps. Some apps will also track your progress so you can identify mistakes and misconceptions to support children on an individual basis.

- *Note-taking* – taking notes can be a useful way to support the learning process. Write your notes, take photographs of the work created on the board and then use this to reinforce a concept when learning at home.

- *Responsibility for learning* – when children have a device they become more involved in their learning. They have a device in their hand that becomes their study buddy. They will enjoy recording thoughts, writing notes on a topic, taking pictures to support a project or inspire a piece of creative writing or reading an interactive book.

- *Dematerialisation* – Sugata Mitra raised this point during his 'Thinking Digital' Conference presentation in 2012 (http://thinkingdigital.videojuicer.com/sugata-mitra-educational-technologist/index.html). He spoke about how objects which were once individual gadgets and tools (the Walkman, the computer, the video recorder) are quietly disappearing into a single device. Your mobile device can be your notepad, your internet browser, your music player, your video player, your computer and your education in the palm of your hand. As Mitra comments, the disappearance of ordinary objects '…that's dematerialisation'. Children have access to a vast array of resources for learning which now can fit into their hands.

- *I now have a photographic memory* – well sort of! Devices have a camera which is incredibly useful to take a picture to support understanding of a topic or concept. It encourages children to take photographs of key points in a lesson.

How does mobile learning affect whole-class teaching?

- *Role-reversal* – when using mobile devices in the classroom, everyone becomes a learner. The classroom changes into a hub of research with all users with devices generating information. It changes the stance that the teacher is the font of all knowledge.

- *Teacher as signpost* – the teacher becomes the facilitator and they guide children in their pursuit of knowledge. This use of the mobile device is supported by the vision of the flipped classroom. Children are able to search for a wealth of information and they now need teachers to make that searching stronger and safer by focusing on what is the essential information. You could, for example, be researching what it was like for children to be an evacuee. The children need to find out what an evacuee is; what they took with them and how evacuees were identified. They need to research whether all children were evacuated and where were the main areas in the UK that they were sent to. On the board, group these questions into large areas. When the children find out a piece of information they write it down on scrap paper in their neatest handwriting and then stick it on the board. No one is allowed to write up the same fact. The researching pair or group with the highest number of facts on the board is then awarded team points.

- *Global access to web resources* – children are able to connect to a wider range of resources. A cautionary note should be attached to this point though. Just because they are able to browse does not mean that children should not also have the experience of searching through books and other sources of information. They too can provide information and generate interest so children should be able to access the broadest scope of resources.

- *It's good to share* – collaboration works incredibly well when people work with mobile devices. It mustn't be under-estimated how important the use of email is on a device. The mobile age is the age of sharing and not being protective with a 'this-is-mine' mindset. Teaching openness at the same time as respect can foster a moral obligation towards someone's work. Teach children about the use of licences from Creative Commons (http://creativecommons.org/licenses/) and encourage children to think about how they would like their work to be treated. If this is fostered at a class level then it also feeds in to your Rights, Respect and Responsibility agenda.

How does mobile learning affect the wider school community?

- *Challenging thinking* – at a one-to-one level, challenging pedagogical questions are raised:
  - How should we record learning?
  - Do we need to print every piece of work a child produces?
  - Do children need the skill of handwriting in an age where the written word is generated by the keyboard?
  - Are exercise books necessary in the modern classroom?
  - What are our printing costs and what are the types of information we are printing? Can these be reduced?
  - Do we want children to be able to take their learning with them at any time and anywhere we choose?
  - What do we want a mobile learner to look like?
  - How do we want a mobile learner to act?
  - Are my teaching team ready for mobile learning?
  - Can my senior management/leadership team lead by example?
  - What are the considerations we need to put in place for children who may be disadvantaged?

These are a few of the questions to engage in at a school level when considering the use of mobile devices. Some of these are big questions which everyone needs to own. For example:

Do we need to have exercise books in Key Stage 2?

Explore any of the notebook/paper apps and you can see the flexibility of these compared to the paper that is available (lined, graph, blank, music manuscript). With the use of a stylus, can you reduce the amount of paper your school consumes and work smarter in the way you ask children to present their work? Why not consider a trial group with one of the classes in your school and evaluate the positives and negatives?

We know that the children in our classes like to learn in different ways – visually, auditorily and kinaesthetically. However, consider the new mixed style of learning that mobile tablets are also creating in respect of how a user interacts and learns through the tactility of interaction with a touch screen. The use of tablets is a 'visual kinaesthetic' way of learning.

What practical considerations are needed?

- *Investment in Wi-Fi* – a mobile solution in your school needs the same type of consideration as your fixed laptop/desktop computers. If you have laptops or netbooks then your wireless system needs to be able to support the additional mobile devices at the same time. Have a word with your technical support company and ask them to carry out a wireless survey on your existing network.

- *Email becomes king* – mobile devices need a transportation system. Create a document, photograph, sound or a short video recording and there is a need to get it out of the device and into another system or device. Email is one of the ways in which this is achieved. Although devices can be used for just the apps there comes a point where you also want the information to leave the device.

Looking for evidence of impact

- *Improvements in results* – interventions in schools when focused and coupled with encouragement and feedback can produce great results with children. The use of apps can provide daily reinforcement of tables and spellings. If children are missing phonic sounds, then they can plug in some headphones and access different apps to help them with the development of learning these sounds. While the normal process is for these activities to be paper-based in primary school, these apps can track much of this data and display a child's progress and errors.

- *Reduction in printing costs* – Essa Academy, a secondary school in Bolton, promotes a solution where every child has their own iPod Touch device. Through sustained use of the devices, they have seen a dramatic reduction in their photocopying cost. When you create a document you don't need to photocopy it for children to use. It can be emailed round so that students have the resource at their fingertips.

Are you ready?

Readiness for the integration of mobile technology is an important factor. Although the devices are easy to pick up and use in the classroom, ask yourself why you want to use the device? Tick in both columns if the answers apply to you.

A	✔	B	✔
So children can have instant access to technology.		Because I want it to work like my computer network.	
I want devices that turn on quickly… instant on.		I want to be able to connect to the my files on the network.	
I want flexibility in terms of software I can purchase.		I want the children to be able to sit at a computer with a mouse.	
I want an all-in-one device which is able to photograph, video, email and access the internet.		I want children to access the software we have installed on our network.	
This technology supports our learning-outside-the-classroom agenda.		We teach the skills of Microsoft Office, Word, PowerPoint, Excel and Publisher and want the devices to echo that.	
Children are able to come into school using this technology so why not use it?		I want to teach children how to log on with a username and password as this is a skill they will need to know in the adult world of work.	
It teaches flexibility in using different pieces of software.			
The mixture of old and new forms of learning is interesting through the medium of this device.			
We want to work towards a more paperless school. We want children to be able to record their notes on a device and use these at home to support their learning and homework.			
Mobile devices will all help to promote individual learning. We don't want children to be tied down to a space to learn.			
We see this as a complement to our existing laptop/desktop computer infrastructure.			

From the table above, if you ticked mostly the B column then perhaps your school may not be quite so ready for a mobile solution just yet.

During a discussion once with a friend, we were debating the merits of teaching some ICT topics later in a child's school life. My colleague commented that although we can break topics down so that younger children can achieve concepts, sometimes when children are older they can understand the topics at a quicker pace and that's when we should teach the more complex topics within ICT. Mobile technology helps to do things in a different way. Apps allow the children to carry out simple tasks without having to know your way around software and menu bars. This means that children can very quickly understand how to use one app as they make it easy to do just one thing.

Planning

So you think you may be ready to begin the process? Where do you begin and what do you need to plan for to ensure that you get the maximum benefit and smooth integration? Below are some starting points.

- *Curriculum integration* – take a good look at your curriculum and the type of teaching staff adopt. Is it chalk and talk? A creative curriculum approach? How confident are your staff in using ICT? Nervous or nutty about the technology? Tablets are really easy to use. These are great tools so if you have willing staff who are ready to have instant access to the internet and can plan the use of different apps into the classroom then half the job is nearly done.

- *Infrastructure* – mobile devices rely on accessing a wireless system. Do you need to upgrade any of your infrastructure? Ask your technician team to conduct a survey on your system. You may need more access points or to upgrade your controller and system if you are looking to invest in more devices. Think about your long-term vision for mobile devices and computer hardware as it may be an idea to upgrade the system so it has the capacity to support a more mobile vision.

- *Apple approved reseller* – unlike computers, there is little variance in terms of Apple device. However, make sure that you look out for Apple approved resellers which are dotted around the country. Although it's possible to walk down to your local shop and purchase devices, an approved reseller will also be able to put you in touch with training and advice to support you through the process.

- *Look for school advocates* – find out who are the most confident users of ICT and mobile technology in your school. Who has their own device at home? Consider a trial with these ICT champions.

- *Are finances available?* – the integration of mobile devices can be implemented in a cheap way or with investment. The less expensive way involves just buying up to five devices and syncing these to an account using the cables and putting an app on each device. The larger investment involves the purchase of a syncing cart (to sync a large number of iPads at one time which certainly makes the management easier), multiple iPads and volume licensing. Whichever method you select, finances are important to ensure that you can firstly implement your investment once the kit is purchased and then sustain it in subsequent years.

- *Which devices?* – ask yourself if you are looking to introduce one type of device (iPads, iPod Touch devices or Android) or different multiple tablets.
- *How many devices?* – I began using just one iPad in my class as a piece of action-research to see how it could be used to support teaching and learning. Some schools purchase a small set of six devices for group work and some schools purchase 16 or a class set. Again this links to your finances, however, each purchase works differently.

Training

Training is a necessary part of any ICT investment. It builds time for staff to become familiar with software and how it can be used in the classroom. This time is crucial. Consider how you might train staff and children including your digital leaders:

- *INSET training* – schedule INSET time to allow training on how to integrate the devices into the curriculum. Ensure that the day is as practical as you can make it. One of the best ways is simply to allow the staff to be in the role of the child and to work out in small groups all the things they can find out by trying certain apps and exploring how they work. Provide each group with a large sheet of sugar paper and ask them to record top tips they have discovered. This way everyone is a learner. After this session have a focus on a curriculum subject. Throughout the day have short reflection spaces where staff can write down their next steps and what they need to do.
- *Home training* – send a few of the devices home over a weekend or a half-term holiday with some of the staff who are less confident so that they can play and become more familiar with them.
- *Refine a focus* – during the introduction of the devices, choose one curriculum focus for them. Encourage staff to share that focus. For example, the use of maths apps to support maths concepts and times-table work. Look at some relevant apps and discuss as a staff the additional support of resources that using the app will create. For example, will you need a personal record card for when the children complete each stage?
- *Display and promote* – create a display in the staffroom and around the school. Share the latest app for staff and children to explore on the devices.
- *Invite children into staff meetings* – our children do know more than we do when it comes to how devices work. Why not put out an advert for knowledgeable children

to come and share their knowledge during a staff meeting and foster a teaching and learning philosophy?

- *School Genius Bar* – once you have your set of iPads in school, set up a 'Genius Bar' in the style of Apple which is available during one lunchtime for children and staff to ask questions about how apps work. Staff this with digital leaders and ask them to think of their top five iPad tips. Tell the children that everyone who comes into the school Genius Bar to ask for help should also leave with one of their tips as well. Each week the bar is active, the children have to think of new tips.

- *Let the children show the way* – children have great potential to lead with mobile technology. Let them show the way. Involve them and encourage them to reflect on how they see the technology working.

The process of implementation

Let's take a look at how you go about implementing a tablet solution in your primary school. Below are some ideas which you could use as a checklist.

- *Timescales* – take between half a term to a term to strategically plan as a team how you want to introduce them to your school.

- *Accounts* – consider how you are going to manage school accounts. Different schools have different set-ups. Some schools have two accounts. One main financial account linked to a school credit card and one account the rest of the tablets connect to and receive their apps from.

- *People* – who will you involve from your school community to help you achieve this goal? Who has the vision, the enthusiasm, the time and the commitment to see this project to a satisfactory conclusion?

- *Parents* – are your parents knowledgeable and on board with your aims?

- *Finance* – have you worked out your sums and how you can commit to supporting this project successfully until the system is embedded?

Firstly let's explore two semi-fictional schools and look at some of their reasons for using devices as they implement a solution across their school environments.

Muddyfield Primary School

This is a small one-form primary school trialling out a set of six iPads. The senior managers decided to focus on one curriculum area to begin with so they could assess the impact. As a school, writing has been cited as an area for development, specifically boys' writing.

As well as having different catch-up interventions, the school wanted a resource that was perceived as cool by the boys as well as having the ability to download certain apps to help the children write, spell and create more easily. It was decided that within the budget there was scope to afford six iPads, with cases. The school wrote down their priorities and aspirations for using the devices:

- To have a core of boy-friendly and engaging books for the children to read.
- To have a device which is portable, lightweight and easy to use in a small group setting.
- To have a device which makes it easier to take notes.
- To use a drawing app so that children can create their own story maps to scaffold their creative writing skills.
- To use apps (Comic Life, SpellBoard, Word Wizard, Puppet Pals and Toontastic) to improve the children's written skills in a variety of different approaches.

The ICT coordinator was tasked with ordering the equipment and setting it up. She located a supplier and was able to order through school. Along the way there were other pieces of equipment they founds they needed. Although the iPad came with a case they opted to purchase cases that were more robust. They also invested in screen protectors.

In conjunction with her school finance manager, she decided that it was a good idea to have one account linked to the school credit card but then to purchase iTunes vouchers for books. They explored the range of books from the Oxford Reading Tree as they already had these in school. They also explored the range of PDF books available from Rising Stars.

They browsed the publishers' websites of the books they already had in school in hard-copy and discovered there were online versions. They found that some of the books were just replicas. While researching they also found a selection of digital books as well. These books push the concept of the book to incorporate the unique features of the tablet. For example:

- There was the ability to use the microphone and record the children speaking the words of the text. This was useful for the children to hear their own voice so they could work firstly on the fluency of their reading and then the expression.
- Some of the books had additional activities. *The Fantastic Flying Books of Mr Morris Lessmore* app (http://morrislessmore.com) based on the book by William Joyce and Joe Bluhm is one such example. It is a beautiful book, which challenges how a book should be viewed and experienced. It includes animation of the pictures with clips taken from the animated movie as well as additional activities linked to the text of the books. The activities also use the touch-screen technology so children can point and press the screen.

Once the iPads arrived in school they were set up, the screen protectors and cases applied and they were ready to begin. The children were excited by the technology and enjoyed using the iPad to read their stories. They begin at first to look at different ways of reading information. The teacher used the camera and then the Comic Life app to create speech pictures for the children to read. To support them with their spelling, they used the Word Wizard app to help them spell out the word.

The iPads are used in different classes and once a week the ICT coordinator calls the iPads in so she can sync them to the computer for the necessary updates.

Barndance Junior School

Barndance Junior School is a three form junior school which is looking to implement a different solution to Muddyfield Primary School. Barndance wanted to implement a one-to-one solution across the whole school with the vision of every child having their own iPad which they bring into school as a resource. As a school, they were well-advanced in terms of their ICT provision, with a large computer suite, two laptop trolleys, interactive white-boards in each classroom and they had obtained their ICT mark as part of their on-going evaluation process. The school was well known locally for technology and was developing a national profile. The headteacher and senior staff passionately supported the use of ICT and actively looked for how it could be used at the best times to extend and support teaching and learning. Parents were supportive of the school and it was situated in an affluent area.

The school was looking for the next steps in children using technology. Their aims as a school were to:

- Change the access children have to the web in order to develop research skills.
- Enable teachers and children to work in a more flexible way.
- Allow children to record their work in different ways.
- Reduce the amount of printing in the school and use technology to support this vision.
- Allow teachers the opportunity to display books and apps as well as having access to the features of a tablet. (Through the implementation, the school purchased one iPad for each teacher to use and become familiar with the technology. They were expected to bring it every day to school and to staff meetings. Minutes and agenda items would be circulated by email.)
- Transform the use of technology in education, in their school.
- Join up the way children learn so that they have access to a device they can learn with throughout the day.
- Have a device that connects to the school services – email, shared calendars.
- Involve parents more through the use of technology.

The headteacher and senior staff at Barndance Junior recognised that the vision was a momentous one. They saw this as a whole-school initiative but decided a snowball approach would be best to introduce the scheme at the end of Year 3 and then each subsequent Year 4 intake that followed. Children would be expected to participate in the initiative and a finance payment plan was created, in the same spirit adopted for residential school trips. They adopted a project management approach and began by setting up a mobile learning and technology task group. The group comprised the ICT coordinator, headteacher, ICT technical team from a local company, finance officer/business manager, an ICT governor and two parents. There was a sub-group comprising mostly of the Digital Senate (digital leaders, the ICT coordinator and additional school staff) who met separately so the children could also own the initiative.

They decided that although the vision was large, it could be achieved through breaking it down into areas to consider:

- Assessing the reliability of the school system.
- Aligning the learning strategy to the School Development Plan.
- Looking at the total amount of finance available for the physical kit, accessories and student bursaries for those on low income.
- Creating a clear structure of roles throughout the project.
- Making links with an Apple Approved Reseller and the local Apple Store who could provide workshops to schools.
- Looking at training needs for staff (INSET time and allocated staff meetings specifically to explore their use.)
- Looking at training for children and agreeing with the Digital Senate what is acceptable in terms of using mobile devices across the school.
- Providing a number of parents' information evenings so that parents could:
  - Try out the devices.
  - See how they can be used for learning in the classroom.
  - Ask technical questions about the devices and talk about insuring them.
  - Talk about e-safety implications and how the devices will be managed in school and at home.

The task group then set regular meetings to continue planning the implementation. They divided the tasks and assigned the roles. The initial stages took between one and a half to two terms to make the necessary changes in the school. During that time two parent information evenings were held to introduce the project and to offer the option for parents who wished to pay for the device over the whole academic year. Further parent evenings were held in the first week of the summer term.

After these parents' evenings, the one-to-one scheme was softly launched in the second half of the summer term where the children (if they had the devices) were able to bring them in and use them in the classroom with the view that the whole year group would have a device ready for September.

These two schools are very different both in terms of the number of devices they chose to implement and also in their approach. Both approaches fit the particular school and their aims. Remember the golden mobile rule... the more devices you have in a school the more structure and planning you will need.

Managing the day to day

Once you have mobile devices in your school then the following section provides you with some advice on how to manage these within a school setting. Some of the management can be 'quirky' and at times difficult due to the fact that these devices are still seen as personal individual devices, but which need managing. Below is some advice for managing your devices on a day to day basis.

Making the personal fit for business

Mobile technology is personal in its nature. We adapt the smartphone or tablet to suit our personal needs. These often vary from person to person. However, in a primary school setting, if the set of devices is organised in a similar way to a bank of laptops then there are a few considerations to bear in mind:

- *Make everything the same* – just like computer laptops and networks, the aim of the game is to make everything look the same so no matter which tablet device you pick up staff and children can use the same app.

- *Mobile access* – these devices are great for creating content (film, photographs, documents and anything else created in an app). Once children create something new they will then need somewhere to put that information so they will need to push the content into or onto a system. Will the children email the information to themselves so they have a record? Will they upload the information to a cloud-based storage facility like Google Drive, Box.com or Dropbox? This will allow users to store their work and also gain access to it when they are not using the device.

- *Think like a network* – networks have shared areas to store work. When you start to use the devices then you need to think about the mobile access described above and how you might set up a structure within that, for example, having class folders and Year group folders.

- *Consider the basics* – can you manage all the basics on your device: Can you manage email? Can you store your work when you have finished? Can you publish your content to a place when required? (whether that is on a blog, wiki, website or learning platform).
- *Similarities to a network* – mobile devices connect into different apps and cloud-based services which you then need to use for your work. Sometimes when you purchase these devices into your school teachers want them to work like a computer network. Mobile devices need to be thought of in a completely different way.

Involving the whole school community

Mobile technology in a primary school involves all staff getting used to the equipment. Whether you have six devices or 60, at some point you will want everyone to understand not only what to do with them but also the vision for their use. Here are some considerations:

- *Involve the Digital Senate* – children lead the way in making decisions about their school. They can provide a valuable direction in the type of technology they want to use in their learning. They can help with training, creating the advice on the best way of using the devices in the classroom.
- *Training* – invest in training. Encourage the sharing of ideas for apps – the good, the bad and the ugly. Share tips for teaching with the iPad: how to use it within the classroom and how to use it with children.
- *Acceptable use* – just as schools teach children how to use a computer to browse the internet safely, they also extend this to teaching children how to use a computer in an acceptable manner. The same is true with mobile technology, even more so due to the way it can be used wherever you are. For example, when you're in the classroom and you are talking, have an understanding that says that the screens should be facing up and off and that the children should be concentrating towards you, the teacher.
- *Morality* – mobile devices have several tools in one. This reduction of several devices (the camera, music player, video player, computer and so on) has meant that children also need to understand the conventions of how to use the separate devices. In the 'good old days' when the devices were separate, children understood the boundaries for using each device. For example, when using a camera the pictures you took on your own were yours to keep. You had to frame your subject and make each shot count as you would only have 25 pictures to take on a roll of film. So you would spend time not wasting film. With the ability to take and retake unlimited photographs some traditions can be forgotten. Now the devices are all in one, more attention needs to be

paid to the ethics of how each is used. When you take a picture with someone else in it, do you have to ask their permission? 'Is it ok to take your picture?' 'Would you mind taking part in my video?' Children also need to get into the habit of explaining what will happen to the picture or video, 'I'm then going to use it to make into a film so I can show the class.'

- *Manners* – develop an understanding in your school about where work is shown so that children understand the boundaries of where their work will go. Look at the table below for examples.

What will happen to my work?

Class	School	Individual children
What happens to the work that is taken in class for lessons?	What happens to the work that is taken by the school?	What happens to the work that is taken by another person in the school?
Work is deleted after the lesson from the camera roll. It is the person's responsibility who took the photo/video to make sure it is deleted.	Digital work that is taken during the school day will be used in the same way teachers create displays around the school. It may be used in assemblies and school-connected presentations and conferences. Some clips may also be used on the school website.	When a person takes your image/video, then they are responsible for what happens to the footage they have taken. If you are happy for your picture and/or video to be taken then be involved if they photograph or film you. If you are not happy, then you must say that to the person but remember to say thank you for asking you. You can change your mind each time you are asked depending on the topic or activity.

Managing the investment

Whether you purchase six or sixty devices for your school, the supporting equipment and software can also add to the final bill. Below are some points to consider as well as purchasing the actual devices.

- *Budgeting to include software* – devices using the operating system developed and distributed by Apple (iOS) run software applications called apps. They can be purchased through the Apple App Store. There is a scheme whereby schools can buy software at a reduced discount for each machine (http://www.apple.com/uk/education/volume-purchase-program/). Remember to find out the price of app so you can multiply it by the number of devices you have. The price is usually reduced when you purchase for over 20 devices.

- *Additional resources* – there are a number of different peripherals which can be added. For the classroom, a basic iPad should have a good case and a screen protector. If you search the catalogues then you will see an array of different additional resources. Remember that you normally get the quality you pay for and a tablet device is a large investment not to protect properly.

- *Rules of the classroom* – consider having a rule which children are aware of when they are using the device such as 'Make sure that you are sitting down with the device when you are working and the iPad is not near the edge of the table'. 'Make sure that you have a good grip of the iPad with both hands when filming or taking pictures.'

- *Cases and screen protector* – when choosing a case, ensure that you choose one that is sturdy, fits all the way around the iPad and is a good recognisable colour. Look out for the corners of the case as well, as when iPads are dropped they tend to fall on the corner and break if the whole corner is not protected. A screen protector is also essential in the modern classroom. It is so easy to break a device when it is dropped from a height. The screen protectors can be fiddly to apply and can result in air bubbles. Don't worry if it does not look perfect as it's just good to have some protection given the number of hands the device will pass through. If you are going to use a syncing trolley or case then check that the device can still be charged with the screen protector on as some can come off or get dislodged and dirt and grime start to appear under the corners.

- *Stylus* – typing words is ok using the on-screen keyboard but sometimes tablet-users can miss the feel of a pen. Most stylus pens are the same. They have a rubber end which means you can type much more quickly and it also makes drawing and sketching a more enjoyable process. Unfortunately the size of a stylus does not change, so finding a stylus that is like a pencil is impossible at the moment.

- *Brushes* – there are some clever art brushes which are being created. The Sensu Brush (https://www.sensubrush.com/) and the Nomad Brush (http://www.nomadbrush.com/) are two examples. These brushes work with apps such as ArtRage, Brushes and Procreate. They look and feel like real brushes and provide budding artists with the opportunity to paint digitally in a more natural way. They can be quite expense but a great experience for an after-school digital art club.

- *Stands* – stands can help to support the device and make it more comfortable to work on while typing. They can also be an excellent resource to ensure that the device does not slip around during group work. Some schools have been inventive in the way they have created stands using small rectangular plastic baskets with a soft padding to support the iPad as it is rested against the back of the basket. Some schools choose to invest in a more sturdy frame.

- *Keyboards* – a keyboard can make the typing process much easier when children have a large story to type up or a large piece of writing to complete. The same issues connected to children using a keyboard on a laptop or desktop computer apply here. They need to be able to locate the keys quickly, know how the shift, space and enter bars work and be able to type quickly at speed with two hands instead of the one-eyed finger tapping. Although the screen keyboard can be used just as well, a connected keyboard is excellent. There is much variance in types of keyboards. They connect through Bluetooth and the Apple keyboards are superb and easy to type on. The function keys will also control many of the other features on the iPad.

- *Photo for the desktop screen* – when you have a set of iPads they need to be recognisable as school property. Consider creating a background for each iPad. Use a computer to design one and then print it as a jpeg file. Send it to the device and then open the file up on the iPad. Save the file to your Camera Roll and then go into the Settings icon. Choose the Brightness and Wallpaper menu, press on Wallpaper and select your image. It will then ask you if you want to save it as the Lock Screen, Home Screen or Both. This can be a quick way for children to remember which exact device they have been working on especially if they have work stored on the device in a previous lesson.

- *Label the back of the devices* – using a permanent pen, remember to label the devices clearly with a large number. This can be extremely useful when counting back the devices as you can see which iPad is missing. It also means that if other year groups borrow the devices then you know which numbers are where. When things look the same in school, some mix up is bound to happen.

- *Security* – as well as numbering the back of the device, ensure that you have security tagged your devices. Search on Google for security labels for school and you can even get printed ones with the school logo on and additional details for clearly labelling it the property of the school.

- *Find My Phone* – ensure that you register the devices and install the device so you can locate where they are if you need to.

- *VGA cables* – invest in some VGA cables for your projector. This is a great addition to the classrooom so that everyone can see on your interactive whiteboard what's on your iPad. Just remember to look at which connector your iPad has.

- *AppleTV* – if your projector/whiteboard/flat screen has an HDMI port then you can plug in an Apple TV. This little device allows devices on the same wireless system to show photographs or play videos or music through the device. Don't worry if you don't have a HDMI connection on your displays. You can buy a HDMI to VGA converter so it can connect to your whiteboard.

Apple Volume Purchase Programme (VPP)

Apple operates a scheme in certain countries which allows schools to purchase apps. In effect it is a two-tire system that operates with administrators (programme managers) and teacher users (programme facilitators).

The programme manager – this person is responsible for managing the programme. They add the teacher users to the system and administer the purchase of the volume vouchers. They sit at the top of the organisational tree. They use a special web-based Apple tool to run the programme and set up programme facilitator accounts with new iTunes accounts. This would typically be the ICT coordinator along with the school business manager who is responsible for the financial aspects of the scheme.

The program facilitators – this role would typically be fulfilled by a class teacher or an individual who is responsible for ensuring that they download the apps for the devices they use on a day-to-day basis. It is worth considering setting up generic accounts, such as Class 1, Class 2, Puffins, Giraffes. As teaching staff move on then it is easier to still keep the accounts and therefore still keep the process moving along.

You can have as many programme facilitators as you need, however in a primary school you may have one for each set of iPads (Upper School and Lower School). To use an analogy – think of a tree, the trunk is the programme manager, each branch is a programme facilitator and at the end of each branch are the leaves – the devices connected to each branch. Things to remember:

- The programme manager will also need to have a new iTunes account but if they are also a facilitator as well, then they will need a separate new iTunes ID as well.
- Find out more information on http://www.apple.com/uk/education/volume-purchase-program/. The VPP works very well once it is set up.
- Most importantly it allows you to see how much you would pay for an app between the 0-19 range as well as how much it would cost over 20 devices.
- If you normally purchase for a set of 16 iPads then it can be worth seeing how much the total amount would be for 20 devices even though you may not have them. You can make quite a saving just by buying those extra few licenses.

Using apps

When it comes to searching for and purchasing apps, then the saying is quite true, there is an app for everything you can possibly imagine. So where do you begin? There are humorous apps, apps to enable productivity, apps to enable just pure creativity as well many educational apps designed specifically for primary age children. Many apps will allow you to select a 'lite' version so you can try it out before committing money. The App Store has a good search facility with reviews and screenshots so you can see what the apps look like. Below is some guidance about using apps.

- *Think creatively* – apps don't always have to be educational apps for a teacher to use them in the classroom. Sometimes the best uses can be the apps you wouldn't think of. WordFoto is an app that lets you take a picture using your camera and then you are able to enter a certain amount of words. These appear on the screen and merge with the photo in an artistic way. Consider how it could also be used to explore adjectives in an object or scene, or learning about synonyms or antonyms.

- *Try before you buy* – it's worth looking at the lite versions. Remember to read the small print so that you can look at the features that are missing or disabled. Some apps will allow you try out features on a trial basis but not be able to save.

- *Educational versions* – some app companies recognise the challenges schools have in managing the devices. Apps such a Puppet Pals or Toontastic allow you to download the free version and then you have to unlock or download a different content pack which is handy when it's your own device but multiply that process by a school set and it can become tedious. Educational versions of the apps allow schools to purchase the app once with all the content unlocked therefore making the install process smoother.

- *Pre-task/during/post-task* – because apps are so flexible it allows you as the teacher to think about how the app will integrate into a lesson. Will it be used as part of a pre-task? Will it be used to demonstrate a concept or record a process of what to do so that the children can play it back later during the activity or after to support their thinking? Is the app going to be used as part of a group task? Will it be used to consolidate new skills? How will the children record this once they have finished the task? Will it be used as a post-task, for assessment or for further work which links back to the class lesson?

Sync-ability, manage-ability

Whether you are a managing a couple of devices or sets of devices, being able to sync them to ensure they have up-to-date information is worth considering. Software always needs to be updated as bugs, new features and fixes to the software are released and can make a difference to the way a program runs. So consider the following advice:

- *Over Wi-Fi* – when plugging each of the devices into the computer, each device is listed in iTunes. There is an option within the summary section to sync over Wi-Fi. Once this is ticked then separately you can update the device through the Setting icon under the General tab on the device.

- *Syncing/charging carts* – having a few devices to manage is manageable within the day but larger numbers require a different approach. One way is to use a syncing cart. There are two versions – carts which just store and charge your devices and carts which plug into your computer and sync the devices in iTunes as well. They do tend to be expensive but for managing class sets of devices they make the job much easier.

- *Syncing cables* – some schools that have a few devices use a USB hub to plug in all the devices instead of syncing the devices one by one.

- *Use your digital leaders to update* – digital leaders can be a great support when updating software or apps. A simple exercise of synchronised 'syncing and updating' with your digital leaders can reduce the amount of management time you have to invest.

- *Use the force of the cloud* – try to work as much as you can in the cloud using content storage sites like Dropbox and Box. Just remember to keep all sensitive documents (children's data, anything with personal information or details) off a synchronised server.

Apple Configurator

This is an app available through the App Store, and is designed to make life easier for schools, technicians and coordinators deploying iPhone, iPad and iPod Touch devices. It is a good start to helping you manage the devices update and put apps on in a similar way that you would if you were managing a network using a Windows Server.

This configurator allows you to load free and paid apps on to your devices. The only rule is that the paid apps require a redemption code provided through the VPP program when you purchase a set of apps through the VPP Education Store.

Once the configurator is installed, there are three different modes: Prepare, Supervise or Assign devices.

Prepare
- This allows you to set up many devices at the same time. The design is very simple. In this mode all the connected devices can be seen.
- In this mode, it allows you to update the iOS. If you have ever had to manually update them individually then you will know what a time-saver this is!
- Apps can be imported so that you can sync them across the devices.
- There is also a profile manager option so you can configure the identical look for each device through the profile manager if you have the know-how.

Supervise

- Once the devices have been prepared, the supervise option allows you to put them into groups, apply and reapply device configurations.
- You can assign a name for each device, for example, your school name or initials and number the devices in sequential order.
- You can change and lock down different common settings.

Assign

- In this mode you can apply tweaks such as the wallpaper for the device and the lock screen – useful for placing the school logo or a jpeg photo with the school rules for how the iPads should be used.
- You can import/send documents to the assigned devices.

The whole system once set up is quick to use. There is an app counter telling you how many app codes you have redeemed so you know how many you have left. If you have VPP and have multiple devices then this free little app is worth exploring.

Operating each day

Finally, there are the day-to-day ways of managing the devices. Below are some further suggestions.

- *Timetabling* – consider how you might timetable the devices in your school. Will you have a central timetable? Will they be kept in a designated place within the school? So that each class has a turn using the technology, will each class be assigned a timetabled slot and then other slots are free? It may be an idea to have a rolling two-week programme so that teachers are able to use the devices in a core subject taught in the morning and then a foundation subject the next week.

- *A smooth take-off* – it is a good idea to begin with your more confident teachers of ICT and enable them to team-teach with less confident members of the teaching team. Are there advocates in your school who you could join up with for a lesson? This is also a useful exercise for peers observing other techniques.

- *Putting on new apps* – consider having a system of putting new apps onto the devices so that you keep the ethos of 'Every device is the same wherever you go in the school'. You can set up an individual email address for app requests so you escape the scenario of getting caught in the corridor and forgetting what the app was called. When staff find a good app in the App Store, there is the option to share the link in an email. This way, you know you have the correct web address for the app. It's a good idea when describing the process to also encourage staff to consider that if the app they are requesting is a paid app, then they will also have to multiply the cost by the number of devices you have in school.

- *Removing photographs and video because of storage* – encourage the practice, that when children have finished using the devices, if they have finished with the content they have created then they either (a) delete it from the device they were using, (b) email the finished project to themselves as a record or (c) move the content to the online storage as images and videos can be re-downloaded at a later stage if needed. When we purchase a personal device, we will often choose the highest size of storage we can afford. However, when purchasing devices in a school setting, we tend to purchase more devices with lower storage so we can get more technology into children's hands. Therefore, devices can fill up quickly if images, videos, documents and email are not removed routinely. Encouraging this practice is a good way of getting children and indeed staff into the mindset that these are not personal devices so they require managing differently to their own devices.

Using Apple devices in the classroom

You've thought about the pedagogy, the management and you now firmly have the devices in your hands. Now for the fun part... using the devices with your class and discovering the world of apps. Staff and children who have the devices at home will have enjoyed exploring different apps and each of these will bring new and exciting benefits to the classroom.

Sit next to someone with an iPhone or iPad and ask them about the apps they use and the similarities and differences will emerge. Mobile devices are personal, unless they are used in a school setting and then the purpose changes. Enter 'apps for spelling' for example, into Google and up will come a list of different suggestions. So the aim of this section is not aggregate all the apps for all subjects under one roof but to really answer one of the questions I get asked the most: 'What are the basic apps to install and where do I start now I have the devices?'

Getting started with apps

So your device has arrived, you've set it up and you're ready to go. Packed inside your iPad are some core apps ready for you to use before you even begin buying any more. So let's start at the beginning…. Here are a few ideas of how you can use them:

Camera/video

A picture can really tell a thousand words and a video can explain or show what is sometimes difficult to write. It can be used support children in many more ways:

- *Instructions* – consider giving a demonstration to your class. Ask them to use the devices and then to take photographs at crucial stages. Teach your class to make a simple dish from the meals cooked during the Second World War (making cakes works equally as well). The children have to photograph the different stages. They then have to use the photographs to write/type the instructions. If the devices are their own, the children can then take them home to make the dish with parents supporting.

- *Remember to set the rules* – before the children begin using the camera set the rules of how they should be in classroom. No teacher wants to feel like they have the paparazzi sitting in front of them snapping at inappropriate times! So have a visual prompt such as a camera icon and a green tick by it to train the children in the class when it's OK to take pictures using the devices. This will also help the children to understand that there are different modes to learning – times when we have to listen, times when we have to take notes to help us in our work, times to photograph work as an assessment or record. It is a using ICT Assessment for Learning strategy for children develop this awareness.

- *You're in the driving seat!* – during a lesson, teach a technique or a concept. As you explain ask the children to photograph key bits of information to use to support their independent work.

- *What is it?* – ask the children to photograph an unusual texture. Then allow them to ask ten questions (which require a yes or no answer) to guess what the object is.

- *Just an iPad minute* – based on the BBC Radio show, over a couple of days take some interesting pictures of objects or places around you. Place these photos in an album by creating a folder so you can use them again. Choose one child from your class. They have one minute to talk about the subject from the photo you show them from your iPad. Connect your iPad to your interactive whiteboard. If the other children have devices as well, then have the The Ultimate Buzzer app downloaded. During the minute, if the child repeats themselves, pauses as a hesitation or diverts off the subject then the rest of the class can use their buzzers to challenge the speaker. You act as moderator. If it is a correct challenge, then the child who challenged correctly can take over. The person who finishes when the clock hits zero is the winner and is awarded team/table points.

- *Scavenger photo hunt* – set the children the challenge of finding different photographs around the school grounds. For example, find the most interesting pattern you can in our playground. Find a stone with a hole in it and take a photograph of it. You can also include compass directions and paces to add an orienteering slant to the activity.

- *Assessment* – we tend to underestimate the power of the voice in favour of written work. Ask your children to film their feedback to a class task. It will support the children who struggle with writing and getting their thoughts down onto the page. This works well when combined with the strategy of two stars and a wish.

- *Evaluation* – record an evaluation of a maths or design and technology activity. Introduce a book to the class using video. Show who the main characters are and their characteristics.

Email

Email is the way of passing your content around the system and is a crucial function of using a mobile device. Below are a few ideas for using email.

- *What is it?* – connect your iPad and use it to teach children about the features of email. You can create a help guide as you go along by snapshotting the iPad screen. To do this press the home button (the round button with a square in the middle at the bottom of the device) and then the on/off button at the top of the iPad for a second. The snapshot is then stored in your camera roll. Just be careful not to hold both buttons down for more than six seconds or the device will reset.
- *Email settings* – get to know the email settings. Locate the Settings app and then scroll down to Mail, Contacts, Calendars. This tab will allow you to add an account.
- *Addresses please!* – ensure that you have entered an email address into each device. Some schools have one email for each separate device while other schools will have one email for each group set.
- *Set up work* – by having a group email it means that you can enter in one address and the same information goes onto each device. Consider how you would use this. You could email starter questions so the children can be reading and thinking about the topic before the main teaching of the lesson begins. Another way would be to attach group tasks to the email ensuring that you clearly write the group name in the email subject field. At the end of the lesson the children just need to delete the original email.

Internet

There is so much great content available on the internet. Websites do vary when viewing them on a mobile device. Some websites will be optimised for mobile devices and some do not work so well because they have different web plug-in or flash activities embedded in the page. Apple's default browser is called Safari. Below are a few ideas of using the internet:

- *Email web address* – the days when we asked children to type in long web addresses into a web browser should be well and truly over. If the children are researching a topic then it is a good idea to email the web addresses to the devices as a way of signposting children towards safer websites. The children then have to click on the web address they need and because this is an email, it means that you can also insert focus questions or success criteria if you wish as well.

- *Share* – locate the share icon which looks like a square with an arrow coming out of it. When pressed, you are presented with many different options such as sending the link to email or to Twitter.

- *Create a web clip* – frequently used or favourite websites can be created into a web clip. This is similar to bookmarking a website. When you select the option 'Add to Home Screen' then it will be added alongside the other apps. This is particularly useful for younger children for reducing the amount of time children spend browsing for useful learning websites.

- *Different strokes for different folks* – enter the text 'internet browser' into the app store and you will see that there are a host of different internet browsers for you to choose from. From Google Chrome through to child-friendly internet browsers such as Olly Browser: Protecting kids which blocks over 660 million pages that are considered to be sexually explicit. Another example is Browser for Kids. This is an iPhone and iPad web browser app which enables the parent to choose and decide what is and is not displayed in their specific browser. It also has a handy optional feature whereby parents can set the number of hours the browser can be used for in a day. After the time is up the browser locks and the parents have to type in a password to unlock it or wait until the next day when it unlocks automatically.

- *No Flash* – there is a misconception that Apple devices cannot run flash. Whilst this is true when using Safari, there are other browsers which work around this issue. Puffin Web Browser is one such example. If there is flash content on the website, a red Flash icon will appear allowing the user to press on it to load the content.

Maps

There is an atlas with a difference in the children's hands. The Maps app allows you to browse for places around the world. Switch on the 3D feature and explore the area. It is also great to look at places in detail. Just like Google Maps, if you click the right hand corner of the map where the page turn is, it will provide you with options to look at different views such as the satellite view or a hybrid version. Below are a few more suggestions for using Maps:

- *Pinch and zoom* – Using a thumb and a finger, allows you to zoom in and out of an area. With one finger, you can then move the map around.

- *Getting to know you* – Why not set the children early morning tasks using the app. Supply the children with a map of the United Kingdom. Label some parts of the map with partial words, for example, L_ _D_N for London. Can the children use the app to locate the places? This type of activity can be made as complex or simple as you wish.

Notes

Notes is a basic app for jotting down ideas. These can then be emailed or printed out. Notes can be used for children to type up basic story work or could be used as a way of improving sentence work or trying out new ideas and descriptions. Notes can also be searchable, so they are a great way of collecting minutes for staff meetings. Remember that if you are typing for a prolonged time then the on-screen keyboard may need to be substituted with a physical keyboard which is more comfortable.

iBooks

The iBooks app enables you to buy books from the iBookstore. Books read through your iPad are changing the way we use and look at text. The books purchased through iBooks tend to be more traditional in that they are a digital representation of the original book. However, iBooks allows you to use additional features. Children can bookmark important pages, highlight sections of text and use the embedded dictionary to look up unfamiliar words. If you have the speech accessibility sections turned on, then the word can also be spoken. iBooks will also allow you to organise books into 'Collections' and to open up and store PDF documents. There are also various settings that allow you to change the colour of the pages, size and font of the text. All of this aims to provide a more enjoyable reading experience for the child.

Why not download some samples to read to your class over a fortnight. Read the front covers, the blurbs and then the sample text. Your class can then decide which book they enjoyed hearing the most and would like as their class reader.

Using and organising apps

Now that you have looked at some of the basic apps that accompany your device it's time to explore the App Store. The rest of the chapter will explore useful apps for the classroom. They have been grouped into apps relating to classroom activities along with some suggestions on how to use them as a starting point. Below you will find some last words of advice:

- *Paid or free?* – the App Store is a mixture of free apps to download and apps you have to pay for. The free or 'Lite' versions allow you to get a taste for what the app will do. There will be drawbacks such as only a few of the tools or functions are available or a watermark is imprinted across content you then share. Everything comes at a price and the hard work a person has put into the design has to be paid for somehow. There will be occasions when paying for the complete version of an app will enable you to do things in an easier way.

- *Open in another app* – some apps have a dual purpose. They are able to link to different services and store work. For example, the Dropbox app is one such example. The app itself allows you to browse the files you have stored. However, if a colleague sends me a Word document in an email, by holding a finger on the attachment it will then open up and upload in that program as well so you then can get access to it on a computer. Some of the media apps such as the VLC player can play media that some other players cannot.

- *Folders* – Once you have downloaded your apps, remember to keep them in an order. To organise apps press down on an app until the icons wiggle and crosses appear. Then drag one on top of another app you wish to combine. A folder will be created with a sample folder name. You can delete this and replace it with one of your own: 'Puffin class', 'Maths apps' and so on. If you do not wish to have the app in that folder just drag it out.

- *The home screen* – consider how you might organise and customise the home screen on the iPad. Page 1 could contain all the generic apps most commonly used by all users (Photos, Notes, Camera, Email), Page 2 and 3 could contain all the apps children need to access for their curriculum subjects and Page 4 could contain apps the teachers use.

- *Availability for different devices* – remember to check whether the app you are purchasing is for the iPad or iPhone/iPod Touch or is it available for all devices? Scroll down to the bottom of the app blurb and it will tell you the compatible devices.

Apps for presenting information

Looking for something different to Microsoft PowerPoint? Then take a look at these alternatives:

- Keynote is Apple's equivalent to Microsoft PowerPoint. There are different templates and animations for children to use. It can import photographs and videos from the camera roll, mask objects, insert tables, 2D and 3D charts as well as different shapes. If you have the same iCloud account linked on each set of devices then the same presentation will appear. You can also purchase additional background templates which work with the app.

- Prezi is a presentation tool that zooms in and presents information in a non-linear way. Text and media can be added and information can be grouped and framed together so children really have to think about the information they are including in their presentation. You may want to consider having a class or iPad set Prezi account so that presentations can be uploaded and then accessed or shared with the rest of the school community at a later date.

- SMARTBoard Notebook also have an app which is similar to their interactive whiteboard software and provides another alternative to presenting information as well as building up an interactive element as well.

- Flowboard is a good alternative to presenting information. It provides the children with a template and they can change the pieces of information to suit their own presentation. Different media objects can be added on to the page. This includes texts, images and video. The great aspects about this app are the different sources you can import into the presentation. You can use the template's graphics, photographs from your camera roll or Instagram or from a folder stored on Dropbox or Box. You can even conduct a Google image search directly from the app and look for a suitable image (notwithstanding the copyright conversation of course!). Complete selections of images can be combined in a 'Gallery' so in the middle of a presentation you can flick through a collect of photographs. In the classroom, the fact that it has a Google search reduces the amount of time children spend browsing and coming out of a task and on to the internet browser.

Presentations

Explore the presentation technique of PechaKucha (www.pechakucha.org). This was originally a business presentation methodology. Developed by two architects who worked in Tokyo, they wanted to streamline presentations to avoid the 'Death by PowerPoint' scenario so they developed PechaKucha.

The concept is a simple 20 x 20:

- Your presentation must only last for 20 slides.
- Each slide must only last for 20 seconds.
- You must set the timer on each slide to automatically move on after 20 seconds.

This means that a presentation will last for six minutes and 40 seconds in total. Most people find that talking to images works more effectively than pages of text. This is a great strategy to keep children focused in a group and to build the discussion of how to present information succinctly. It also means that as a teacher, you know how long each presentation will be. Children tend to need longer when practising this technique as the first few goes can throw them when the slide moves on so quickly. Twenty seconds is definitely a short amount of time!

Apps to support 'office-type' working

Mobile technology is great when you're away from your computer but how do you make sure you can still continue to view and work on documents and other 'Microsoft Office' type files? Below are some suggestions.

- Quickoffice Pro HD – this is a great app for working with Word documents, spreadsheets and presentations. While there are different apps such as Documents To Go, Quickoffice is clean and easy to use and has the ability to track changes and add comments in an easy way. It connects to different multiple cloud applications like Dropbox, Box, Google and Evernote.

- Google – if you have Google in your school, then there are a range of different apps that help you to connect. The Google Chrome app provides a useful alternative to the Safari internet app. Use the Google Drive and iDocs HD Pro for viewing and editing your documents. The Google+ app will allow you to set up Google Hangouts which allows you to video conference with other Google users.

- PDF documents – want to read and annotate PDF documents? PDF Expert, Adobe Reader and Cabinet are some apps to take a look at. If you are serious about the paperless school, then apps like this can help the process. Email a worksheet in PDF form and then use the annotation tools to write answers in. The annotated document can then be send to an individual email account as a record.

- GoodReader, Dropbox, Box and CloudOn are apps for seeing and managing files and are great for those moments when you need to see documents you have stored there.

- Pocket is a useful app that works like a clipboard. Websites and useful links can be attached and then viewed later through the app.

Apps for writing

There are different ways of getting children to write using apps. Here are a few to load on first:

Book Creator

What is it? Book Creator is a great app for supporting children in creating their own books. Children can create multimedia books and then publish them to iBooks. Text and images can be combined together on a page. Children can easily record sound clips and place them around the page. Use the app to create project books, storybooks and non-fiction books. A very easy app to use.

Why is it a great app to use? Book Creator provides the children with a blank canvas to write their own books. The ability to include their own voice in sound clips and insert photographs and video makes this a great multimedia aid. Use it as a record of assessment for children to track their progress in music or a project they are building up. Or use it to produce a simple talking book.

Comic Life

What is it? Comic Life is the app version of the popular comic book software. Use the app to take photographs and then insert various call outs, text boxes and speech bubbles. The lettering looks like it's from a comic.

Why is Comic Life a great app to use? This is a fun way for the children to produce comic strips from scratch and using traditional templates. Why not produce a school tour in a comic strip or use it to explain a science concept and write up an experiment? It is great that you can use your own photographs you have taken with the camera roll and you can even colour the image to look more comic-like.

Word Foto

What is it? WordFoto is an app that allows you to take a photograph and then add ten words to the picture. The words are then wrapped and morphed against the photograph.

Why is WordFoto a great app to use? A simple app which can be used for descriptive writing, poetry and for exploring the concept of words and pictures together.

Lifecards

What is it? Inside the app are different writing templates like postcards and newspapers. The children can then type in their work.

Why is Lifecards a great app to use? Sometimes when using an app it can be useful to just have a template to get the children started and so they focus on the work rather than the look. You could use it when the children return from the summer holidays. The children have to use a holiday picture and use the template to create the card. Print these off and create a holiday display at the beginning of the new academic year.

Apps for rote learning and drilling

Some apps can make the business of learning your times-tables or weekly spellings fun. Provide the children with a paper-based score card so they can track their progress. Place these in a zippy wallet and attach them to your maths display so children know where to access them. Here are some apps to begin with:

Percy Parker.

What is it? Percy Parker is the app version of the software with the same title. The app sets each of the times-tables to music. The songs are very catchy and were a firm favourite with some of the children I used to teach.

Why is Percy Parker a great app to use? Setting times-tables to music is a great way to begin learning them. Children can plug in their headphones and sing away at home or link the iPad up to the interactive whiteboard and the whole class can sing along.

Early Birds: Times Tables Training

What is it? Early Birds is the app for training children on their times-tables. Choose a table, press all the multiples in that times-table and see if you can beat your time.

Why is Early Birds a great app to use? This is a colour app and great fun. Provide the children with a record card so they can track their progress. If the children are using the same device then there is also the option to add themselves as a player. This will store their data and produce a best times sheet from the 2x table to the 12x table. Very useful for looking at the speed of your children's recall.

Squeebles Times Tables

What is it? Squeebles Times Tables works in the same way as Early Birds except it displays the multiplication question and the children enter in the answer.

Why is Squeebles a great app to use? Just like Early Birds, Squeebles provides a colourful way of practising times-tables. You are able to load different players and it will track your scores. It has a nice option called 'Your Tricky Tables' whereby it will provide you with more questions based on the tables you answer incorrectly. As you progress, you win different Squeebles, medals, stars, spins, themes and trophies which all add to the fun. A great addition to varying the children's paper-based routine.

SpellBoard

What is it? SpellBoard is the great app for learning weekly spellings. Enter your spellings in and it will generate a test for you.

Why is SpellBoard a great app to use? Very much like the times-table apps, you are able to load different children so it stores a record of their progress. You can enter your weekly words, place them in a sentence and record both the word and sentence using your voice so you can place the word in context. You can also attach a picture to the word as well. The app will mix the words up and also the iPad app has three different activities (word scramble, word search and missing letters). So no more having to create these out of paper and it is personalised to each child. You can enter your own words as well as use the word lists already loaded.

Apps for video productions

There are some easy-to-use apps for making videos apart from just pointing your camera and shooting. Here are five video apps to get you going:

iMovie

What is it? iMovie is Apple's own version of its movie editing software. You have two options – create your own video project following the more traditional ways of editing film on a timeline or create a movie trailer using a template.

Why is iMovie a great app to use? Video editing is great fun and you can be up and making films in no time. Although the app is simple to use, it presents the basics of film editing. There is a timeline and children can trim and add clips and play around with the sequence just by dragging and dropping the clips in the correct places. Audio, video and photos can be inserted to create the finished product. There are some pre-determined theme templates such as reporting the news, which can be incredibly useful in the classroom.

VideoFX and 8mm

What are they? VideoFX and 8mm are two apps that can apply different effects to the video footage you are shooting.

Why are VideoFx and 8mm great apps to use? Some software is specially created for multiple platforms. With the rise of mobile devices, cut-down versions of the software are produced. The video editing software, iMovie is one example of this. The iMovie app has some of the features of the full version such as the ability to import footage and then trim clips however there are a number of limitations when it comes to effects, titles and transitions. There are a number of different apps that can apply an effect to footage you shoot using the camera on your device. Two examples of these are VideoFX and 8mm. I particularly like the black and white television screen on VideoFX for the classroom. Set the children a television report to complete during a World War II topic explaining key events. 8mm works is a similar way. Both export or save to the camera roll so you can then import them into an iMovie project.

I Can Animate

What is it? I Can Animate is a great app for getting started with animation. Point the camera and then just press the camera icon and you are animating from scratch.

Why is I Can Animate a great app to use? This app is simple and easy to use. I especially like the fact that onion-skinning is included. Once you have taken a frame, the second you move the camera it displays a ghost image of the previous frame. This helps children to produce a smoother animation. Within this app is also a function to produce time-lapse animation whereby you can set up a camera to take a photograph every 'x' number of seconds or minutes over a given time period. At the end you can replay the video and see an action which took hours to create in minutes.

VideoScribe HD

What is it? VideoScribe HD provides a blank canvas where you drag images and write words to explain a concept. The great aspect about this app is that it draws out the process for you in the order in which you placed them on the page. This is a great way of explaining a concept and thinking carefully about the things you wish to say in a visual way.

Why is Video Scribe a great app to use? This is a technique made popular by the RSA Animate (www.thersa.org/events/rsaanimate) series. Watching one of these will sum up the concept behind VideoScribe HD. Ken Robinson's 'Changing Paradigms' is particularly worth a look. It is a good idea to watch the first minute or two so the children can understand the idea before trying out the app. The divided brain is one such example (http://www.thersa.org/events/rsaanimate/animate/rsa-animate-the-divided-brain).

Apps to explain learning or for assessment

There are some apps which provide you with a blank whiteboard, pens and will record every action, movement and word spoken by the person. Here is just one example:

Explain Everything

What is it? Explain Everything is a great app for assessment. The children can play text, insert photographs on a canvas and then annotate or describe what is happening. Multiple slides can be inserted, making this an ideal way to produce video podcasts. The finished video can then be exported to the camera roll, YouTube and a host of cloud-based storage facilities.

Why is Explain Everything a great app to use? This app allows children to assess their work and visually demonstrate their understanding. Use this app for children to talk about a concept or get the children to take a photograph of their work and then visually point out the different elements they would improve as part of their Assessment for Learning strategies. Due to the fact that multiple slides can be created beforehand, the children can create talking presentations, books or 'What I know about… (a topic)' type tasks in maths, history, geography and so on. It is an incredibly versatile app to use in the classroom and one in which it is lovely to hear the children talk about their learning.

4 Using ICT in English

ICT can play a powerful role in supporting all children with their literacy work. In speaking and listening, for example, children can uses their voices to record their stories and instructions or explore how they can add expression when reading aloud. Children can listen to recordings of stories as well as following the text in the book. ICT can also fully support the writing process: from mind-mapping thoughts to exploring the different ways ideas and stories can be represented. Apps can also be used to help in drama lessons, by placing children in the role of director, producer and actor all rolled into one. Below are some suggestions for how you might incorporate ICT across the different aspects of the English curriculum.

Speaking and listening

ICT can be used very effectively to enhance and extend the speaking and listening opportunities of the children in your class. We learn to communicate effectively through the power of speech from a very early age before we develop the skills of the written word. ICT can be an effective way to capture the children's ideas if they struggle to convert their thoughts into writing and can be used as a vehicle to develop speaking and listening skills. Try the following ideas:

- *Adverts* – as part of work on persuasive writing, ask the children to create their own adverts, for example, for a chocolate bar, the school fete or the school production. Using a program such as Audacity or a podcasting piece of software, the children can then add music and other effects. Some regional grids for learning do provide access to music clips at little or no cost to the school. For example, the South East Grid for Learning (www.segfl.org.uk) provides access to a schools' version of Audio Network (www.audionetworkplc.com). This is a professional production music library with music that has been used in many popular television programmes. Creating adverts can also be a great way of teaching children some of the skills of marketing and promoting themselves and their product.
- *Radio shows* – listen to various radio shows aimed at children. Explore the podcasts on iTunes or the BBC website. Explore with the class how a radio show has been created. What does the presenter do? Where do they use music and why? What types of questions are they asking? Are they asking them to gain more information or illustrate

a point made? There are many cross-curricular links that can be made. As part of a topic on the Romans, for example, the children could plan their own show live at the Coliseum. They could interview the gladiators just before they enter the arena and then afterwards if they make it out alive. The children could make their own moving chariots to race, and the winner's story could then be told. They could also compose some Roman pieces of music to use as a soundtrack.

- *Talking displays* – there are some great tools around to develop communication (www.talkingproducts.com). These are products children can talk into and can then be stuck on to displays or used to support English work. These products range from microphones which plug in to a USB socket, to specially crafted recordable speech bubbles where you can record a 10 second clip of information and then the whole speech bubble can be stuck onto a display. Why not record the learning objective/ instructions to support children or ask the children to talk about the display in their own words and then attach that to the display?

- *Recording stories* – after planning a story map for a creative piece of writing, ask the children to use this as a scaffold to record their story. Alternatively they could use a well-known fairy tale and adapt or embellish the story as they go along. The children could also record a few pages from their current reading book. As a teacher it provides you with valuable feedback on how their fluency and expression is developing. It is also useful for the child themselves to hear how fluent they are when reading.

- *Providing instructions to support group work* – using your interactive whiteboard and the sound recorder, set up a group task on the board with the instructions on what to do. The children can record their feedback on how the task went or if it is a task to be completed over a few days they can record their progress. You can also record some 'Don't forget…' types of questions. Use talking tins (see 'Nervous beginner' section on page 115) or postcards to record what the children need to do then those that need to can re-listen to the instructions as necessary, helping them to become more independent.

- *Using dictation software* – there are some great pieces of software which are now becoming more sophisticated at listening to a child's voice and converting it into text. Dragon Dictate by Nuance (www.nuance.co.uk/dragon/index.htm) is one such example. There is still a need to train the software to recognise the words but the accuracy is improving. This type of software is useful in giving a voice to and helping those children with extremely poor fine motor skills, handwriting difficulties or specific learning needs.

- *Creating audiobooks/stories* – listen to some examples such as *A Bear Called Paddington* by Michael Bond (HarperCollins) or the *How to Train Your Dragon* series by Cressida Cowell (Hodder Children's Books). Ask the children to tell you what they notice about how the story is read and what the reader does to keep the audience listening and at times in fits of giggles. By modeling how a story is read, it can support the children in their reading.

- *Recounts of school trips* – use software such as Photo Story to import photographs taken on a school trip and then record what is happening in each picture. Different effects can also be added.
- *Recording speeches* – why not try recording an alternative Christmas speech? Or when it is time for the school council elections, the children could record their speeches for the children to playback.

Speaking and listening

Try these simple ways of combining ICT and speaking and listening in your classroom:

- Set up a listening corner with CDs or digital audiobook downloads.
- Provide a flip video camera for the children to use to retell their stories. Ask them to look back over the footage. Give the children an evaluation card so they can look at their work more critically. For example:
  - What was the best part of your story to watch? Why?
  - Write down two ways you can improve your story.
  - Re-record your work again. Watch both clips. Which version is better? Why?
- Explore 'Talking tins' (http://www.talkingproducts.com). These are small tin cans that contain a recorder which allows you to record a short clip. These can form part of a display where children record their thoughts, ideas or descriptions. They also produce many similar products including postcards, talking albums and talking invitations.

Talking books

Create talking books using presentation software such as PowerPoint or using your interactive whiteboard software. Encourage the children to storyboard their work and to break down their story into pictures. Either get the children to draw the images on paper and photograph these with a digital camera or use a painting software package. Record sound clips using Audacity (http://audacity.sourceforge.net). Save these clips and then embed them on the slide along with the image.

This doesn't need to be reserved just for talking books. The same technique could be used to support written work in science or instructional writing.

Interactive whiteboard tip!

Explore the use of sound on a Promethean interactive whiteboard. Locate the sound recorder in the special tools menu. This is one of the easiest tools for children to use. When the icon for the sound recorder is clicked a simple recorder is displayed with two buttons – a record button and a stop button. To record, just press the button, speak into the USB microphone (or the internal microphone if your laptop has one). Once you have finished recording just hit the stop button. A sound icon will appear and can be dragged onto the page. Begin by recording:

- Instructions for a group task.
- Classroom observations of what the children have been doing.
- A general knowledge wall full of facts, each day the children have to reveal a fact for the day much like an advent calendar.
- Sound clips for new styles of music. The children have to identify the instruments they can hear.
- Descriptions of a character with audio descriptions all around the page. The same could also be applied to a description of a plant or an explanation of how the water cycle works.

The great part about the sound recorder in Promethean's software is that the files can be saved altogether with the flipchart so there's no need to link them!

Using a sound recorder

EXPERT

Take the use of inserting sound into your interactive whiteboard file one step further. Every time a sound is inserted the icon appears as an object which means that you can adjust the transparency settings. The following techniques will allow you to create the effect so when an picture is clicked it plays a sound:

Select the sound icon. Stretch this over a picture by clicking the icon and then making it bigger in the same way you would with a picture in Microsoft Word. Ensure that the icon fills the whole of the picture. You will just be able to see your picture behind the icon. Click on sound icon and look for the transparency slider or use the transparency settings. Slide the slider across so that the image of the sound icon disappears.

- Use the above technique to make interactive flipchart pages. Take a photograph of a school trip. Using a sound recorder, ask the children to record their impressions and highlights from the day. Stretch the sound icon over the child's face and then make it transparent.
- Set up an online folder (box.com, Dropbox or Google with Drive Tunes installed) for your class to save their finished interactive stories to. Use this as an online book library. Some of these websites will allow you to create a special link to these folders so there is no need to log in. Alternatively, use one of the dedicated apps to access these and then the children can listen to the stories other children have created.

Sound stories

Ask the children to retell a story through using sound.

1 Begin by either drawing or finding an image to use as a story map background.
2 Ask the children to write the setting of their story in their planner books.
3 Explain that they are going to record story 'hot spots' on the map or background.
4 (For Promethean users) Click the icon of the hammer and the spanner to bring up the special tools bar. When the icon for the sound recorder is clicked a simple recorder is displayed with two buttons – a record button and a stop button. To record, just press the button, speak into the USB microphone (or the internal microphone if your laptop has one). Once you have finished recording just hit the stop button. A sound icon will appear and can be dragged onto the page.
   (For non-Promethean users) Use a sound recorder like Audacity to record the children's story clips (then follow instruction 5 and 6).
5 Ask the children to record their story in small sections using the sound recorder. As they record each section the children drag them to the correct sections on their map.
6 At each stage place a number beside each sound clip so the listener knows the correct story structure to follow.
7 At the end of each sound clip include an instruction, for example, 'Go to the castle to continue the story'. Alternatively there might be a question that the children have to answer and write down the answer.
8 Ask the children to place a button which they hyperlink to another slide for when then have finished reading each page.

Reading

The web is changing the way that we read. There is more useful information for people to access than ever before. You can be better informed, educated and entertained at the click of a mouse. We read text in a different way when it is on the screen. Electronic books have transformed the way books not only look and respond but have also challenged the understanding of how we can interact with text. Below are some ways of combining ICT and reading together.

- *Questions for guided reading* – using a presentation piece of software such as PowerPoint or your interactive whiteboard, display a section of text which you have the copyright for. Use this as a basis for a guided reading session. Ask the children to read the text and then, working as a group, the children can record their answers to the questions.

- *Interactive whiteboard software* – make sure that your software is loaded onto your laptop. This then provides you with the flexibility to use the software features. Use the fill tool and, for example, ask the children to fill in the different synonyms for 'said'. Or using the highlighter the children can be story detectives within a text. Ask the children to focus on a character and to find all the evidence relating to that character. Using two different colours, ask the children to highlight the words which give them direct information about the characters in the text and those which lead them to make a judgement on the character.

Using eBooks in the classroom

Books have been used for many years to support teaching and learning and for pure enjoyment. However, just like in Charles Dickens' *A Christmas Carol*, the development of technology, and specifically mobile technology such as iPads, has led to the written word developing its own past, future and present, as shown below.

Past	Present	Future – the book +
• Physical copy • Ability to share and huddle round a book • Various shops and places to purchase and take out books	• Digital copy of a book • Portable • Text can be enlarged • Can bookmark important pages • Can make notes on the book • Can record your own voice	• Links to extra reading • Further activities • Pages can include animation • Pages can include sound clips • Widgets can be embedded into pages with the ability to display HTML, presentations, videos, sounds, 3D pictures and quizzes

eBooks can come in different formats from the industry standard of an ePub through to PDFs and Apple's own iBooks. Through the App Store, iPad users can download books from the iBooks store but can also download the Kindle apps widening the range of books which can be used. Schools are now beginning to explore the potential of using eBooks. Here are some ideas for using them in the classroom:

- Begin by sharing the book together and read through the text. You can either connect up your iPad to your interactive whiteboard using a VGA cable or have the same book on each iPad.
- Use the highlighters in the book to identify the characteristics of characters or main events in a story.
- Explore book apps such as *The Pedal Lady* or *The Unwanted Guest* from Moving Tales. The story is narrated but children also have the ability to record their own voice. This is a great tool for reinforcing reading-aloud skills and reading with expression.
- Younger children and beginner readers can enjoy the timeless classics of Ladybird reading books. These have been updated and children can hear the narration and then read it aloud for themselves. There are also sound effects embedded into the book.
- There are some beautiful picture books such as *Imagine A Night* and *Imagine A Day* by Sarah Thomson (Atheneum Books) which can be used to stimulate creative writing. The accompanying illustrations are stunning. Connect your iPad up to your interactive

whiteboard with a special adapter and it can be used with a starter lesson for creative writing.

- Explore the future of books by looking at the excellent *The Fantastic Flying Books of Mr Morris Lessmore* by W. E. Joyce (Simon and Schuster). Based on a short film, the book has been animated and further activities placed within the book from learning a tune on the piano through to visual effects within the pages.

- Many schools use the Oxford Reading Tree to get children reading. There are a number of digital versions available which can be read online (www.oxfordowl.co.uk/home/reading-owl/find-a-book/library-page). This is a superb resource for parents, especially if their child forgets their reading book or needs more books to read.

- Encourage the children to read. There are books, comics, newspapers and a host of different things to read which are available through a computer or on a mobile device. Rising Stars produce pdf ebooks (www.risingstarsebooks.co.uk/your-ebooks) which are well worth exploring to support your library collection.

Using an iPad to support reading activities

- If you have access to a mac computer then explore iBooks Author. This software enables the user to create their own eBook.

- Explore other apps in the classroom. Word Cloud enables children to type in words to generate a visual word cloud in the same way as Wordle. Ask the children to think of their main character and to type words to describe that character. For example, use Roald Dahl's *Fantastic Mr Fox* to describe his character and his feelings towards the three farmers.

- Ask the children in small groups to record the story with accompanying sound effects using a voice recorder app.

The future of the modern eBook on the iPad certainly looks exciting with many possibilities pushing the boundaries of what books may look like in the future. As well as the pictures being conjured in our head they may also come alive before our very eyes!

Create your own books

CREATIVE

There are a number of different websites and pieces of software that enable you to create reading books of your own:

- My 'e' book (www.myebook.com) allows you to create a book online. You can begin by using basic templates; although they are limited it will get you started.

Alternatively, you can begin with a blank canvas. From here you can then begin to type the text of your story. You can add subsequent pages and then enhance your book with various multimedia items such as sound clips and images. Once you have finished your creation you can publish the book. You are provided with a URL/web link and more importantly HTML code. This may look like a lot of jumbled text all in one place but it really is the computer code for the books you have just published. Copy this code and then you can embed it into your school website or blog so people can read your books and turn the pages just like a real book.

- iBooks Author is Apple's own solution to publishing your own book/textbook (https://itunes.apple.com/gb/app/ibooks-author/id490152466?mt=12). This is a Mac only piece of software but provides some great opportunities for experimenting and looking at how books can be created. Teachers or indeed children can have a go at just trying to create their own book. As well as text, many different elements can be incorporated into the page to make the content engaging for the reader.
  - *Templates* – you are provided with different templates to use for your iBook. You can insert an introduction video and glossary.
  - *Drag and drop information* – text, Word documents, images and videos can be dropped in.
  - *Interactive Widgets* – drag these into your book and add a little interactive touch to your documents. These widgets embed into your book and allow the user to interact with the content you have embedded. There are different types, for example:
    - *HTML* – this is code from an internet web page which enables you to embed it into your book. For example, look up a place on Google Maps and it provides you with the HTML embed code. You can then embed that code into your iBook.
    - *3D images* – these images enable the user to rotate a 3D image whilst reading text within the book to support their learning.
    - *Video and audio* – sound clips and video files can be inserted in the page to illustrate your point.
    - *Chapter reviews* – At the end of a chapter, a review can be placed with questions to test the understanding of the reader. Questions can be multiple-choice, choosing the correct image or labeling an image. It can also contain a mixture of all three of the different types of questions.

Use your finished eBooks for guided reading. Tasks for the children to complete whilst they are reading the book could be included as well as a review section after each chapter.

Writing

The ability to word process and communicate using digital text can make the writing process easier for some children. By using spelling tools, a thesaurus and reorganising text, they can produce work to a high standard in a shorter space of time. Below are some suggest for how ICT can support children's writing:

- *Story maps* – story maps are a great way to get children thinking about different ways of planning a story. Pie Corbett in his storytelling book *The Bumper Book of Storytelling into Writing* (Clown Publishing) suggests that, based on storytelling research, a way to support children's writing is to ask them to draw a story map and then use this to tell their story. On a blank interactive whiteboard flipchart, collect different examples of images the children might use in their work. Have a different page for each genre – fairy tale characters, dragons, 'baddies', 'goodies', princesses, methods of transport, buildings and so one. Using the copy and paste function, ask the children to then create their own story map.

- *Using a word processor* – take the word-processing of stories one step further. Although the word processor can provide a blank space to work it can also be used as a structured writing frame. Type headings for the children to use as a writing frame. They can use the mouse to select the text and drag sentences around and edit their work in a more fluid way. Using tables is also a great way of supporting writing. Insert a table with two columns. In the left-hand column type in the main heading and then write questions for the children to answer. These could be based on a character or the setting. The children can then use the other column to compose sentences for their answers.

Typing skills

NERVOUS

- Improve your children's typing skills. Draw or take a photograph of a computer keyboard. Reduce the picture down on the photocopier so it will fit inside the back of the children's spelling book. Each week when you provide the children's spellings, encourage them to write out their spellings and then turn to the page at the end and 'type' them out. Can they type out just the letters and then place a capital letter at the front of the word using the shift keys?
- Let the children type their stories up on a simple word processor. This provides them with the opportunity to edit, improve and retype their work.

Story writing

ENTHUSIASTIC

2 Create A Story is a piece of software by 2Simple (www.2simple.com). The aim is to make the process of using ICT within another subject simple to use. The software is great for Key Stage 1 and into Key Stage 2. The 2 Create A Story software is a simple story-writing program. Children are able to draw a picture with the fat or thin colouring pens and then type text into a box below to write their story. New pages can be added so children can create their own books or rewrite a favourite story of their own. Animations, sound recording and sound effects can also be added, all enhancing the effect of the text.

Tools for writing

EXPERT

Encourage the children to use different tools for writing. Writing on the internet or blogging can encourage different forms of writing. Create a blog that the children write with adult supervision.

Brainstorm different types of writing the children could create, from book reviews, to story writing and journalistic writing. Explore how these are already written on the web and how they also include different forms of media. Ask the children to compare different styles of writing. How are cookery blogs written and how do they differ from a fashion blog or a games blog?

Teach the children how to write a blog post and embed accompanying photographs to support the points they are making in the post.

If you host your own WordPress.org blog, the editor also allows the children to toggle between visual writing and text code. This will enable the children to create writing but also see the code behind a post and develop an understanding of how embeddable media like YouTube is placed into a post. This way of enhancing their writing with different forms of media should also help children to see how they can communicate their ideas more effectively.

The Jolly Postman

CREATIVE
ICT

This book can form the basis of a great cross-curricular English project, culminating in the children making their own Jolly Postman book.

Begin by reading *The Jolly Postman* by Janet and Allan Ahlberg (Penguin). Tell the children that they are going to create their own version of the book. In the book they will need:

- A map showing who the Jolly Postman will deliver his letters to.
- To choose between 3-6 people to deliver letters to.
- To work out what each person will receive through the post.
- To think of a gift the whole village gives to the Jolly Postman when he returns home as a thank you for working so hard delivering all his letters.

There are many different uses of ICT which can then be incorporated into this topic. Here are a few ideas:

- One of the letters could contain an exercise, cookery or instruction DVD. Ask the children to film a short clip and burn this on a DVD. The children need to write the instructions or the script and then organise themselves to create it.
- Use a painting package to create the map of the Jolly Postman's route.
- Use collaborative writing tools to collect ideas about the different things that each person could be given. There are often many characters that the children want to put into their books like a wolf, a witch, a giant or a gingerbread man. Ask the children to work together on Google Docs, PrimaryPad or Twiddla to suggest the ideas. This will support the children who find contributing ideas difficult.
- Once the book has been created, ask the children to write an author review and then post these as separate blogs. The children then have to read one of the books as part of their reading tasks throughout the week and leave a comment under that author's review.

Apps for writing

- Comic Life – is a great way of introducing comic writing to children or presenting a story in a different way. Comics come in a couple of different styles. Children can insert photographs from the iPad's camera to illustrate their comic. They can add text as well as groovy cartoon writing to really provide their comic with an authentic feel. The app also has a unique feature whereby children can share comics they have created over Wi-Fi.
- Lifecards – is an app which has various blank templates for children to use to structure their writing. There are templates for newspapers, postcards and various others. These can be filled with photographs from the iPad's camera and text can be typed straight onto the template.

Drama

Drama is an excellent vehicle for providing speaking and listening opportunities. Different types of media can be used to stimulate discussion and be used as a springboard for drama work in the classroom. Below are some ideas for how ICT can be used to support drama.

- *Performance poetry* – there are many excellent examples of authors and poets performing their work on You Tube. Take a look at Michael Rosen reading his poem 'No breathing in class' (http://www.youtube.com/watch?v=z1cfVQyrQ3Q). Showing the children examples of how to perform poetry can be a great way for them to look at tone, pace, expression and communication skills.
- *Using digital clips and DVDs* – use different clips to begin a lesson or a timely clip can illustrate a specific learning point. There are some great 'Starting Stories' DVDs produced by the British Film institute (BFi) which can be used to work into a freeze frame/tableaux activity (http://filmstore.bfi.org.uk/acatalog/info_3962.html). The clip entitled 'Baboon on the Moon' (http://ftvdb.bfi.org.uk/sift/title/747538) is a wonderful example of how an animated clip can support children with empathising with the concept of loneliness or a sense of duty. The story is about a lone baboon character who has the sole task of lighting the moon every day. Right at the very end of the clip we witness emotions from Baboon that support us as teachers to pose questions to the children such as, how would you feel if you had the job of lighting the moon each day? How do you know that Baboon misses people back on Earth? Coupled with different active drama strategies (http://dramaresource.com/strategies), the clip can produce some powerful work.

Apps for drama

Puppet Pals

Puppet Pals is a stunning app to use to support creative writing and speaking and listening. Puppet Pals creates a stage for children to use to retell their story. Children can choose to use characters that can be downloaded in genres to use on their story as well as backgrounds. When children have selected their characters and their background they press the record button and then act away, moving the characters around with their fingers whilst narrating at the same time.

The most impressive feature is that children are able (with the director's pass edition) to cut out characters and backgrounds from photos. This means that children can paint, draw or use backgrounds taken by the iPad's camera. They can also cut out characters in the same way. Children can literally place themselves on the stage. They could transport themselves back to World War II and talk about what life was like then.

The finished film can be exported to the camera roll for use in other programs.

Toontastic

Toontastic is similar to Puppet Pals, in that children can record a story they have created using characters and backgrounds. Here, however, the characters are cartoon–like and their arms and legs move as you animate them, which the children enjoy. Characters are arranged in different genres. However when it comes to selecting characters all the different characters are displayed for you to use. There are static backgrounds or children can draw and use their own background created with simple painting tools within the app.

The story is semi-structured through a basic 'story-arc'. This helps to structure the children's thinking in creating a story. More sections can be added to the basic story arc so the story can be made as simple or complicated as needs be. One really great feature is that each stage is explained to the children so they understand about the different stages of the story. Because the app allows you to design your own background, it can be used to describe things in different subjects as well, for example science – how the water cycle works or how a bee pollinates a flower. The only two slight minor drawbacks are that the instructions are provided in an American accent and when exporting finished stories they are saved on the Toontasic website so there isn't the ability to download your masterpiece. However, you can link to it as it will have a web address.

Using your ICT resources

As well as the use of ICT to support different areas of the English curriculum, there are also ways that ICT equipment can support English activities. Take a look at the equipment you currently have in school. Below are some suggestions to get you started.

Digital camera

A digital camera can be used to support English in the following ways:

- *Literacy stimuli* – photographs can be great for generating ideas about a scene. I use the Pixar character of Mr Potato Head to support the children's written descriptions of a scene. What are the things you can see, hear, touch, taste and feel in the picture?
- *Handwriting* – use the video function to record younger children forming their letters. Record children making each letter in the sand and then place these on your learning platform for children and parents to watch and copy at home.
- *Create a story for creative writing* – combine the use of storyboarding and drama to create a short narrative story, which the children have to make into freeze-frame 'still' photographs. These pictures can then be inserted into a storyboard with a description of the action and the characters' words written by the children below the images.

Overhead projector

An overhead projector can be used to support English in the following ways:

- Explore making silhouettes or creating shadow characters as part of drama work. Using the completed characters, ask the children to tell a story they have created and written during an English lesson.
- For a MFL/maths/English starter activity, place an object on the screen and ask the children to describe it to improve their vocabulary.

USB microphone

A USB microphone can be used to support English in the following ways:

- *Instructions* – support your less able children by recording the instructions for a task. Some children have difficulty retaining instructions because of short-term memory problems. These children can then play the instructions as often as they need.
- *Creating stories* – using a microphone, ask the children to record their stories onto

tape. When children speak their stories they will often add embellishments and improvements to the story. Before recording their story ask the children to jot down the main points in words or pictures to help. This will provide them with a structure to talk to.

- *Literacy* – using the microphone ask the children to read a short extract or talk about the best parts from their favourite book or the books they are currently reading. Tell the children that they will also need to say the title of the book and who the author is. Using Audacity (http://audacity.sourceforge.net) insert all these short extracts so they are one after the other. Publish these as a class 'books of the week' podcast so that other children can listen and get inspired about the books they should read next.

- *History/literacy* – in pairs, place one child in the role of a historical character or a servant of that character and the other as interviewer. Combining the use of microphones with editing software creates an obvious curriculum link with literacy. For example, the children could create adverts to launch products or school events or create radio shows on a chosen topic area.

Digital video camera

A digital video camera can be used to support English in the following ways:

- *Instructions* – ask the children to create instructions for making their favourite sandwich in the style of a 'How to…' guide.

- *Drama* – ask the children to take on the role of a character and then to film an interview with that character. In the trial of Goldilocks and the Three Bears, for example, one child could take on the role of baby bear and the group could film an interview after he has discovered Goldilocks has eaten all his breakfast.

- *Literacy* – create a video diary. Instead of the lethargic, egocentric talk that pervades many of the reality television programmes, why not ask children to research a famous person from history or a famous scientist, writer, artist or musician and then present the facts in a different way. The children could combine this with drama and take on the role of that character and provide information or facts about themselves.

Visualiser

A visualiser can be used to support English in the following ways:

- *Editing skills* – use the visualiser after or during a creative writing lesson, or for demonstrating a good plan or diagram someone has drawn.

- *Reading books* – use the visualiser so that all the children can share the book.

- *Work in progress* – encourage volunteers to work in real-time under the visualiser. Children can borrow great ideas they see while the child is working.

Scanner

A scanner camera can be used to support English in the following ways:

- *Homemade books* – create your own digital library for your website or to put on your Learning Platform. Collaborate on making a book together, then take this a stage further and scan the children's work in and ask them to narrate the book too. The children could design the front cover or create illustrations using some free online software such as Sumopaint (www.sumopaint.com).
- *Literacy writing* – as anyone in the classroom knows, when a child produces a great piece of work it is an opportunity to celebrate and to share this with others so they can learn from it. Scan a child's piece of work into a flipchart and then using the pen tool on the whiteboard, ask the children to improve and edit this work. At the end of the exercise print out the work and the child can use this as a guide to improving their work.

Interactive whiteboard

An interactive whiteboard can be used to support English in the following ways:

- *Creative writing* – using the pen tool, draw a map of an imaginary land and mark the different places where various make-believe characters might live. Discuss with the children what other features the imaginary world would have and draw those in too. Use this to support creative writing or a geography discussion on settlements.

Superheroes

The topic of superheroes creates a superb theme for rich English work. Just think of your favourite superhero. Is it Superman, Bananaman or SuperTed? This is a really exciting topic in which lots of strands of ICT can be included and many different curriculum activities planned. The main idea is that the children have to create their own superhero. Begin by using voting devices to 'seed' (collect from the whole class) ideas of what makes a superhero super (see below for more information about voting devices). Ask the children to name superheroes they like and then say why they like them.

Introduce the following English and ICT activities to support this theme:

- *Write a story* – use a word processor to create a story that involves the superhero the children have created.
- *Superhero comics* – using Comic Life (http://plasq.com/products/comiclife2), encourage the children to create their own comic with their superhero as the central character. Scan in the children's hand drawings or use the web camera to place into the comic strip.
- *Playscripts* – teach the children how to create a playscript using a word processor. Show the children how to use the tab key so that all the dialogue is all in line. Ask them to create a short scene involving their superhero.

Below are some additional curriculum activities to support the topic.

- *Superhero badges* – using a design or art package, ask the children to design a logo for a 'goody' or a 'baddy'. Explore the different colours that could be used. Ask the children to draw a circle and then create their badge in the middle of it. This could then be printed and either pressed into a proper badge or stuck on to card.
- *YouTube* – stuck for superheroes? Take a look on YouTube. There are many great examples of superheroes and also clips from cartoons which may help the children to collect different ideas.
- *Design a costume* – ask the children to design a superhero costume in groups. Each group then has to create a display and take digital photographs. Use tricider (https://tricider.com/en) which is an online voting tool. Enter a question such as 'Which is the best dressed and designed superhero and why?' and the children can add their ideas. They can add a description but also upload an image of their character. Everybody can then leave constructive advice and then vote for their favourite either online or offline during a secret class vote. The winning design with the most positive feedback then receives the 'Superhero Designer of the Year Award'.
- *Superhero theme tune* – using musical instruments, ask the children to create their own theme tune for their superhero. Download theme tunes for the children to listen to from iTunes or other music download sites and then ask the children to identify the elements of a good tune. Record the children's own version.
- *A wanted poster* – using publishing software, such as Microsoft Publisher or Pages for Mac, ask the children to design a wanted poster for a superhero. What would they put in their job description?

5 Using ICT in maths

Using ICT in maths offers opportunities for looking at mathematical concepts in different ways. There are children who struggle with the leap from concrete apparatus to the more abstract areas of number, shape and space. ICT can really support you in demonstrating some of the trickier maths concepts, and as the ICT offers the opportunity to change and then manipulate objects or undo actions, children can explore without the fear of getting things wrong.

There can be an assumption that the only ICT to use in relation to maths is the calculator. In fact, the world of apps and the internet has brought maths alive with technology.

So where do you begin? Below are a few ideas for incorporating ICT into your maths lessons.

Using spreadsheets

Spreadsheets are really underused in primary school. They can help children to find the sums of amounts quickly as well as graphing results. There is also the extended challenge to stretch children to apply formulas to their work so that the computer works harder. Below are some suggestions for using spreadsheets with your class:

- *Party planning* – tell the children that they are going to plan their own class end-of-term party. Collect ideas on the board for the types of food they would like to make: sandwiches, cakes and so on. Explain to the children that they will be preparing and making the majority of the food. When the ideas have been collected, ask the children to draw up a shopping list. This can either be carried out as a class or each table can be responsible for drawing up separate areas such as deserts, sandwiches, fruit and so on. In groups and using computers, ask the children to then research how much each item is going to cost using a supermarket website. Give the children a budget and encourage them to look for bargains and offers where they might be able to make a saving. Show the children how to create a simple spreadsheet listing the food items and their price. The children can then use the autosum function or enter a formula for adding up the total amount.

  Using a different graphing package, create a pictogram or for upper Key Stage 2, the children could produce a pie chart based on the percentage of each food type. The data can then be interrogated. Talk to the children about the various ways data can be displayed. How can we make our results easier to understand? Use voting devices, if you have them, to answer question such as, 'Which area did we spend the most on?' and 'Out of the 16 pieces of fruit we cut up, what fraction would be apples/strawberries?'

- *Christmas lists* – firstly ask the children to create their own Christmas present wish list. Then, using a catalogue, encourage the children to search for gifts for family, friends and hypothetical gifts they think you or their headteacher might like. Enter the data into a spreadsheet. How much have they spent? Using a word processor, ask the children to then draw up the definitive list. Extend this by asking them to write a letter explaining why they believe they have been good enough for Christmas presents this year!

Numbers and the number system

Simply 'playing around with numbers' is a necessary skill in learning about numbers and the number system. Children need to practise counting forwards and backwards, reading and writing numbers so that they take on board the transference between physically counting objects to more abstract forms. ICT can be very useful in supporting this process and motivating the children with sound effects such as people applauding and visual stimuli. Here are a few ideas and resources to support children's learning of number:

- *Counting* – on your whiteboard, there is the possibility to clone an object so the same object is repeated time after time. Begin by either placing a shape to represent a coin or import a picture of a coin. When that object is dragged on to the page, right-hand click and look for the menu. Depending on the whiteboard you use it will either say drag a copy or infinite clone. Use this as a tool for counting money.

- *Sorting numbers* – bring up a timer on the board. Draw different-coloured squares around the board. Provide a label for each one. For example, even numbers, numbers under ten, multiples of five. Bring up the number cards and drag different ones on to the board. The children have to race against the clock to sort the numbers into the correct place. Then press the refresh button or undo all the actions to get back to the beginning. Can the children beat their previous time or the time of the previous child?

- *Vocabulary/word of the week* – using the random name picker from Classtools.net (http://classtools.net/education-games-php/fruit_machine/), type in the mathematical vocabulary for your topic. Throughout the week, spin the fruit machine and talk about the term with the children.

- *Place value body motion* – use a simple random number generator like the one found on http://primary.naace.co.uk/activities/. Set the generator to make a three digit number by setting the maximum number to 999. Explain to the children that the computer is going to generate a number between 1 and 999. When the number is generated, tell your class to read out the number (guide them in your loudest reading-aloud 'teacher' voice). Tell the children that they are going to say the following phrase each time, for example, '463 (insert number) is made up of...'. Tell your class that they are going to:

- pat their head for each hundred
- bend their knees and slap the top of their thighs (gently!) for each ten and finally
- for each one, turn and face a partner (in the same way for playground clapping songs) and clap their opposite hand and say one, two, three and so on. In between each number they have to clap their own hands together. You then generate the next number.

This is a really good activity for getting children active and their bodies moving. Early counting is an essential skill. Explore some of these mobile apps to help children improve and practise their number skills.

Number and place value apps

MOBILE

- Montessori Numbers – this app allows the children to learn their basic numbers up to ten by exploring a variety of different activities. From tracing the numbers to using numbers rods, counters and blocks.
- Montessori Place Value – the children are given a number to make out of place value number cards.
- Place Value by Quantum Victoria – a variety of different numbers fly around the screen. At the bottom of the screen, the children are given an instruction such as 'Find numbers with a 4 in the hundreds column' and the children need to then press on the correct numbers.
- Place Value by Joe Scrivens takes an alternative approach to place value. A number is displayed on the screen with a place value question written above such as 'How many tens?' The children have to look at the number and place the correct number of fingers down on the screen.
- Place Value MAB (Multibase Arithmetic Blocks to you and me) – is part of a collection of maths apps by Aleesha Kondys which are worth exploring. The place value app has different activities involving counting the tens and units blocks and then typing in the answer, through to making a given number by dragging up the correct blocks on to a whiteboard.

Basic maths apps

There are a number of apps available which cover general areas of maths all mixed together. Here are a few examples.

- MathsBoard – this app sets column addition, subtraction, multiplication and division questions. There is a 'workings' area where the user can try out the questions before inputting the answer.
- Ladybug Addition/Ladybug Subtraction – add up/subtract the dots on the ladybugs' backs and then tap the answer in.
- Jelly Bean Count – count the different coloured jelly beans. There are four different colours. If there are three green jelly beans then you place three fingers on the green colour bucket.
- DoodleMaths – this is a very comprehensive app to support one child's maths development. It's like having your very own maths tutor. The app covers the majority of the curriculum. The work is based around an assessment the child completes first. There are seven-a-day questions on the range of different topics and a new this week tab to learn a new area of maths. There are also some games the child can play. This is a great app to recommend to parents wishing to support their child with their maths work. There is even a parent's page where the program can be tweaked and where parents can read useful advice for support their child.
- Fraction Circles 2.0 by Hooda Math – allows you to build up different fractions which would be a good resource to use when connected to a projector for whole-class teaching.
- MathBoard Fractions – similar to the app immediately above but focused on fractions with enough challenge for your upper juniors.

Mental maths

There are a number of useful resources that can be drawn upon when testing children's mental maths skills. ICT can be used to record different tests for the children to listen to and then take as many times as they wish. This can be useful practice in the run up to SATs. Below are a few ideas for developing their mental maths skills using ICT.

- *Tests and quick fire questions* – consider using Audacity or podcasting software to record your mental maths tests. When reading questions aloud as a teacher we tend to be quite forgiving with the time. Prepare the children for listening to mental maths questions being fired at them at a fast pace by recording a test. Allow sufficient time for each question, including instructions and then record the whole test. When you begin recording the counter will count on up. This will enable you to time the length you give the children to answer the question accurately. If the software allows, you could then put the test on your learning platform for the children to practise different tests. When providing this type of test for the children, begin by playing it through a couple of times so they get used to the speed before they answer. After a couple of attempts, the children will be flying!

- *Explore the web* – Kent ICT (http://www.kenttrustweb.org.uk/kentict/kentict_sub_math_iwb.cfm) have some excellent short web resources for all aspects of your maths lesson. So do ICT Teachers (http://www.icteachers.co.uk/resources/resources_numeracy.htm)

- *Interactive mental maths display* – use some of the Talking tins (www.talkingproducts.com) to create a maths starter display at child level. Record questions for the children to answer and attach these to the wall or if you are being especially inventive an old coat you no longer need. Choose a child or children from your class who have been especially good or worked hard in maths. They have to choose a tin while the rest of the class listen for the question. If your talking tins are on a display, ask the children to make the answer using number cards or if the tins are attached to the coat the children have to write the answer on mini-whiteboards. You can re-record the questions each week or get some child 'helpers' to do it for you.

- *Link to tools* – one of the great ways to enhance interactive whiteboard resources is to link to different tools:
  - *Random number generator* taken from http://primary.naace.co.uk/activities/.
  - One of the best countdown timers my children used to love was from Classtools (www.classtools.net/education-games-php/timer). As you run out of time, the colour even changes to red.
  - http://rupertcollins.com/educationwebsites/numeracy/ provides some useful resources including the old Interactive Teaching Programs (iTPs) which are always helpful resources.
  - Woodlands Junior School (http://resources.woodlands-junior.kent.sch.uk/teacher/maths.html) always has great resources to use.

- *Sing and find out* – there are many novelty warm-ups that you can use. Take a look at the pop group Keane singing a maths problem to the tune of their song 'Everybody's changing' http://youtu.be/VzXEJh9wzx4. Challenge the children to find a current pop tune they enjoy. Can they make up their own mental maths problem to the tune?

Shape, space and measure

Visualising shapes, especially 3D shapes, can be difficult for children when they first begin. Most schools will have a box of the physical plastic shapes but ICT can support children's understanding further. There are some great pieces of software, like Poly, which can help children to understand how shapes are connected together. ICT provides the opportunity to rotate, reflect and visualise shapes in different ways.

- *Poly* (www.peda.com/poly) – This is by far my favourite program for exploring 3D shapes. I must confess, I do not have an A Level in Maths and this program helps to extend my own knowledge on how different 3D shapes are constructed. Do you know your rhombicosidodecahedron from your elongated pentagonal rotunda? No – I didn't either but with this little program you can explore these with your children and get them to choose different shapes and then tell you what they see and how this relates to the work the are doing on cuboids, prisms and pyramids.

- Primary Games (www.primarygames.co.uk/evalindex.html) are just superb maths warm-ups for all areas of maths. There are trial versions on the website but games such as Top Spot, Multiple Wipeout, Sid's Swimming pool and Balloon Burst were always favourites with my classes.

- Although not strictly an ICT resource (www.superteacherworksheets.com) provides an excellent source of worksheets to support the busy teacher. It's a great help as it provides the answers and is especially good for times when you are caught short when a supply teacher has not shown up.

- There are a number of good apps to support the teaching of measures alongside the children's practical work. ICT can support the teaching of measures by making it visual so that the children can see how to measure liquids or how to draw lines using a ruler. Many interactive whiteboards have specific maths tools such as protractors and rulers so you can demonstrate this to the children. Mostly Postie (www.ictgames.com/mostlyPostie.html) works by giving the children a parcel to weigh which they put on the scales and then have to read the amount and enter the weight on an on-screen calculator. Dial Scales from TeacherLED (www.teacherled.com/resources/dialscales/dialscalesload.html) also provides the same type of activity.

- The Measuring Cylinder iTP (http://rupertcollins.com/educationwebsites/numeracy/numeracy/measuringcylinder.swf) allows children to pour out a liquid and stop it at a certain amount.

- Interactive Resources (www.primarygames.co.uk/index.html) design a range of different measure games and activities which can be used during class inputs and to support group activities (www.teachingmeasures.co.uk/menu.html)

Shape and space apps

- Bloki – an app for making different shape pictures out of the bloki blocks.
  You could challenge the children to design the most creative picture using
  just quadrilaterals or shapes with internal angles ranging from 60–90 degrees.
- Tangram – use different shapes to create your own freehand tangram or the children
  can copy some of the predefined tangrams using templates.
- Math Geometry by Vinta Games – a useful app to test children's shape and space
  knowledge.
- Measurement HD by Emantras Inc provides different measurement activities based
  on time, measurements and capacity.

Data handling

Collecting data using technology can speed up data handling tasks so that children can
have more time to interpret the data. Ask yourself the question, when was the last time
you had to draw a graph? Technology can make the task of collecting and producing
information much quicker and easier.

- *Use the protractor* – using the full protractor, some interactive whiteboard software will
  allow you to select a colour and draw an angle. If you have selected for that angle to
  be filled in when you have finished, it will fill it in in the colour you were just drawing
  with. Repeat this process with different colours to create a pie chart you can use to
  measure different angles.
- *Use voting devices* – collect simple numeric data for data handling by using voting
  devices connected to your interactive whiteboard. How many children's favourite meal
  is pizza? The voting devices can collect the information and display it in a graph for the
  children to interpret. If the children work in small groups and use the device software,
  they can create their own questions and collect the data quickly from the class instead
  of the laborious and time-consuming way of individual children going round to every
  child in the class.
- *Unleash the Furbles* – when the software Furbles (www.ptolemy.co.uk/project/furbles)
  was released, I thought it was simply brilliant! Furbles is a piece of data handling
  software that can be used for teaching how to take data and turn it into tally charts,
  bar graphs and pie charts. Furbles are small creatures that come in different 2D shapes
  and colours. They also have different numbers of eyes (for even more fun, move your
  mouse around a Furble and look what happens to their eyes!). You are presented

with a set of these Furbles which you then need to sort into an order, be it by colour, shape or the number of eyes they have. This is the first stage. You can select it so the computer sorts the Furbles for you instead. So if you select to sort the Furbles by shape, it will then animate the sequence and sort the Furbles and then animate them into a bar graph as well. At any point you can pause the animation and explore with your class the sequence from actual numbers to tally chart to bar graph.

- *Get healthy and use ICT* – why not use the idea behind The Global Children's Challenge (http://socialinnovation.ca/node/1672) to inspire some maths and ICT work. The Global Children's Challenge was a school initiative to encourage children to walk more. It provided every child in the class with a free pedometer. Over a period of time, the children would wear their pedometer to measure the number of steps they took. Each day they would record the number and then the class total would be entered into the website. The number of steps then moved the children, as a class, around different places in the world. The class would find out more information about different countries as they arrived at each one. The more steps you took the further you would go.

  There are cheap pedometers available if you do not have any in school. The mobile app Moves acts as a mobile pedometer to support children with measuring the number of steps they take in this task. Ask the children to enter their own data into a spreadsheet and use a formula to calculate the total number of steps. Alternatively, if you use shared documents in the cloud, you can create a shared spreadsheet with the children's names down one side and the children then enter their own number of steps. Each day as a class, you calculate the total.

- *Use online tools* – if you are a subscriber to 2Simple's online platform, Purple Mash (www.purplemash.com/) then consider using some of their online tools like 2Graph to collect some results and produce a very simple graph. 2Simple (www.2simple.com) has a range of simple software to use across the curriculum which is particularly suited to infants and lower juniors.

Using digital photographs for maths

One of the greatest strengths of using an interactive whiteboard is that information can be presented clearly. Words and pictures can be combined in a variety of interesting and colourful ways. Many schools have digital cameras for recording school events and achievements but how can they be used within maths? The first step is with the humble digital photograph. A picture can be used to stimulate a mathematical word problem or for shape work, for example. Look around you. Take a photograph with your camera and look carefully at it. How many different maths questions could you ask from this one photograph? Could you ask multiplication questions? Shape questions? Percentage questions? Data handling questions? Once you begin looking at photographs in a mathematical way, there will be no stopping you using them as a maths warm-up or group activity. Below are some suggestions.

- *Car number plates* – if staff do not mind, take a picture of each of their number plates. On the board write the letters A–Z and then underneath the letter A write the number 1, under B write 2, under C write 3 and so on. Ask the children to look at the number plates and convert the letters first into numbers and then to work out which member of staff has the highest total based on their number plate.

- *Coloured flower pots* – can inspire ratio, number sequence and capacity work – If the blue bucket holds 2L of sand, the red bucket holds 1L and the yellow bucket holds 1.5 times more than the blue bucket, how much sand is there in this picture?

- *Road signs* – look out for signs which have different distances on them. Use these photographs as a basis for maths questions. For example:

Winchester	10
Southampton	15
Portsmouth	20
Chichester	35

How many more miles is it between Winchester and Portsmouth? If it takes me seven minutes to travel ten miles and the time is 15.00, how long will it take me to get to Chichester?

- *Food and money* – if you have a very kind shop owner nearby, they may allow you to take a picture of a display. I once took a picture of chocolate bars with their respective offers attached. Chocolate eggs were sold in groups of three, which of course lent itself to practical applications of our three times table. It could be an early morning challenge in which, for example, the children have to work out how many eggs are on one shelf.

- *Best maths digital photograph* – set a class competition to find out who can take the best maths digital photograph at home. The children should devise a maths question for others to solve. Display all the photographs and questions for other children to work on in pairs. Finally choose a winner.

- *Let's go shopping* – there are examples of practical maths all over the environment. Use a digital camera to snap shot these and then use them as a stimulus for talking about maths. For example, a photograph of a shop window during the sales and say, 'This shop has 30% off during its summer sale; what would a coat cost in the sale if the original price was £110.00?' Another example would be to take a photograph of the section where vegetables are sold. Ask the children to work out the price if they bought a bag of carrots and onions together. How much change would they receive?

- Take a photograph of a room in a house. Ask children to identify the 2D or 3D shapes.
- Begin a shapes topic by taking a photograph of your kitchen cupboards with the doors open. Which real-life 3D shapes can the children spot?
- Take a photograph of the kitchen cutlery drawer. Lay out the forks. Ask the children to count them. Write down the number of forks there are (on the interactive whiteboard). Tell the children that there are the same number of knifes as forks – how many is that altogether? Explain that four knifes, four forks and six spoons have been used during dinnertime and ask how many pieces of cutlery are still left?
- Use a photograph of the school hall or another building with windows. Ask the children how many lines of symmetry the windows have.

Using digital photos with a whiteboard

One of the great advantages of having an interactive whiteboard is the way in which children can draw or put a circle around objects they see. This helps to promote good discussion and is also a great way of developing concentration. Below are some maths ideas for using two different photographs with an interactive whiteboard.

Photograph 1: In the school hall	<ul><li>Use the whiteboard pens to draw round all of the 2D shapes in the photograph.</li><li>What is the time you can see on the clock?</li><li>Look at the tessellation of the floor tiles – can you design a different tessellating pattern?</li><li>If the door is 160cm in height, estimate how tall the plant next to it is?</li><li>In the board showing colour teams, which group has the highest score (data handling skills)? How many more points has the red group than the blue group?</li><li>Twenty tiles fill one row on the ceiling. There are 22 rows on the ceiling. How many tiles are there in total?</li></ul>
Photograph 2: The courtyard	<ul><li>The school pond holds 100 litres when it is half full. How many litres are needed to fill the pond to full capacity?</li><li>A lemonade bottle holds two litres of liquid. How many bottles would be required to fill half the pond? How many for the whole pond?</li><li>How many squares can you see in the fence panel?</li><li>Look at the wall. 100 bricks are needed to build one side. How many bricks have been used? What fraction/percentage is coloured? What would this be as a decimal?</li><li>Look at the picnic tables in the courtyard. Eight children can sit at one table. How many children can sit in our courtyard?</li></ul>

Photograph 1 *In the school hall*   **Photograph 2** *The courtyard*

Further maths ideas for your interactive whiteboard

- *Interactive Teaching Programs* (iTPs) – during the introduction of the government's National Numeracy Strategy, a series of mini-programs were designed to support the teaching of maths. There are some great tools you can use to teach different concepts: (www.taw.org.uk/lic/itp/) or (www.nationalstemcentre.org.uk/elibrary/collection/1034/interactive-teaching-programs). Further guidance can be read here within this document (http://www.nationalstemcentre.org.uk/dl/0aedc3ff9a0ad0f262ac6d7f1b48d451a38108a3/1034-ITP%20index%20and%20guide.pdf). Although these are getting old now, with focus and sharp teacher questioning, these iTPs are great visual resources to support children's mathematical understanding.

- *Sorting diagram* – provide the children with a collection of objects to sort. Using the line tools, create a branching database or use the circle shape tools to create a Venn diagram to sort the shapes.

- *Clip art* – use clip-art images to create simple mathematical sentences to help younger children practise their counting skills. For example, look at the number of cats on the page. Five are missing, how many cats do I have altogether?

- Takeaway maths – scan in a takeaway menu (targeted research will obviously be necessary over the weekend). Use the voting devices and ask the children questions, such as the total for the order, the delivery charge and any discount required. The children could then work out the change from different amounts.

Make a start

Explore the web resources created by Interactive Resources (www.interactive-resources.co.uk). Many of the resources and activities are still available for evaluation through www.primarygames.co.uk/index.html. Although the 'Evaluation Only' word is splashed across the screen, they still provide a wonderful start for anyone beginning to use and see the potential of maths games with their class.

Games and activities

Explore the range of iTPs (www.taw.org.uk/lic/itp/) and maths flash-based games on ICTGames (www.ictgames.com/resources.html). There are so many different activities to explore and work into your maths teaching and bring a hint of ICT to each lesson.

Explaining a concept

ICT can also be used to create helpful instructional videos, a concept Khan Academy (www.khanacademy.org) is founded on. Use a screen recorder like Screencast-o-matic (www.screencast-o-matic.com) to record some 'what to do' tutorials for your children. Just click the 'Start recording' to begin and you're away!

Use the app Explain Everything to explain a maths concept. Explain Everything provides a whiteboard and the ability to insert photographs. The children can press a button and record anything that is on the screen. Challenge the children to explain the weekly maths concept using the app.

6 Using ICT in science

The use of ICT in science brings about the interesting combination of using technology during sessions, alongside practical experiments and learning about theoretical scientific concepts. ICT can be used within science to:

- Capture and gather scientific data using special data-logging equipment which can register on the computer.
- Model how things work or strategies the children might need to use to conduct an investigation. Some concepts which are difficult to see or understand can be simulated, making them easier for children to visualise.
- Act as a stimulus to lessons and promote discussions. This in turn can then be used to encourage the children to make predictions or to support them as they explain their thinking.
- Help record what happened during an experiment.
- Help the children develop and share their own ideas.
- Present findings and conclusions from investigations.

Investigative work

Investigations offer exciting ways for children to explore the world of science. ICT can support children in writing up their investigations as well as the recording what happens during an investigation. Some children can struggle with organising their thoughts and structuring the write up. Technology can make things a lot easier for them, as well as offering different ways for them to present the information. Below are a few suggestions for using ICT during the investigation process:

- *Design a leaflet* – ICT offers different ways of presenting written work whether you use a word processor or a piece of publishing software. Launch a desktop publisher like Microsoft Publisher and choose a style of writing. Ask the children to design a leaflet or even make a poster with their science findings. Challenge the children to write their findings in a different way. For example, can the children write a short newspaper article about the disappearance of Sammy Solid, Leah Liquid and Gregory Gas on a summer's day.

- *Combine drama, science and ICT together* – dress up as a science expert/personality and give yourself a fictional scientific name like Dr. Bunsen or Professor Hydrogen. Record the investigation question 'in role'. Ask 'Have you ever noticed about…' type questions. Challenge the children to investigate the question and report their findings.

- *Make a video diary* – during the process of an investigation, ask the children to make a video diary of their work. To take this a step further, ask the children to create a how-to guide, for example in the style of a television cookery programme.

- *Moving objects* – when exploring plant growth (for example, cress), set up a web camera and then use animation software such as I Can Animate or Animate It! (www.kudlian.net/Kudlian_Software/Product.html) to film the process. On most pieces of software, there is a function called time lapse. This tool tells the computer to take a picture at regular intervals, such as every couple of seconds. You can set the interval of time at which it takes the pictures and then when you play all the pictures together you have a real-life animation of the growth process. You can also use this to record fast-moving objects like cars on a ramp or parachutes falling through the air. Another idea is to show how shadows move throughout a sunny day.

- *Collection of results* – use data loggers (see below for definition) to take measurements throughout an experiment, allowing the children to also work more efficiently during their work while the sensors are recording.

- *Results* – use different graphing packages to present results. Some software such as 2Simple will allow children to create graphs using basic tools. This could be used to support your less able children in sharing their work.

- *Use a dictaphone to support investigation write-ups* – record sentence starters, audio-prompts or audio-writing frames to support the children in their write-ups. The benefit of using a dictaphone means that children can replay the prompts to support them. For example:

First we took _____g of water into a cup. We used a _____ to measure how much heat was lost when no **thermal insulation** was wrapped around the cup.

This way the children can use the scaffold of the words to record their work.

- *Explore special educational needs (SEN) software* – some SEN software and mobile apps can be a useful resource to support the writing process. Clicker (www.cricksoft.com/uk/products/tools/clicker/home.aspx) allows the creation of word banks and sentence-builder grids. The children can type the words they know already and use the grids of words to help them. By pressing on the word it is then inserted into their sentence. Clicker Sentences and Clicker Docs are also available as iPad apps which work in the same way.

ICT/science equipment to explore

Certain pieces of technology equipment can enhance the teaching of science:

- digital microscopes
- digital cameras
- torches and overhead projectors
- data loggers

Below are some suggestions for using them.

Digital microscopes

- *Zoom, zoom, zoom* – there is often great excitement and awe at the use of a microscope. Use it to explore parts of the human body close up – a hair, teeth, ears, a finger nail and so on. There is nothing like the reaction from a whole class when they see inside the human mouth and realise that the same thing is happening at the same time in their mouth!
- *Explore different objects* – explore different metals and objects under the microscope. Use it to ask questions which probe more into the qualities of materials rather than just what they are made from.
- *You're on camera!* – make use of the still image and video options to capture the movements of minibeasts or of the objects being studied.

Digital cameras

- *Starting points in a discussion or investigation* – take photographs of the window steamed up by the kettle or when the shower is on. Ask the children why droplets of water appear on the window. Take a photograph of a puddle and ask the children to explain why a few days later the puddle disappeared after the sun came out.
- *Labelling* – ask the children to label an image taken with the camera – habitats, shadows on the playground, a chocolate bar which has melted in the sun and so on.

Torches and overhead projectors

- *Light sources* – these provide a strong light source for teaching elements of the science curriculum. Demonstrate different materials to see if they are transparent, translucent or opaque. How will we know? What will we see? Place the different materials over the torch or OHP light source. Ask the children to look at how much light comes through the material either by placing it over the torch or by looking on the dry-whiteboard if you are using an OHP.

Data loggers

Data loggers measure a variable and present the data in a graph so children can then use this data for their investigation. Data loggers offer a quicker way of collecting data over the sometimes slow methods people use. Data loggers can also measure very small amounts of time, with increased accuracy, that would be impossible for people to measure. Time intervals can be set for measurements and charted over longer periods of time. Measures are, therefore, more accurate.

- *Get to know the sensors* – data logging units can measure a variety of different things, mainly temperature, light and sound. Experiment with how to work the device. Where does the sensor need to be placed? How does it connect to your computer? Does it require a CD-ROM to be used to run the software or does it need to be installed?
- *Tea time?* – use a temperature sensor to find out which material would be the best thermal insulator to keep a cup of tea the hottest for the longest amount of time.
- *Save the neighbour's ears!* – set the scenario that one of your neighbour's children have just begun to learn the drums which they have put in their garage. His parents are keen not to disturb the neighbours and want to minimise the sound. Challenge the children in small groups to make a small cube model of the garage and line it with a material of their choice. Link this to work on 3D shapes and nets. Place a buzzer inside the garage (can the children use their electricity knowledge to create a circuit with a switch?) and then place the sound sensor outside the garage. As a class, hold a competition to see whose garage reduces the sound level the most.
- *Sunny* – challenge the children to find the best material to make sunglass lenses from. Using pieces of material and a light sensor, they can measure the amount of light that comes through different materials.

Life processes and living things

ICT can help children explore and record living things from the natural world. Use it to help them find out about the human body, the world of plants, where animals live and more. Below are some suggestions for using ICT for exploring living things:

- *Food chains* – make an animation beginning with a food chain producer that is then gobbled up by a caterpillar which is then eaten by a bird which flies away… and so on.

- *Teeth* – use a digital microscope to explore the teeth inside a child's mouth. Use the snapshot feature to take pictures which the children can then label.

- *Food diaries* – ask the children to make a food diary using a word processor. Can they create a table? They could have one column for the food they ate, one column to insert a digital photograph and one column to explain which food group it belongs to. Ask the children to collect their ideas over a week and then to add an evaluation at the bottom of the diary. These can then be presented to the class or put up on display.

- *Digital photographs and video* – create a Horror of the Human Body video or photo story. The rather gruesome aspects of the human body can be made into an Inside the Horrible Human Body Museum. Divide your class into groups. Each group has to produce a short video on how the stomach digests food, or the nasty effects of not brushing your teeth, or what happens if you eat too many sweets and so on. Ask each group to present their video and transfer these on to separate laptops. Set up your classroom so that you have to walk around your 'museum' in one direction. Place the videos on the laptops and position them at various points around the learning walk. As the children to move around the walk, they can press the play buttons of the various videos to learn more. Ask the children to make photo cards with extra facts or details of where to go to find additional information. The children can pick these up as they go around.

- *Made for iBooks* – Apple's iBooks (www.apple.com/uk/education/ibooks-textbooks) allows the reader to view books on a device. Digital books allows the reader to collect notes, highlight important lines in the text, change the size of the font and colour of the page as well as place bookmarks at certain points. Apple now has a tool called iBooks Author (www.apple.com/uk/ibooks-author). These are iBooks 'plus' in a way and can have embedded content on the page:
  - Entire keynote presentations can be inserted.
  - Photographs can be inserted to illustrate points.
  - Images can be interactive so the user can zoom around an image to learn more.
  - Pop-overs on an image can provide extra information which can be read.
  - Video, audio, quizzes and HTML content (embeddable content made from the web) can be included to enhance the learning experience.

There are a number of books with enhanced content from Dorling Kindersley which explore living things, such as their *March of the Dinosaurs* enhanced iBook which looks at ten different dinosaurs. There is a good amount of detail included as well as narration for struggling readers.

Life processes and living things apps

- Inside Nature's Giants – this app allows the children to explore 12 different animals. Videos, information and images are all included. See through different layers from muscles to the skeletal structure. Some parts are gruesome which older children may enjoy but make sure you explore the app first for younger children.
- Science360 for iPad – this is a collection of videos and images (mainly American) about different aspects of science.
- Dorling Kindersley's The Human Body app – this app allows children to explore parts of the human body.
- Food Chains for Kids – in this app children are given a muddled food chain which they have to put in the correct order.

Materials and their properties

Studying the use of materials, their properties and the changes they undergo involves practical observations and investigations. Even though this area of science is practical, there are some uses of ICT:

- *Using digital video stimulus* – because of the more practical nature of looking at materials and their properties, set the children an investigative task through a digital video stimulus. These could then be put on your learning platform for the children to explore with their parents at home. Make sure the children work with an adult to supervise them. Questions to investigate could include: How can you separate the baked bean juice from the beans? and How can flour and rice be separated?
- *Animating changes* – use animation software such as I Can Animate to animate the properties of solids, liquids and gases.
- *Irreversible changes* – provide the children with a fairy cake recipe using a melted chocolate bar as a 'topping'. At home or as a class with adult supervision, ask the children to make some fairycakes. Can they describe where the sugar has gone after they have cooked the cakes? What happens to the chocolate when it is heated (either in the microwave or in a bowl placed over a pan of hot water? (Note: ensure there is parental/adult supervision.) Once melted, can the children turn it back into the bar of chocolate, or what has happened?
- *BBC Bitesize* – the BBC has some excellent resources to support teachers (and children) in their learning of different scientific areas. There are games to play, further information for the children to read in class or at home and even quick quizzes. Apart

from the design and appeal to children, one great advantage of these resources is that they can be embedded into your website, Virtual Learning Environment or blog using basic HTML code (www.bbc.co.uk/schools/ks2bitesize). There are also literacy and maths activities available for the various key stages.

Physical processes

The abstract world of physical processes can be challenging for children to grasp. Through the use of simulations, the interactive whiteboard and the internet, ICT can help children's understanding of physics. Below are a few uses:

- *Simulations* – there are many CD-ROMs available which simulate different physical processes, such as how a circuit is made or the effects of putting too many batteries in a circuit. The activities on these CD-ROMs can provide great independent tasks on the interactive whiteboard. With targeted questions based on the simulation, the children can then use the sound recorder to record their answers. Sherston produce some good examples http://shop.sherston.com/sim3-mlt-cdrm-1.html

- *Flash cards* – www.easynotecards.com provides a simple way to create flashcards which can be used in class. Video, digital photos and voice recordings can be used within the cards to enhance them. Once these cards have been created they can then be embedded on a blog or in your learning platform using HTML code. Look for a HTML button when editing text on your blog or learning platform. Create revision cards with an image for a topic or for SATs revision.

- *Using sensors* – use different data sensors to collect data, for example, the patterns sound waves make when you play a note or hit a drum, or use a light gate sensor to measure the speed a toy car travels at different slope inclinations. A good place to begin is with Data Harvest (www.dataharvest.co.uk). They produce sensors and data logging equipment as well as other science ICT equipment.

- *The Children's University* – provides some excellent resources for the children to learn about different aspects of science. There is a collection of activities on Earth and Space and other areas of science for the children to explore (www.childrensuniversity. manchester.ac.uk/interactives/science).

- *Explore BrainPOP UK* (www.brainpop.co.uk) – this is an outstanding resource to use in the classroom. It centres around two characters, Tim and Moby, who answer questions on a range of topics which the children ask. BrainPOP then produces an animated video on the subject. The children really enjoy watching and learning through the videos. There is a large number of videos for the children to choose from. You could allow your 'star of the day' to choose a topic they are interested in! Some of the videos are free, while some require a subscription. This is a great resource for those spare five minutes.

BBC science

Explore some of the BBC science clips (www.bbc.co.uk/schools/scienceclips/index_flash.shtml) to support your teaching. These are great resources to use on all interactive whiteboards. They contain several flash activities on all areas of science and can be useful home activities. Why not consider 'flipping your classroom' by asking the children to watch the clip before they come into class and then design activities around the learning they are bringing into the classroom.

Electrical circuits

Try out the Yenka Basic Circuits program (www.yenka.com/en/Yenka_Basic_Circuits). It allows children to drag in different components on to a page to create an electrical circuit. What is really nice about this software is that all the components look realistic and behave in the way they should. For example, the more bulbs you enter into the circuit the dimmer the bulb gets.

Looking at physics

Explore Algodoo with your gifted and talented scientists. This is a piece of software as well as an app that lets you explore and simulate how physics affects different objects like fluids and springs. You can play around with different parameters of objects and apply the effect of gravity and friction on the objects. This is one to explore first before using in class.

Space apps

There are some really lovely science apps available for looking at space, the stars and for exploring the human body (e.g. 3D brain). These also bring interest to science in a different way. Many of the apps focus on space and enable the children to explore and read about the physical process of the universe and beyond. Below are some ideas and apps.

- Use iPad and iPod apps in a different way – try using the PuppetPals and have two of the characters to explain a scientific concept.
- Brain Cox's Wonders of the Universe – a huge amount of the content is included in this app. It is a super app for exploring the universe.
- Star Walk or GoSkyWatch Planetarium – two apps that allow you to gaze at the stars in the universe. Hold up your device to the sky and the app will tell you the stars you can see in the sky.
- Rocket Science 101 by NASA – allows children to learn more about NASA's rocket work. Find out about different missions and even build your own rocket and then launch it.
- Solar System – is a combination between a book and an app. Touch Press produce beautiful and stunning apps that are highly visual as well as full of information. This app could be used during research time or just for the fun of exploring the universe. Touch Press has also created The Elements which explores the different elements in the periodic table. This was one of the first apps to gain the 'wow' factor when the iPad was released just by the way it has been produced.

Useful web resources for science

- Birmingham Grid for Learning has a range of interactive whiteboard science links that are worth exploring covering all aspects of science (www.bgfl.org/bgfl/15. cfm?s=15&p=249,index).
- If you are a Promethean interactive whiteboard user, then explore the store on Promethean Planet. There are a number of free resources as well as specially designed interactive whiteboard files such as the 100 Interactive Whiteboard Lessons where you can purchase separate files on a range of different topics including science (www.prometheanplanet.com/en-gb/Products/PublisherCreatedResources/Series/Item/47992#.UhyHgBb3D5Y).
- Yenka is a software company that creates some interesting pieces of software around science, mathematics and computing. The design is not all-singing-all-dancing but they are full of learning potential and free for students to download at home. Explore their 'Free stuff' page. (www.yenka.com/en/Free_stuff_from_Yenka). Although some of the resources look Key Stage 3 in nature, they would make a good teacher resource and group activity.
- The Science Museum offers a number of different resources teachers can use in the classroom (www.sciencemuseum.org.uk/educators/teaching_resources.aspx). There are some great activities to use and games children will enjoy playing.

7 Using ICT in humanities

ICT can be used to explore and open up new worlds; to find out about different cultures and localities which are hard for us to visit as well as helping us to discover more about people, places and their environments. You are no longer confined to the parameters of your local environment but given a global stage in which the possibility of building international links is no longer just a dream.

ICT can make historical characters come alive and enable children to relive and re-enact scenes from the past and understand how history is about people, places and the way they used to live. The use of ICT in RE can encourage the children to understand the beliefs of other cultures and develop tolerance of other people's views. Below are some ideas of how you might use ICT to support your teaching of the humanities.

Geography

ICT can help you to collaborate and communicate more effectively and create projects that not only allow your children to develop their geographical understanding but also their cultural understanding. Below are some suggestions for ways that ICT can enhance the geography work you do.

Map work

Geography involves a huge amount of map work. Using ICT children can discover where places are and not only see villages, towns and entire countries but they can also zoom out on the map and put everything in context. *How long would it take me to get there? Which countries surround the one I am currently looking at?* Here are some suggestions for using ICT to explore the wider world:

- *He's got the whole world in his hands* – Google Earth (http://earth.google.co.uk/) is a great resource for introducing different places to the children and for generally increasing knowledge of where places can be found in the world. Install the software and then you can search for places or you are free to roam. Use this to challenge the children with questions – I'm looking at the United Kingdom on the map at the moment. Can anyone tell which country I would find if I continued flying to the left?

Look at the board which shows a picture of the Mediterranean Sea. Can anyone tell me the rest of the countries around the sea?

- *Exploring the world* – the beginning of term is always a great opportunity for children to explore where others have been on holiday. Collect a list on the whiteboard and then ask the children to use Google Earth (http://www.google.co.uk/intl/en_uk/earth/index.html) to locate a country and find out what the capital is.

- *Google Street View* – use the 3D street view (click on the yellow man) on your interactive whiteboard when using Google maps (http://maps.google.co.uk/) so that the children can explore their local area. Bing maps is an alternative to using Google Street view. There is also an opportunity to explore places and fun things to do that are nearby to a location. Why not use it to locate places and then to develop children's understanding of what a town needs to offer? They could compare this with what a village offers.

- *Navigation skills* – use a digital camera take photographs of common places around the school grounds and then place a letter at those points. Ask the children to orientate themselves to the various points and then collect a letter at each point to make up a word. As an extension, the children could use a portable microphone to collect the sounds they hear at different points.

- *I'll send you a postcard* – using some publishing software like Microsoft Publisher or Postcard Creator (www.readwritethink.org/files/resources/interactives/postcard/), ask the children to design a postcard with an image from their local area. These could then be printed out and sent to a link school or another school in a contrasting area.

- *Find a map?* – need to find a map of a specific place. Take a look at (http://geology.com/world/) as a starting point.

Atlas app

MOBILE

Barefoot World Atlas is a beautifully made app based on the hardback version of the Barefoot Books World Atlas. The app allows children to explore the globe in a creative way. When the app loads, the globe looks slightly unusual as there are objects littered all over the surface of the globe. Tap on any of the objects and more information is displayed along with a real photograph of the object. Realistic sounds and music plays in the background. Select the 'Regions' and information is given about the region's physical features, climate, weather, environment, wildlife, transport and people.

Other uses of ICT in geography

As all geographers will tell you, the best geography is taught by the soles of your feet. Geography is about bringing places to children to study, learn and experience. Much of this is easier with the internet. Below are a few ideas on how you can use ICT to support other activities within geography:

- *Top Trumps* – explore the National Geographic for kids website (http://kids. nationalgeographic.com/kids). Ask the children to collect some new geographical facts each week. They can collect information on capital cities, size of population, food they export and more. Using PowerPoint or interactive whiteboard software, the children can create their own TopTrumps.

- *Link with others* – use video conferencing equipment or software like FlashMeeting (http://flashmeeting.e2bn.net/) to build links with other schools, either in your local area or further afield, and find out how they are different. The children could use a digital camera to take photographs of their local area and around their school.

- *Don't knock down our woodland!* – your class has received a letter from your local council explaining that they are going to build new shops over your local playground and woodland. Using digital cameras or mobile devices and adult support, ask the children to take photographs and record video clips to find evidence for why the shops should not be built.

- *Digimaps* – (http://digimapforschools.edina.ac.uk) provide schools with the opportunity to use electronic versions of Ordnance Survey Maps. A subscription is required to access the full service but under the 'Free resources' section there are ideas for how the maps can be used in the curriculum.

- *Geocaching* – is like a treasure hunt that uses the GPS on your mobile phone to search and find what are called caches. They are hidden all over the country in different locations and placed in plastic containers. Once you locate the cache there is usually a stamp to say you have found it. You then put the box back so that other geocachers can find it. Explore the website (www.geocaching.com) to find out more and download the mobile app for your phone. Great fun!

- Developing enquiry skills – use digital cameras to explore your local area. Plan a trip to explore your local surroundings around the school. Ask the children to photograph their local area as they walk around. Supply the children with question prompt cards to take with them. For example: what is the place like? How has it changed? What shops are available to the community? How is the space organised? What areas around you are there to relax and enjoy the environment?

- Geographical Association – (www.geography.org.uk) this is the subject association for geography and provides some superb resources for primary schools to use. With a specific 'Early Years and Primary' section to explore, it is a good place to begin whether you are a geography coordinator or a class teacher.

- Data loggers – use dataloggers to explore the temperature around your school. Ensure that the children use the equipment to take accurate measurements.
- National Geographic for Kids (http://kids.nationalgeographic.com/kids/). This website has different activities for children to carry out. Two areas worth exploring are the 'Photos' and 'Countries' sections. The information doesn't go into a lot of depth, but there is certainly enough for the children to find out facts and discover more about a country.
- World music – look at examples of music (www.worldmusic.net) from other countries, including different instruments. Create a display with a world map and then mark off the different countries each time you listen to a track from that place.
- Barnaby Bear (www.barnabybear.co.uk) – is a website dedicated to the travels of the bear. Barnaby Bear, created by the Geographical Association, travels around to different places having his picture taken. This then helps children to begin a discussion about where the bear has visited and what the place is like. On a similar theme, you might consider having a class mascot that travels around the local area or nationally. Ask friends in different schools from different areas to have your class mascot for a visit and then wrap them up carefully and send through the post. When your mascot arrives, the children can use Skype (https://education.skype.com) or Google Hangouts (www. google.com/+/learnmore/hangouts/) to link with your partner school and get to know a different class and their surroundings.
- Create a new virtual village (http://www.bekonscot.co.uk/fun-and-games/virtual-village/). Place different buildings and discuss the features of a settlement. What types of buildings does a village require?

History

Exploring the events of the past leads children on a fascinating path of discovery about what life was like. What were people like in the past? Who were the characters? How did they live? What did they wear? What did they do for history and how has what they did made a difference to the way we live now? History is about getting children to look at evidence and different sources to piece the puzzle together to build, understand and create a picture of what life was like. ICT can support history by allowing the children to:

- get at the evidence
- create a response to what they discover
- look at a simulation to see what life was like.

Below are some ways ICT can be used:

Getting at the evidence

ICT enables children to look at elements of history through different sources. First-hand experience is obviously one of the most valuable ways to place history in context but where this can't be so then allowing children to use ICT to see the evidence in other ways will help them to build a partial picture.

- *Exploring film* – British Pathé (www.britishpathe.com) is a fascinating site to explore. The site collects historical film clips which are available to watch. These include Martin Luther King's iconic 'I have a Dream' speech; Churchill; The London Blitz and the Titanic. With over 90,000 clips available it makes a great resource.

- *Examining artefacts* – some visualisers have the ability to zoom in really close to an object so you can see it in incredible detail. This can be useful when exploring history artefacts or different RE resources.

- *The Evacuation Learning Experience* – has a number of resources which are useful for exploring the experience of an evacuee (http://microsites2.segfl.org.uk/view_project.php?id=128).

- *The National Archives* – tis is a great resource for allowing children to see different sources. The National Archives (www.nationalarchives.gov.uk) provides information and images to help people understand more about the historical evidence that is stored. There is also an education section with relevant resources for different key stages.

- *English Heritage* – there are a number of resources on the English Heritage education section of its website (www.english-heritage.org.uk/education/) which are useful for seeing aspects of history. Their Heritage Learning magazine is full of interesting articles that may inspire you with other ideas for your classroom.

- *Record offices* – do you have a local records office near you? For example, Hampshire Record Office (http://www3.hants.gov.uk/archives) has a number of resources for schools and access to information about real people.

- *Explore the library* – The British Library (www.bl.uk/) helps you to 'Explore the world's knowledge'. Again this may be useful for providing resources you may need.

- *The Mary Rose* – the website of the Mary Rose Museum (www.maryrose.org) offers a fascinating look around the famous Mary Rose Tudor ship. Explore this website with the children, as there is lots to discover here even if you cannot get to the museum.

- *Explore different museums* – there is a wealth of experience children gain from visiting museums. First-hand experience always adds to the learning. However, if this is not possible then there are many museums dotted around the country. Many will have education sections to their websites. For example, The Museum of English Rural Life (www.reading.ac.uk/merl) has a number of images about agriculture through history.

Other useful history websites

- *The National Portrait Gallery* (www.npg.org.uk) – although not truly a history website, it does include portraits of historical figures. Type in Henry VIII, Mary Seacole or try out different historical figures and see if there is a portrait.
- *The Great Fire of London* (www.fireoflondon.org.uk) – a resource to use with activities about The Great Fire of London.
- *The Museum of London* (www.museumoflondon.org.uk/schools/classroom-homework-resources/) – has a number of different resources which are useful and feature all aspects of historical life.
- *The Historical Association* (www.history.org.uk) – has resources for primary schools on its website and even podcasts which it has created.
- *BBC History* – The BBC (www.bbc.co.uk/history) has quality resources that can be used within the classroom. The main site for adults can also be used with older children to provide a useful overview without being too jargon based. They also have a page entitled 'History for kids' (www.bbc.co.uk/history/forkids/) with excellent animations and links to resources ideally suited to the classroom and for primary schools.
- *Neil Thompson's site Key Stage History* (www.keystagehistory.co.uk) – has a number of resources. There are some samples as well as resources you have to subscribe to. As a past local authority advisor/inspector and OfSTED inspector, he has a wealth of knowledge and resources available from his site.

Creating a response

During the course of learning about different periods of history, children can explore the use of ICT to create a response to the history work they have been undertaking. Below are some classroom examples:

- *Radio shows* – using Audacity, ask the children to create a Tudor radio show about Henry VIII. They will need someone to be in role as Henry VIII and someone to ask him questions. They could then interview his wives. What did they see in him? Can they tell the listener all about their family? Where did they come from? Can they shed some light on some of the other sides of Henry? Which sports did he enjoy? What are his favourite foods?

- *Evacuation messages* – ask the children to research what times were like during the Second World War. Ask the children to think like an evacuee. Point out that there was little communication between parents and evacuated children. If those children had owned a mobile phone at that time, what would they have texted home? Can the children provide a recount of aspects of the war in text messages?

- *A snapshot of history* – invite grandparents in when studying evacuation during the Second World War. Ask the children to interview any grandparents who experienced what it was like to be evacuated. After the interview, ask the children to make a short video clip introducing their evacuee.

- *Timelines* – help children to gain a sense of chronology by using Timetoast (www. timetoast.com) or Tiki-Toki (www.tiki-toki.com) for building timelines. You can insert an image, links to other information and websites, dates for the event and a description. Like many of these web-based tools, it can be embedded by taking the HTML code and putting it into a website or blog.

- *Kar2ouche* (www.immersiveeducation.eu/index.php/kar2ouchepg) – is a piece of software that provides a stage for the children to animate a story. You drag in characters on to the main area and can move them around, add narration, backgrounds, additional characters and historic props. Kar2ouche has a range of historic titles and draws on many cross-curricular links. It is a superb tool which puts the children in the driving seat as content creators instead of content consumers.

Seeing what life was like

Some aspects of history can be difficult to understand. The web and digital media come in very handy by re-creating historical events.

- *Horrible history* (http://horrible-histories.co.uk) – children really enjoy reading these books which are written in a very accessible way. Along with the website, the BBC has produced a wonderful selection of Horrible History songs (www.youtube.com/ horriblehistoriesBBC) about the different historical periods in time. They provide very catchy tunes as well as a task for children. At the beginning or end of your history topic, play the song through a couple of times. Ask the children – 'Is this song historically correct?' The children have to find evidence from either prior learning or through researching using books and other resources. Ask the children to also explain what is missing from the song clip. What has been left out that would be historically accurate?

- *BBC television* – always keep an eye out for various programmes that are shown on the BBC. From 'What was a Tudor Christmas like?' to 'Victorian Farm'. These are great resources that are well made, for example, take the children's classic 'Five Children and It' (www.bbc.co.uk/cult/classic/fivechildren) and it enables the children to gain a glimpse of what life was like in the Victorian era.

- *Video conferencing* – a number of museums are beginning to offer video conferencing facilities whereby an actor is in character and converses with different classes. Take a look at the Janet Community website (https://community.ja.net). Type in 'history' in the search bar to see some of the current and past projects.
- *BBC games/simulation* – the BBC have produced a number of different history simulations through games (www.bbc.co.uk/history/interactive/games) so the children can explore different aspects of history.
- *Use your interactive whiteboard* – locate a black and white photograph of your school from the past. Next, take a coloured digital photograph from the same position. Place the black and white photograph on the bottom of the page and lock it into position. Next, place the coloured photograph on top so the black and white photograph cannot be seen but make sure this is not locked so when you press the object the menu appears. Press on the photograph and then find the transparency slider for your whiteboard software so when you slide it across, the coloured photograph disappears to the black and white photograph demonstrating what life was like in the past.
- *Make your own Tudor house* – www.3dhistory.co.uk/interactive-images/tudor-house. php is a good site to see how Tudor houses were constructed.

History apps

The range of apps to support children learning history is not as developed as other curriculum subjects. Either the apps are too heavy in text or they are not as developed in terms of the activities and then end up just presenting information. Below are a few history apps to explore:

- Encyclopedia Britannica Kids has developed apps on Egypt, Ancient Rome, Knights and Castles. Different facts, figures and information are presented along with relevant images.
- Museum of London: Streetmuseum and Streetmuseum: Londinium are two apps that focus on comparing life now with in the past. For example, there are streets in London where you can look at what it looks like now and then find out more about what they were like in the past.

Professor R. T. Fact

Every teacher has their favourite lesson. This became a favourite 'OfSTED' lesson of mine and certainly an activity the children thoroughly enjoyed. The main objective is to have a real-life archaeologist helping you discover how to look at artefacts. The only way I could get an archeologist to assist me with this lesson was to put myself in role, a drama or 'active learning' strategy entitled Teacher in Role (TIR). So off to the local fancy dress store I went picking up a moustache, some 'professory-looking' glasses and suitable attire. I also stopped at a few charity shops and selected a few items I could use as evidence.

In my kitchen, I loosely hung a poster of Tutankhamun on my wall taken from a copy of the *TES*. I set up my digital video camera on a tripod facing me and proceeded to record instructions and explanations for my class. A transcript of what was said is shown below in the lesson structure.

The intention was to have a normal lesson but to have (live) video clips interjected throughout the lesson to make the children think and further their understanding of how an archaeologist looks for clues using artefacts.

Before the session you will need:

- A numbered bin bag for each group filled with artefacts about a person. Ask members of staff to bring in suitable objects from home that would help children to explore more about them. (Within my bin bag, for example, I included: some musical manuscript paper; an ICT magazine; a children's toy; a clay piece of artwork a friend had brought back from a trip to New York; a broken conductor's baton; an empty pack of hot chocolate; a glass paperweight a mentor had given to me as a gift on my final teaching practice; a small empty bottle of Eau de toilette and a torn page from on old school diary.) You will need about eight of these bags, depending on how small you want the groups to be.
- A key questions sheet. On the sheet were questions to help probe discussion among the group, such as:
  - Can you see any distinguishing features on your artefact?
  - Does your artefact belong to a male or female and where's the evidence to support what you think?
  - Can you date your artefact? Is it modern? Old? Antique? Or can you not say? What made you make up your mind?
- A trainee archeologist record card for every child. On the card the children had to write what the object was, a description of the object and then draw a picture.
- A siren sound on the interactive whiteboard.

- Three A4 envelopes for each group containing Clue A (the key questions sheet, above), Clue B (a small part of a photo of the person to whom the artefacts belong) and Clue C (the rest of the photograph).

Learning objectives:

- To understand some of the skills an archaeologist carries out.
- To be able to use artefacts to voice an opinion confidently within a group.

As the children come into the classroom, project an invitation on the interactive whiteboard inviting the class to take part in archaeologist training for RSTA (Royal Society for the Training of Archaeologists).

Starter

Explain to the children that you have signed the class up for archaeology training. In a minute you are going to go live with your first session. Explain that at the end of this session they will have practised some of the skills of being an archaeologist. Ask the children what they think an archaeologist is. Collect these ideas on the whiteboard.

Play part one of the video:

Narrator: *(Over the top of video)* Welcome to the RSTA Archaeology training session – Archaeology for beginners. Live with Professor R. T. Fact.

Prof. Fact: Good afternoon and welcome Class 6 to this live training broadcast. By the end of this training you will have learnt and practised some of the skills archaeologists use.
Have you ever wondered about the past? What was it like? How do we find out about this? The word is archaeology.

When you think of archaeology, most people think of buried treasures or lost cities, and yes some archaeologists have discovered these things. But archaeology isn't about fame and fortune. It is a way of learning about people who lived in the past: where they lived, what they ate, what they believed and the effects they had on the environment. I'm going to see you in a little while but now a little task to get you started.

After part one pause the video. Tell the children that they are going to practise some of the jobs archaeologists carry out. Explain to them that every time they hear a siren sound they will receive more information to help them solve the mystery of their rubbish bag. Explain that in each of these bags are artefacts that belong to a person and they have to guess who that person is.

Task 1

Place a bin bag on each table. Ask the children to spend two to three minutes looking generally at the artefacts.

Sound the siren for clue A. This will be key questions on looking at artefacts. Give out a copy to each group. Show part two of the video.

Prof. Fact: Great! You've found my first clue. Every so often you can be looking at an artefact and a new piece of information will come your way to help you come closer to solving that puzzle and answering those questions. Archaeologists study the remains left behind by people. This is called evidence or sources.

The evidence can include artefacts, man-made movable objects such as pottery, tools or jewellery which can be made from materials like clay, bone, stone, wood or metal. Like these.

Task 2

Tell the children that this time they are going to use the key questions to look more carefully at the artefacts. Tell the children that they will have between 10–15 minutes to talk within their group and to fill in their record cards. Remind the children that archaeologists work in groups and often have to share their ideas with others; by doing this everybody's thoughts and ideas are used.

Sound the siren. Provide Clue B, a small fraction of the photograph so the children can just about work out some more information about that person. Be careful not to give it away completely though!

Prof. Fact: Great! You've found my second clue. Pictures help us to date evidence by telling us about the clothes people wore and the transportation they used to get around. Pictures can even tell us about the type of art people liked and how they decorated their home. Look at these pictures. What do they tell you?

Give the children time to discuss their new piece of evidence and to draw conclusions from it. Give each group the opportunity to feedback on their rubbish bag.

Play part three of the video – congratulations and revealing the answers to each of the bags.

Prof. Fact: Great! We've nearly come to the end of our training. It's time to reveal which bag belongs to which person. I hope you've reached a conclusion. Here are the answers and why.

Sound the siren. Provide Clue C, the rest of a digital photograph of the member of staff whose artefacts the children are examining. Conclude the lesson by providing a checklist of objectives the children should have mastered over the lesson. Review as a class – are they ready to become archaeologists? Ask the children to describe two things they found difficult and one thing they really enjoyed.

Religious education

ICT can help children to understand different cultures as well as different religions. Children can experience some aspects through film clips on the internet, and, in the same way as history, can use ICT to respond to the RE work they are doing. Below are some ideas and websites to help:

- *The BBC* – has a number of resources to use. There are numerous short clips (www.bbc.co.uk/learningzone/clips/topics/primary.shtml#religious_education) on different aspects of RE as well as their normal resources (www.bbc.co.uk/schools/websites/4_11/site/re.shtml).

- *Let's celebrate!* – make a celebration video or slideshow of a religious ritual, such as a wedding, Diwali or Christmas. Ask the children to either make these into a video documentary or use software such as Microsoft Photo Story 3 or Photo Peach (http://photopeach.com) to create a slideshow and narrate what is happening over the top of it.

- *Use the web* – there are some good resources such as Embedding ICT in RE in the primary classroom by Paul Hopkins (www.mmiweb.org.uk/microsites/primaryreandict/index.html) which provide ideas for using ICT and also links to other resources. Andy Seed of Cracking RE (www.crackingre.co.uk/htdocs/crackingre/secure/teachSupp/ict.html) also has a list of good resources.

- *Use of music* – music can have a wonderful power to create spiritual moments and spaces of calm in the classroom. Listen carefully and choose a song than has a slow BPM (beats per minute). So that the children have relaxing and reflective music to help them when praying. Ludivico Einaudi's 'Le Onde' (www.einaudiwebsite.com) and other tracks he has composed make an excellent background to thinking music within assemblies. There are also specially made CDs (http://advancedbrain.com/soundhealth/sound-health.html) with classical music for your classroom produced to facilitate different ways of working.

- *The National RE Association* (www.natre.org.uk) – has a range of useful resources.

- *Teacher's Media* (www.teachersmedia.co.uk/videos/resource-review-primary-ict-special-primary-re) – provides a number of free resources from the old Teachers TV site. These are useful resources to develop the teaching of RE and it is always great to see real teachers in action.

- *The Religious Education CPD Handbook* (http://re-handbook.org.uk) – has some useful resources and links. Although mainly aimed at RE coordinators, it can provide a good start point.

- *Use your digital camera* – visit a place of worship and ask the children to take pictures (with permission) using a digital camera. Once back at school, ask the children to make a presentation or use video editing software to create a multimedia slideshow. The children can also use the photographs and interactive whiteboard software and insert audio clips of them explaining the different places and how they are used within the worship.

- *Use animation to retell stories* – use animation software such as I Can Animate (www.kudlian.net/products/icananimatev2/Home.html) to animate religious stories. A top tip is to look out for cake decorations. One year I managed to pick up an entire nativity set of characters. Children in Reception were able to retell the story using the characters without the fiddly task of making them from scratch.

- *Cumbria and Lancashire Education Online archive (CLEO)* (www.cleo.net.uk/index.php) – has a wonderful selection of resources for teachers to use and explore, not just in RE but across all curriculum subjects.

- *Create a Voki* (http://www.voki.com) *to retell religious stories* – I once used the Jesus character to retell the Easter story through a number of Vokis I made.

- *The Miracle Maker DVD* (http://www.imdb.com/title/tt0208298/) – retells the Easter story through animation. It is a great film to watch and use to illustrate your teaching.

Bible app

MOBILE

The Children's Bible (www.childrenbible.org/nouwp/?app=childrens-bible-books-movies) is a lovely app. It retells the Bible as a comic version as well with video clips. There are numerous stories from the Bible and care and attention has been taken over the production of this app, as there is so much to see and read. It is a super resource to support the teaching of Christianity and the children loved seeing RE from this perspective.

8 Using ICT in music, art, design and technology, physical education and modern foreign languages

Finally it's time to draw the curriculum chapters to a close with a look at a few more subjects including music, art, PE, design and technology (DT) and modern foreign languages (MFL). ICT has the potential to be used across different subjects to enhance your teaching. Never be afraid to also find a balance between the traditional classroom methods that develop children's social and emotional skills and using the technology to breathe new life into topics. ICT keeps us on our toes and sometimes gives us a glimpse into what learning will look like in the future. However, it takes a teacher to recognise the potential it has in children's learning.

Music

There are a limited number of software titles written for the subject of music and sadly, within the primary sector, there have been very few updates. However, there are many different ways that ICT can support the teaching of music. Music is a creative expressive subject, one that enriches the soul and engages all people at an intellectual, social, emotional and spiritual level. Although a very practical subject, ICT can make the teaching of music visually easier and enhance the performance. Mobile technology has added a separate dimension to the music. Many apps are available to compose, listen and perform music in new ways. Below are some ideas on how ICT can support the teaching of music.

Class teaching of music

- *Music equipment* – take a look at all the music equipment you have around the school. Do you have a device to playback music on? An MP3 device or another portable device? Do you have keyboards children can use? Do you have computers with installed software and internet access? When you locate this equipment, take a look at how it works. How does the device turn on? Are there any special cables needed? If it is software that is needed, make sure you also make time to play with the software so you can be comfortable with how it works.

- *Rhythm work* – use the interactive whiteboard shape tools to create a four by four grid. Label each column from one to four. Use the circle tool to create rhythm beats that the children then need to clap back. As an additional hint, draw a circle at the bottom of the page and then set it to 'Drag a copy' or 'Clone' depending on your software. Now that shape will produce an exact replica each time, making it easier for you to just drag a rhythm up on the board.

- *Lyrics* – type the words up on a PowerPoint page for the children to see. Make sure that the font is clear to read and large enough. Usually you should be able to fit a verse and a chorus on each page. Make the chorus different to read, either in bold or italic font works well. Create a template by saving it as a template.

- *YouTube* – since the introduction of YouTube there are now many clips available to show to develop discussion with children. For example, ask: Why do people listen to music and how does it affect their lives? Use '500 Miles' by The Proclaimers (www. youtube.com/watch?v=69AvNm8zubo) and 'The Streets of London' (www.youtube. com/watch?v=DiWomXklfv8) as examples. Discuss how they make the children feel. Want to learn how to play an instrument or watch examples of music from around the world? The chances are that YouTube will have an example of it. It is a fantastic resource to use in the classroom. Just remember to screen the clips to check that there are no inappropriate surprises. When watching YouTube clips, you may want to start the clip at a certain point in the video. A quick tip is to click the 'Share' tab under the video and then find the exact place in the clip. Then copy the URL web link and paste it into your whiteboard flipchart. That way when you click on the link it will take you to that exact point therefore not affecting the flow of your lesson.

- *Singing games* – get the children used to using their voices by playing singing games like 'Take a line on a walk'. Select a colour or if you are using the SMARTBoard one of their funky effects pens. Draw a line from top to bottom that the children have to copy with their voices (their voices should also go from the top to the bottom. Use your finger to guide the children). Experiment with wiggly lines, lines that circle and then climb up or lines that go up step by step and down the opposite way.

- *Use resources to build confidence* – music schemes such as Music Express (http://pages. bloomsbury.com/musicexpress) can help support music teaching for teachers who are non-specialist. Many of the activities come with CD, web and whiteboard resources.

- *Web based resources* – there are a number of online resources which provide ready-made activities, lesson plans and backing tracks. Some examples of these are Charanga (http://charanga.com), Trinity Music Tracks (www.trinitycollege.co.uk/ site/?id=1068) or why not set up your own mini-band for your more gifted children using Rock School (http://trinityrock.trinitycollege.co.uk/instruments/groups).

- Use keyboards – keyboards provide a great opportunity for children to explore different prebuilt sounds and rhythms. They can be used as part of a music lesson. Why not use them within a class 'call and response' activity. You play a rhythm and the children have to play back the rhythm on the notes you specify or to a particular scale like the pentatonic scale (CDEGA).

- Explore software titles – there are a few software titles that are available for classroom music: below are some of the more well-known titles.

    - 2 Simple Music toolkit (https://www.2simple.com/music/) – is a suite of different programs to develop different musical elements. The children can record and play sounds by clicking different musical instruments. They can organise different musical sounds into a sequence as well as begin to explore different things.

    - Compose World (www.espmusic.co.uk/composeworldinfo.html) – is a software title that has been available for a long time in schools. It presents different musical building blocks to the user. Behind each one is a musical pattern. The children drag down the different musical blocks to create a tune.

    - Dance eJay (www.ejay.com/uk) – allows children to build up music by stringing together samples of dance music to create a music track.

    - Musical Monsters and Mini Musical Monsters (www.busythings.co.uk/cd-rom-musical.php) – is a colourful piece of software for composing. The main screen has a blank grid in which the monsters are placed. At the bottom of the screen is the control box where the children select the monster they would like to hear. Behind each one is a different musical sound played by an instrument. You can adjust the pitch so it sounds higher or lower and you can change the tempo of the whole piece so the music is played more quickly or at a slower speed. Mini Musical Monsters relies just on pictures for children to create their music and allows very young children to explore musical sound.

    - The Dums (www.espmusic.co.uk/thedums_desc.html) – allows children to explore different instruments. It introduces them to the sound of different instruments and the children select them to find out more information. There is also an international version in which children can learn about gamelan, Indian Raga and African music amongst other styles.

    - Rhythm Maker (www.espmusic.co.uk/rhythmmaker_desc.html) – presents a number of percussion instruments down the left-hand side of the screen. By entering different beats by clicking on the timeline, the children can create rhythms. This can be played together, creating a percussion background that can be exported.

    - O-Generator (www.o-music.tv/index.htm) – takes an alternative look at composing music using software. It presents a musical bar which would normally be read in a linear way and converts it into a circle so the beats in a bar go round in the same way a clock hand does as it counts time. You choose the combination of musical instruments and then you turn off and on different 'pads' to make the music. Set your drum, set your guitar rift and then as the counter arm rolls over the pad it will play all the sounds. A different but exciting way to compose more modern pieces of music.

- *Audacity* (http://audacity.sourceforge.net) – is not really a dedicated piece of music software but it can be used within the classroom. Use it to record compositions, singing or instrumental backing tracks that can then be played in class and used to support colleagues who are not so confident. Audacity provides tools for editing your track and cutting out sections. There are also a number of special effects such as being able to speed tracks up. This software is useful for creating podcasts as the tracks can then be exported as MP3 tracks.

- *Sibelius* – if you run a school orchestra or instrumental groups, then Sibelius (www. sibelius.com) is notation software that will allow you to quickly write out scores and transpose them. This does save endless amounts of time for your music coordinator if they have to rewrite music or transpose it for the clarinets or trumpet players in your school.

Performance

There is nothing like practising a piece of music and then performing it in front of others. Even if the performance isn't in front of parents, ICT can support the overall performance in the following ways.

- *Sing your heart out!* – writing words out on the screen is one way to engage the children. There are some superb resources to encourage children to sing. SingUp! (www.singup.org) was a national initiative that has now converted to a subscription service. It contains a number of excellent resources and songs for children to learn. There are backing tracks, words for your interactive whiteboard and a range of different songs. This is a great resource not only for a classroom warm-up but for whole song practices as well. Out of the Ark (www.outoftheark.co.uk) by Mark and Helen Johnson have always produced outstanding modern songs as well as productions with great music. They have a number of singing resources such as being able to follow the words on screen (www.outoftheark.co.uk/series/words-on-screen) where you can play the track and the words highlight as you sing the song in synchronization with the tune.

- *Recording production songs* – record the children singing the songs they are learning for a special occasion. These can then be played in class time during the day to help children learn and become more familiar with the tunes.

- *Record performance* – use a digital recorder to record performances of the children. These audio tracks can then be put on the school blog for the children and parents to listen to.

- *Backing tracks* – if you are a teacher and a piano player then, just like some instruments in the orchestra you are fast becoming an endangered species! Not every school has a pianist, however there are many backing tracks available including religious hymns with modern upbeat backing. This means that the musical diet of songs used during assemblies can be increased, 'He's Got the Whole World In His Hands', 'Colours of Day', 'Autumn Days' and more can still have a place in school assemblies. Explore the use of professional made backing tracks:

  - *Audio Network* (www.audionetwork.com) has tracks that have been used by BBC drama productions, reality programmes and within film scores (type in Christmas Eve and see where you have heard it before – The Apprentice and The Hotel Inspector). The tracks are inexpensive for individuals and schools to buy and can be used as music within educational productions. Some broadband providers to schools also provide access to AudioNetwork free so that you do not need to pay for the tracks. I have used the tracks in the past during dance and PE lessons for warm-ups; within class for tidy-up music and during school productions for sound effects and for entrance music for different characters.

  - *Ameritz* (www.ameritz.co.uk/) have a number of different styles, some with backing vocals and a number of tracks from musicals, soul, pop and jazz genres to name but a few.

  - *Karaoke-version* (www.karaoke-version.co.uk) does exactly what it says on the tin. It provides standard backing tracks but it also gives the option to customise certain tracks, taking the whole vocals or the bass part out. It is great for your beginner musicians to play to during assembly if it is a relatively simple chord progression to follow.

- *Slow it down!* – if backing tracks are too fast to use in the classroom, then there are occasions when you have to slow down or speed up the tempo. The Associated Boards of The Royal Schools of Music (ABRSM) produce a number of apps to help (http://gb.abrsm.org/en/exam-support/practice-tools-and-applications). Speedshifter is one such app. It slows the tempo without altering the pitch, which some programs can do. It is worth exploring their other apps for musicians as well.

Create an iPod/iPad band

There are now many different devices that can generate sound and music. Why not create your own mini-band. Just take a look at this example from the North Point's iBand (http://www.youtube.com/watch?v=F9XNfWNooz4) for inspiration. There are a number of different instruments available on iPad and iPod that can be combined together. I once ran a workshop at an ICT conference and managed to get a room of adults (some self-confessed non-musicians) to play 'Eye of the Tiger' using just iPods and iPads. Below are a few apps and pieces of advice to get you started:

- You will need the normal selection of instruments you find in a band (guitars, keyboards, drums, etc.). Search for different instruments in the app store. I use the following although it is worth looking around as the quality of instruments varies. The trick is to look for how responsive they are under your fingertips:
  - iAmGuitar (https://itunes.apple.com/en/app/iamguitar/id407752080?mt=8)
  - Six Strings (https://itunes.apple.com/gb/app/six-strings/id374226640?mt=8) This app will also let you adapt the chords as well.
  - NLog MIDI Synth (https://itunes.apple.com/gb/app/nlog-midi-synth/id391268291?mt=8)
  - iGOG: Massive Drums (https://itunes.apple.com/gb/app/igog-massive-drums/id330434150?mt=8)
  - BaDaBing (https://itunes.apple.com/gb/app/badabing/id395952688?mt=8)
  - WI Orchestra (https://itunes.apple.com/gb/app/wi-orchestra/id434371426?mt=8)
- Next you need the Ultimate Guitar Tabs app (https://itunes.apple.com/gb/app/ultimate-guitar-tabs-largest/id357828853?mt=8). Tunes are submitted here with the chord symbols and the lyrics. Using this you then know the correct chords to give to your guitars and chords or notes to give to your keyboard players. There are many different pop tunes and it is always updated so you are bound to find something current that children will really enjoy playing.
- Write out the lyrics on the board and copy the chords just above the words.
- For your keyboard players, I use the idea of an ICT concept keyboard. Find a sheet of clear acetate film (as you would use on the overhead projector) and lay it over the iPad. Load up the keyboard app. Make sure the acetate is secure using sticky tack. Look at the chords in the song. Cut squares of address labels the same size as the keys and then label just the chords you need.
- Practise each separate part at a time and then piece together the tune.
- Finally, invite your singers to join the band.

- You now have your very own iPad/iPod band. Each instrument will need an amplifier. There are some cheap but portable speakers that can plug into the iPad/iPod just using a 3.5 headphone jack.

Producing your own iPad/iPod band can be a great experience especially for the children when collectively they are playing songs from Adele through to The Beatles!

Listening and appraising

Music is full of listening opportunities. It is a fundamental part of the music process. It is useful for reviewing work we have composed, to help us work and to experience new musical genres that we have never listened to. Music is personal and has an emotional connection with all of us. Here are some ways you can use ICT to promote listening and appraising skills.

- *Play music* – train your class to experience different types of music from jazz to classical to music from around the world and times in history. Make a deal with your class that if the music is on when everyone is working then everyone must be able to hear it.

- *Set your rules for listening* – how many times do you actually sit and listen to music? We use music a huge amount as a background soundtrack. Listening to music involves sitting still and listening to it and something that at first children and sometime adults find difficult. Ask the children to listen to certain features:
  - Which instruments do they hear?
  - How does the music tell a story?
  - Ask them questions relating to the different musical elements of pitch, duration, dynamics, tempo, timbre, texture and structure.

- *Around the world challenge* – insert an image of a world map on an empty flipchart. Set your class a challenge at the beginning of the year that as a class you are going to see how many pieces of music from different countries you can listen to. As you listen to a piece of music then you place an image of a dot/shape/cat/plane (whatever you like) on the relevant country to represent that you have listened to its music. Why not have a whole-school competition to see how many different pieces of music you can listen to. That way you can swap music with colleagues.

- *Create a listening grid* – create a four by three grid on the interactive whiteboard. Place headings at the top of each square such as rhythmic, percussion instruments, fast, slow, singer. As you listen to the pieces of music, you either tick when you hear that quality or write the name of the piece in each box. You are then able to see the aspects each piece has.

- *Sliding scales* – using your interactive whiteboard software, draw a number of lines on the page and lock them in to position. From the resources bank, insert an arrow or a pointer or a cartoon character. Use this to assess how much the class likes aspects of the music. For example under each line write a musical aspect such as singing, instruments, drums, woodwind. Then at certain points throughout listening, stop the track and slide the image from left to right depending on how much the class liked the singing/instruments/drums and so on.

Listening and instrument apps

MOBILE

There are a number of good apps to make listening to certain pieces of music more visual and well as introducing children to different instruments. Below are a few suggestions:

- Learn the Orchestra (https://itunes.apple.com/gb/app/learn-the-orchestra/id448760801?mt=8) enables children to discover the different instruments of the orchestra and read more about the instrument and the sound it makes.
- My First Orchestra App (https://itunes.apple.com/gb/app/my-first-orchestra-app-hd/id568583429?mt=8) is written by Naxos who produce classical music on CD. Written for younger children, it has sample tunes, looks at composers who have written for instruments and features whole families of instruments.
- Young Person's Guide to the Orchestra by Benjamin Britten (https://itunes.apple.com/gb/app/young-persons-guide-to-orchestra/id665019589?mt=8) is an app written to accompany the music written by the composer. You can find out about the instruments as well as see the music being played through.
- There are a few apps designed to make Camille Saint-Saëns' piece 'Carnival of the Animals' come alive. Naxos (http://www.naxos.com/feature/The_Carnival_of_the_Animals_App.asp) have produced a colourful app to accompany the music. Aedify (https://itunes.apple.com/gb/app/carnival-animals-music-education/id655525796?mt=8) tie their app more to the musical education side so within the two pieces you find out more about duration and steady beat. Finally, The Saint-Saëns' Carnival of the Animals app (https://itunes.apple.com/gb/app/saint-saens-carnival-animals/id475653515?mt=8) allows you to see other animated aspects of the music as well as being able to see pages of the score.
- The Orchestra by Touch Press (www.touchpress.com/titles/orchestra) is a beautiful app that is incredibly well thought-through. The app shows what it is like to be inside the orchestra with film clips, players talking about their instrument, seeing the music as it is played as well as being synchronised with pictorial references so you know which instruments are playing.

Composing

Composing using ICT used to be limited and in some ways developed a narrow sense of composition. Many older software titles worked on organising samples of music to support the composition process. Advances in technology have made composition much more creative and inventive since the introduction of mobile devices. Below are a few suggestions for how ICT can support composing as well as some apps worth exploring to start you off.

- *Compositions* – when the children are working on composing a melody, record the final or on-going composition. On-going compositions can be used for assessment purposes and to provide children with a way of reviewing their own work and talking about the next steps of how they are going to improve their work. You can also collect excellent pieces of work as samples to play to children doing the topic in subsequent years. All of the final compositions could then be collected together on the school's Virtual Learning Environment or embedded in a blog post for parents to listen to or download on to an MP3 player.

- *Create from scratch* – the body is one of the cheapest instruments children can use to compose with. Composing using the body means that children explore the 'polite' percussive sounds they can make with their body. These include using their hands to tap out a rhythm on their chests; making a popping sound with their lips or rubbing their hands together and then clapping at the end. The list is endless and the children really enjoy creating their own sounds. Ask the children to think of their own body sounds and then record these down the side of the board. Next draw a four by four grid on the interactive whiteboard and enter one of these sounds in each box to form a pattern. The children then sound out the first line and then progress to the second line and so on until the whole composition is complete. Divide your class into four and give each group a line to perform. The children can then make their own versions up in small groups and perform these to the rest of the class. For inspiration take a look at 'The Percussion Show Presents: Body Percussion' (www.youtube.com/watch?v=sb-2VsE2y-U) or the Honda car advert (www.youtube.com/watch?v=DlaK8q5HT7k).

- *Isle of Tune* – this is a novel way of looking at composition. The Isle of Tune (www.isleoftune.com) lets you compose a piece of music by building your own city. Each piece makes a particular sound. The house makes a low xylophone sound; the flowers are the sound of keyboards and the lampposts are different percussion beats. All of these can be customised by pitch and you have the ability to change the different sounds. You're a given a piece of field where you can lay down road and then musically decorate it with the different objects. Finally you place up to three different cars on the road. As the car passes the object it triggers the sound. Isle of Tune is a great resource open to everyone. There are examples for you to look at. Search for

'Don't Stop Believing' and you will see the talent of some people. However, inherent in the notion that the resources are open to everyone does throw up one potential e-safety dilemma. Anyone can upload an island they have created. Unfortunately some people choose to name these islands in inappropriate ways. This either becomes a program that you do not use or a teaching point about etiquette and how you should name files appropriately. You can talk through how the children create their own island and explain the dangers and sanctions if children are found searching during school times. This certainly does stimulate a good discussion, it is just a shame people find it difficult to behave and act appropriately.

- *Graphical notation* – the interactive whiteboard provides an excellent resource for creating a graphical score. This is a way of composing using pictures to represent sounds. It is organised in a linear way and read/played from left to right, from start to finish. Place different icons on the page to create your score and then perform it as a class.

Apps for composing

Below are a few suggestions for apps that can be used to compose with.

- Musyc (www.fingerlab.net/website/Fingerlab/Musyc.html) is a really interesting app. Sounds are made by musical objects bouncing off the lines you have drawn as well as the objects you have placed within the screen. It's great fun and certainly an interesting way to compose.
- SoundBrush (https://itunes.apple.com/gb/app/soundbrush/id577710046?mt=8) allows you to draw lines of the sound on a grid. The longer the line is, the longer the sound is played. There are different instruments that can be purchased through the app and combined together to make a composition.
- Isle of Tune (https://itunes.apple.com/gb/app/isle-of-tune-mobile/id430845597?mt=8) is an app version of the web application listed above.
- StarComposer (https://itunes.apple.com/gb/app/starcomposer/id670221315?mt=8) is an interesting way for children to look at different styles of music and compose their own in the same genre. Get sounds and you can make up your lyrics and then record a vocal track.
- MadPad (www.smule.com/madpad) presents you with a four by three grid. Each square comprises a sound. You can record you own or use a grid that other people have produced. Due to the multi-touch nature of the iPad it means that more than one sound can be combined together. Take two fingers and slide your fingers up and it speeds the sound up while the opposite way will slow things down. You can record your own signing, instruments, rhythms and sounds and then use these to make your own compositions.

Art and design and technology

Like music, art is a very practical subject. ICT can support the planning and can help to create art in a digital way which is very different to the traditional techniques of using a pencil, paper and paints.

Art

Below are some suggestions of how ICT can support art.

- *Websites* – use websites like Sumopaint (www.sumopaint.com/app) to create new digital artwork and discuss the benefits and merits of using a computer to draw, over pencil and paper. Paul Carney, an Advanced Skills Teacher in Art and Design (www. paulcarneyarts.com/index.html), has a wealth of ideas to support how you use ICT in art.

- *Resource packs* – explore your interactive whiteboard software and its attached sites. If you have Promethean software, then type 'art' into Promethean Planet (http://www. prometheanplanet.com/en-gb/) and you will find a variety of flipcharts and what are called 'resources packs' which you can download and install into ActivInspire. This will give you a bank of images to use in your flipcharts.

- *Digital photography* – explore using the digital camera to create art. Take a portrait image of every child in your class and print off each photograph. Then ask the children to rip the photo in half. Explain that they are going to create a different portrait of themselves using pencil, watercolour or pastels. The end results should be a complete portrait with half a digital photograph and the other half drawn in a different medium.

- *Photograph and enlarge* – ask the children to use a tablet device to take a photograph of an object they are going to draw. Then ask them to enlarge it and draw a particular section. The enlarged drawing could also be used as a template for a piece of batik wax artwork.

- *Software to support the curriculum* – software such as ArtRage (www.artrage. com), Revelation Natural Art (www.r-e-m.co.uk/logo/?Titleno=25343) and Dazzle (www.indigolearning.com/indigo2/site/product.acds?context=1935703&instanceid=1935704) can support the art curriculum by providing a range of different tools for children to paint with. They can also use the programs to create repeated patterns and explore how to create art using separate layers.

- *Use the web to appreciate art* – explore websites like The National Gallery (http://www. nationalgallery.org.uk) or type in the name of an artist and there will be work to use to create a stimulus.

- *Let's animate* – use animation software to animate models the children have made. This could then be combined with music to make a short film.

Using your overhead projector and scanner

Below are a few ways that different pieces of ICT equipment can be used to support art and design and technology activities.

- Demonstrate drawing skills by creating each of the stages to make up a sketch and then join them and overlay them during the lesson(s). Then as your drawing progresses, the children can see and follow each stage.

- Use the overhead projector to investigate colour mixing using different coloured films. What happens if we mix the yellow film with the red film?

- Children thoroughly enjoy seeing their artwork when it has been scanned in. I worked with a group of children who struggled with finding positive points about the brilliant artwork they had produced. However, when it was scanned in, their responses were bizarrely quite the opposite. Strange, but when asked what the difference was between the scanned version and their own real-life version they commented that the scanned version made their artwork 'clearer' and 'better'. The scans can then be used in a digital scrapbook of the year or placed as an example of good work within their end-of-term report.

- Scan in pencil sketches the children make and use these as a template for batik, screen-printing or collage work.

Using your interactive whiteboard

The interactive whiteboard provides a huge digital canvas for you to model art techniques to the class. Different colours and pens can be used for drawing and colouring. Try using dedicated software like Artrage, Dazzle or Revelation Natural Arts, which provide you with more specific tools to also use.

- *Become an artist* – your interactive whiteboard can be transformed into a larger than life canvas. Using the art software you have available in school, use the whiteboard to demonstrate different drawing techniques. Use a photograph and select a brightly-coloured pen and trace over to create an outline frame so that the children can see how it would be drawn. Trace over the main outline of the photograph and then remove the photograph so that it just leaves the pencil line drawing. You could use this, for example, to draw a Tudor portrait of Henry VIII.

- *Snip snip* – take a photograph and load it on to the interactive whiteboard. Use the camera tool to snip out sections. Place these on a new flipchart page and use it to create abstract art.

- *Annotate a photograph* – project a photograph of a child from your class on to the whiteboard. Using the pen tools the children can then draw around features on their face or draw extra features.

Using a digital camera

Mobile devices and digital cameras allow children to photograph any aspect of the world they wish. Below are some suggestions for using a digital camera to support artwork.

- *Final artwork* – keep a record of the children's artwork throughout the year. Children could then use an art package such as Artrage, Dazzle or Revelation Natural Art, to add to or improve their artwork.

- *DT through the stages* – assist children when making a clay 'thumb pot' in art or during a DT project. Photograph the different stages and the children can either use these to write instructions based on the pictures for children who were away or to make the final product or their own version at home with their parents. You could also set up an iPad with animation software such as 'I Can Animate' that has the feature 'Time lapse' enabled. Set it to take a picture every three to five seconds and then the children can use the finished video to stop and start and then create their piece of arts work.

Using visualisers

Visualisers offer a unique way to demonstrate different techniques to a class, from cooking to drawing. Demonstrate some of the more complex art or design and technology procedures to the children that can be difficult to see when crowded around a table. When a visualiser is connected to a display it can be easy for the children to understand how to make that join for the moneybox they're making or how to use a knife safely.

Art apps

The creation of digital art has produced a new genre of art altogether. With the development of the iPad, there have been some stunning pieces of art drawn on these devices. If you are planning to use mobile devices, then it is worth investing in a stylus. These, however, tend not to be as accurate as a pencil and it does take time to get used to feeling the weight of the stylus in your hand.

It is really worth exploring the Sensu brush (www.sensubrush.com). They are an excellent investment as they have a stylus in them as well as allowing the children to paint digitally. Below are a few suggestions for art apps.

- ArtRage (https://itunes.apple.com/gb/app/artrage/id391432693?mt=8) and Sumopaint (https://itunes.apple.com/gb/app/sumo-paint-create-draw-doodle/id542324634?mt=8) are both apps of their software counterparts. An alternative to these are Brushes (https://itunes.apple.com/gb/app/brushes-3/id545366251?mt=8), Paper (https://itunes.apple.com/gb/app/paper-by-fiftythree/id506003812?mt=8) and Tayasui Sketches (https://itunes.apple.com/gb/app/tayasui-sketches/id641900855?mt=8).
- 8mm (http://8mm.mobi/) uses the iPad's camera and applies an effect. Many of these effects are particularly artistic such as the ability to film in 1920s or Noir. A frame jitter button is on the right-hand side so the children can film a video so it has an authentic look to it. The finished clips are placed into a reel and then themes can be applied along with accompanying music.
- Enhance photographs with apps which apply an effect. Repix (https://itunes.apple.com/gb/app/repix-inspiring-photo-editor/id597830453?mt=8) Snapseed (https://itunes.apple.com/gb/app/snapseed/id439438619?mt=8) PicsPlay Pro (https://itunes.apple.com/gb/app/picsplay-pro/id527093371?mt=8) and Moldiv (https://itunes.apple.com/gb/app/moldiv-collage-photo-editor/id608188610?mt=8) can create some beautiful effects from the children's photographs.

Physical education, health and well-being

ICT can support physical education by engaging children in learning and helping the transition from learning in a fixed space such as a classroom to a more open space such as a hall or field. ICT can help bridge this gap, especially with the use of mobile technology. Below are some ways that ICT can support the teaching of PE:

- *YouTube videos* – use different YouTube videos to look at how professional sports people play and practise their sport. This can help children to improve posture and technique. Alternatively, use your video recorder and the children can film each other's egg-and-spoon race in preparation for doing their best during Sports Day.

- *Orienteering skills* – take pictures with a digital camera from around the school at unusual and obscure angles (but just enough so the children can work out where in the school that place is). If you have iPod Touch devices or devices with a QR code reader why not provide links in the form of QR codes to fun, games and educational websites. (To learn more about QR Codes and Readers, visit www.whatisaqrcode.co.uk) A QR reader will then read the QR code and take the children to one of the websites. Link to some of the BBC bitesize clips (www.bbc.co.uk/schools/bitesize) to help the children revise a topic in preparation for their SATs test. Create numbered cards that correspond with the pictures you took with a digital camera, make a QR code and then print off and stick these around the school.

- *QR codes* – you can create your own QR Codes by either making them directly from the app or by using a web browser 'plug in' which helps you to generate the QR Code. Firefox users can explore Mobile Barcoder (https://addons.mozilla.org/en-US/firefox/addon/mobile-barcoder), Google Chrome users can use QR-code tag extension (https://chrome.google.com/extensions/detail/bcfddoencoiedfjgepnlhcpfikgaogdg) or QR Code Generator (https://chrome.google.com/extensions/detail/cicimfkkbejhg gfjaabggafffgdnjgjp) or install it into the major web browsers by following this guide (http://www.wikarski.com/cms/content/generate-qr-code-your-web-page-links) .

- *Body monitors* – explore the use of pedometers by looking at the Global Children's Challenge (http://socialinnovation.ca/node/1672). This is a great website to get children active. Using pedometers, there is a race and every day the children enter in the total number of steps they have taken as a class which is then divided by the number of people in the class to calculate an average. The children then move along a route of the world learning about different places. The more they exercise (and don't cheat) the more ground they cover.

- *Make a warm- up DVD* – challenge the children to create a warm-up DVD. This can be used at the beginning of a PE lesson. Can the children think of activities to warm up in pairs? Can they create a warm-up or cool-down routine? They could use the app Tempo Magic created by Lolofit (http://lolofit.com/) to help them if the speed of the music is too fast.

- *Music for PE* – use some of the music apps listed earlier in this chapter to create music that could be used for warm-up or cool-down music at the end of the session.

- *Gaming equipment* – gaming equipment such as Wii Fit and Dance Mat can make a great warm up at the beginning of a session. Use your hall projector and the space in the hall to follow one the warm ups.

- *Starters in class* – use the interactive whiteboard at the beginning of a lesson to introduce the topic to the children. This seems to really focus the children on the objectives before heading out into an open field.

Sports app

MOBILE

Coach's Eye (www.coachseye.com/features) allows children to take a short video of a sports movement and then replay it and annotate over the top of the video. It is great for assessment purposes and for producing feedback for children as they look for ways to improve their technique.

Modern foreign languages

For non-specialists, the teaching of a modern foreign language can be a challenging task, particularly in getting the speech and pronunciation right. ICT, and especially the internet, can be a great support, both to you and the children. Use the internet to allow the children to listen to native speakers and try the resources given below:

- *Speaking and listening* – glance back at the section at the beginning of Chapter 4 and take a look at some of the ideas for using ICT to develop speaking and listening. The same ideas can be used for developing MFL.

- *The Global Gateway* – managed by the British Council, the British Council Schools Online (http://schoolsonline.britishcouncil.org/) provides access, resources, funding and linking with schools across the world as well as many other opportunities for language and cultural development. If you want to link with schools across the world then there is opportunity to do so and get an introduction here. A fantastic resource!

- *TeacherTube and YouTube* – if your skills in French, Spanish, German or other foreign languages are anything like mine then the thought of pronouncing the words with the correct accent and nuances can give you sleepless nights. The internet might provide you with resources in that language but it also throws up many pages that you might not even understand. Try searching on YouTube (www.youtube.com) or TeacherTube (www.teachertube.com) for teaching resources in your chosen language as this can bring up useful resources with real voices to support your teaching.

- *Look at language for the young* – look for websites that have been especially created for very young children to learn a language. The best way to learn a language is through play and immersion in that language. Sites written for little ones will encourage exploration and learning in a fun way instead of a more vocabulary-led way. Poissonrouge (www.poissonrouge.com) is a great example of this. Want to learn Dutch or Japanese? Then take a look at the Miffy website (www.miffy.com) which also been converted into Dutch (www.nijntje.nl/) and Japanese (www.miffy.jp).

- *DIY* – ask the children to use 2Do It Yourself (www.2simple.com/2diy/) to create different MFL resources for younger children to teach them what they have learnt.

- *Google Earth* – when exploring new countries on Google Earth there are tours around places. Why not have a trip around the Eiffel tower and listen to the guide speak in French and try to work out the different things that are being pointed out?

- *Online translators* – explore online translators and discuss whether they are completely reliable and how language changes depending on the everyday meanings that are used.

- *Exploring language* – use word cloud websites like Wordle (www.wordle.net) or Tagxedo (www.tagxedo.com) to create interesting-looking MFL sentences that are then jumbled up. Ask the children to rearrange the sentences to try to work out what is being communicated to them.

9 Using ICT to support all children

If children struggle with aspects of their learning, then ICT can make it easier for them to achieve. ICT can also present challenges. The thrill of learning new skills, taking on responsibilities and solving any problems/challenges along the way can stretch your gifted children.

Using ICT to support children with additional needs

There are many different products, pieces of software and adapted hardware that can be used to support children with special educational needs. The BETT education technology show (www.bettshow.com) dedicates an entire zone to this part of the market. SEN coordinators (SENCOs) have a complex job and ICT can make interventions and action plan targets for children with SEN much easier to achieve.

So how can ICT help support these children? Below are a few ideas of where ICT might be useful:

- *Learning styles* – whatever the area of learning need, all children respond to learning presented in either a *visual*, *auditory* and/or *kinaesthetic* way. Making learning multi-sensory ensures all children's learning styles are catered for. Leaving written instructions on the board; video help guides or using the digital camera to photograph work can all support different ways of learning.

- *Clicker* – if writing is difficult, then the sentences can be supported with Clicker (http://www.cricksoft.com/uk/products/tools/clicker/home.aspx). It works by the children pressing different word blocks in order to create sentences. This method is based on the concept keyboard which was typically used to support children in their writing. Whole sentences and visible word banks can be created. With the support of a teaching assistant helping to edit the work, the children can produce results that are stunning.

- *Explore different media* – if children find it difficult to write, consider that there may be other ways of assessing their learning. The use of the flip video recorder or a dictaphone will also let them share their learning.

- *Speech recognition software* – for children with poor motor skills, an alternative piece of software is Dragon Dictate. This software allows the user to speak their words and then the computer generates this into text (http://www.nuance.co.uk/dragon/index.htm).

- *Interactive whiteboard sound recorder* – this is a tool that isn't used nearly as much as it should be. For Promethean users only, it gives the teacher the ability to record their voice. When you've prepared your flipchart, use the sound recorder to record all the sentences which are on the screen then, if the children do not know what a sentence says, they can have it replayed to them. This also works in reverse. Once the children understand the task, they can record their answers just using a microphone. I once set this task for a child with SEN and their assistant to complete based on explaining how a circuit works. The level of understanding was excellent and demonstrated that just because there is a difficulty does not mean that children are incapable of understanding quite high levels of scientific enquiry.

- *Visual timetables using digital photographs* – take pictures of the daily routines (assembly, PE, lunchtime, tidy time) and create a visual timetable for children who struggle with the organisation of the day. Add a mobile dimension to this by creating a photograph album for each day of the week. Add the correct photographs to each day and then the children can flick through the album each day.

- *Supporting children with Dyscalculia* – JellyJames (www.jellyjames.co.uk) produce two software programs called DynamoMaths and Dynamo Profiler which help to support and identify children who struggle with maths as well as providing some good activities children can use at home as well as school. Numbershark, produced by White Space, is another alternative (www.wordshark.co.uk/numbershark.aspx) schools can use to support children with dyscalculia.

- *Wordshark* – for children who need some support with aspects of reading and spelling, Wordshark (www.wordshark.co.uk/index.aspx) can be used by classroom assistants as an intervention strategy.

- *eBooks* – there are a range of great eBooks available to use in the classroom for children who struggle with generating ideas during creative writing sessions. *Descriptosaurus,* written by Alison Wilcox (Routledge), is an excellent resource for children to use as it provides words and phrases children could use if they were stuck. The great thing about technology and specifically eBooks is that useful sections can be highlighted and read out to add extra support.

- *Shhhh!* – sometimes specific children or indeed whole classes can struggle with making too much noise. If you need to find a way to encourage quiet working, the Child Silence Timer (http://www.keaton.com/) is a fun way of helping children to monitor the level of talk in their classroom. Try linking it to your interactive whiteboard and if your class is too noisy the dog wakes up to remind them! Reward your children with a class star or marble for each time they are successful. Another example is MyClassRules – Noise Monitor (http://enapp.appvv.com/475268.html).

Using a mobile device

A mobile tablet, such as an iPad, can be an excellent resource to support children with additional needs. They are light and practical to carry around and now have a wide range of apps to support children. Below are some ideas:

The camera

- The camera can help children with short-term memory difficulties to record useful lesson content. Encourage the children to take photographs of the key messages from the input and written instructions that you have provided.

- If no sound recorder is installed then use the video camera to record thoughts and reflections on the lesson. At the end of the session, make a short ten-second clip about what has been learned. This can then be used as a good home-school link for the moment when parents ask their children what they learned during the day.

Notes

- Use the 'Notes' function for recording simple sentences. Highlight a word and the tablet can find a definition for you or read aloud a sentence.

Reminders

- When instructions are given in class, children can set short reminders that they can tick off as they achieve them.

The accessibility features on the iPad

There are a range of different settings on a tablet to support complex needs, including 'Talkback' which is a screen reader on android tablets as well as other features such as the ability to zoom in on parts of the screen. These features are built in and work incredibly well and are worth getting to know. As well as helping all children they can support those children with more complex needs. On the iPad these features are located in the Settings under the General tab and then the Accessibility menu.

Supporting visual difficulties

- *Voice over* – this is a screen reader that lets you know what is happening. A voice speaks to you as you place your finger on the screen. One cautionary note however, if you try it out it can be a little tricky to put it back… consider yourself forewarned.

- *Siri* – Siri is your personal assistant to help you do everything on your device. It can launch apps, set reminders, put dates in your diary, make notes and search the web amongst other things. This can help children to get more organised and build positive study skills.

- *Speak selection* – highlight any word or a sentence and several options appear. If you have turned on the Speak selection option then it will read the words back to you. The speed of the voice can be increased or decreased. This is a useful feature for children to use as it will read websites, text in emails and sentences children have typed out.

- *Dictation* – tap the microphone and dictate sentences. This takes some practice with children but it is a good way to record thoughts and take the strain out of writing.

- *Making it easier to see* – there are three options that can make the information easier to read. The first is a built-in magnifier which can zoom between 100 and 500 per cent. Turn the feature on and tap three fingers. Among the settings there is also the option to make the text size much larger as well as to invert the screen colours.

Supporting motor difficulties

- *Assistive touch* – this is a nice feature that provides access to the hardware functions (volume controls, home button) as well as the some of the gestures such as multi-tasking and screenshot. This also helps to save the physical home button getting worn out.

- *Guided access* – this is a useful feature for restricting areas of an app so children do not become distracted. It is not so good for older children but for younger children it can keep them focused on just one task.

Supporting dyslexia

Dyslexic children can have difficulties with several areas: writing, memory, reading, motor control, space-related tasks and listening. Below are some ways the mobile devices can support children with dyslexia.

- *What is dyslexia?* (http://www.nessy.com/uk/) – this app helps children to explain the difficulties they will experience. There are tips for schools and parents as well as explaining what it's like being dyslexic. The app is set out in a bright cartoon way with some useful information.

- *Dyslexia Quest* (http://www.nessy.com/uk/) – this app aims to assess areas dyslexic children find challenging, such as working memory, phonological awareness, processing speed, visual memory, auditory memory and sequencing skills and provides games for the children to complete. Results are presented at the end so parents and teachers can gauge areas of strengths and identify areas for development.

Apps to support children with dyslexia

MOBILE

Area	Difficulty	How technology can help
Writing difficulties	• Getting ideas down to help with writing	Use apps such as iBrainstorm, Popplet, iThoughts or MindMeister to encourage children to brainstorm and collect their thoughts together while generating ideas.
	• Finding the correct word	There are many different dictionaries that are available but DD's Dictionary A Dyslexic's Dictionary is one that is easy to use. You can use the Dysle+ie font, which is an easy font to read. As the children begin to type then possible options appear.
Writing difficulties	• Organisation and structure of writing	Drawing apps such as Bamboo Paper and Inkflow allow children to draw ideas first. SMART have a mobile version of their interactive SMARTBoard which allows the user to enter text, draw and move ideas around the page.
Memory difficulties	• Ordering of numbers, letters and learning timetables	Word Wizard allows children to drag letters in sequence on to a board. A short activity you can do is to drag some letters in a random order and then ask the children to rearrange them back into alphabetical order. The tiles stay where they are so the children can use this for support if they need to.
Reading difficulties	• Knowing where you are on the page. • Letters jiggling around the page • Re-reading information	Read&Write Gold produced by Texthelp (www.texthelp.com/UK) is a PC software program to make reading the web, documents and all the reading tasks children need to do much easier. The PC program installs a toolbar where you can place the cursor by the text, highlight/select sections and then press play and the software will read out the words. A superb feature is that the software double highlights in contrasting colours. Therefore as the software reads the text, each word is highlighted helping children to track what is being said. They also produce a mobile app which mimics some of the main features of the paid software.

Area	Difficulty	How technology can help
Motor control difficulties	• Being able to trace letters	Paint Sparkles Draw is an app children enjoy using. It simply provides a blank canvas with paint pots. As you paint, sparkles are emitted. You can choose a colour and draw a letter. The children then have to choose a different colour and trace over the drawn letter.
Motor control difficulties	• Coordination and fine motor control	BinaryLabs, Inc (http://www.dexteria.net) produce a suite of apps to support children in developing their motor skills. Their Fine Motor Skills apps enable the children to develop their pre-writing skills by tracing lines. Their Dexteria app allows children to chase the letters of the alphabet and pinch coloured crabs to strengthen their motor skills. The app Fingle is a good app for two people to play to improve motor control skills. Using a finger, both people have to match the colour square together. Tap the Frog is an app that tests speed reactions. You have to tap the frog in different games and it then measures how quick you were.
	• Copying skills from the board	Children can use the camera app on the tablet to photograph the whiteboard, giving them a copy in front of them to use.
Spatial/ temporal difficulties	• Telling the time	The clock app can help children to keep track of time. If you have planned events throughout the week then the app Countdown+++ can help children visually see the events countdown. This could either work on a daily basis or by putting in events the children have to get ready for throughout the week such as PE/games or library book change.
	• Finding your way without getting lost.	Mobile tablets have map apps built into them. Some of these will also give you turn-by-turn directions.
Listening difficulties	• Taking notes	Notability allows the user to write notes as well as record audio at the same time. A good app for jotting down quick thoughts.

Apps to support children with complex needs

Apps can support general learning difficulties and make learning more accessible for all children. Some children can have more complex and specific needs. ICT not only supports these children but often transforms their worlds by enabling them to communicate more effectively and successfully and by reducing frustration. While there are a number of apps at lower prices, apps specifically designed for this field can be very expensive but are worthy of the investment. Here are a few examples:

Children with autism

- Autism Apps – provides lists of apps as a starting point. The pricing is in dollars but don't let that stop you, as your tablet will recognise the UK iTunes store. The app tries to pull together apps which are useful for children with Autism Spectrum Disorder (ASD); with Down's syndrome as well as other additional needs. It is a very useful app for parents and SENCOs.
- Timers – there are numerous timers to work in the classroom. Picture Prompt Timer allows you to take photographs in the same way you would for a visual timetable. What is nice about this app is that you can display a photograph of what you want the child to do first and then the activity they will complete next. The timer counts down in the middle where an audio can be played which you can record yourself. iPrompts allows you to set a number of tasks to complete stage by stage, for example, getting ready for PE or home time. It will then present the schedule at each step.

Children with communication difficulties

- Proloquo2Go – this is the gold standard of software for children with communication difficulties. The child presses on the different words to communicate their sentence. As each word is pressed it appears at the top and is spoken. It can be used with switches or by touching the tablet interface. It is an excellent app but expensive.
- Grid Player – this works in the same way as Proloquo2Go, so symbols can be pressed. You need to sign up for a free account to use it. It has some super phrase banks as well as sentence starters.

Children who use signing

- British Sign Language (BSL) – there are a number of different apps to teach BSL. The BSL Level series by Twinkle Fingers is a useful professional development resource for teachers.
- Baby Sign and Learn – this app will help children communicate using signing. Tap on a picture and the animated baby says the word and makes the sign. You can even create useful flashcards and some of the most common words are already there for you to use.

Children with behavioural difficulties

- ClassDojo (www.classdojo.com) – is an online tool which can be used to support not only individual groups of behaviour but also whole classes. Enter the names of all children in your class and each name appears as a cartoon monster/alien. You award points for positive and negative behaviour. The titles of each of these types of behaviours can be modified and you can add behaviours as well. To award points, you simply press on the name, select the behaviour and a large summary 'Well done!' screen appears with the child's name and why they were awarded. There is an attendance screen so children can self-register which is always good for improving independence skills. A mobile app is also available so you can award points on the move.
- Supernanny – Jo Frost from the behavioural show 'Supernanny' has produced an app entitled Jo Frost Rewards which works in the same way as ClassDojo but is useful for parents to use at home as well.

For more information, there is an excellent guide produced by Craig Mill and the CALL Team from Scotland entitled *iPads for Communication, Access, Literacy and Learning* (iCALL) (http://www.callscotland.org.uk/Resources/Books/iPads-for-Communication-Access-Literacy-and-Learning/) which is a must-read for any SENCO.

Using ICT to stretch more able children

One of the perceptions that we have of many of our youngsters in school is that they know much more about how technology works than we do. This is partly true and largely comes down to a few factors which are outlined below:

- *Exposure* – the more children become familiar with how something works the more they will learn how to use it. As the exposure to technology has widened, especially with the internet, the more children are able to research more, read more and refine their computer skills. However, children still need to be shown techniques and tricks for using a computer so they can become more efficient in the world of work. For example we can search the internet by browsing using mobile phones, making it easier to find information but do children know how to use different search engines and how to refine searches so they can extract useful information at a faster pace?
- *Adaptability* – the ability to be presented with information which looks slightly different means that children's 'getting used to using it' phase gets shorter. Working on a laptop requires similar skills to a netbook, a desktop PC or a tablet device. However, all this requires children to change the 'mode' in which they work, which they are able to do quickly.

- *Challenge* – there is a challenge of wondering what a piece of equipment can do. Technology fosters a practical approach to using it and encourages the 'can it do this?' and 'I wonder if I press this what will happen?' type questions. These are great open-ended and higher-order type questions that allow children at a basic level to come out of their comfort zone but within a secure environment.

- *The social talk element* – the more people talk about and discuss technology, the more others pick up hints and tips. Technology does have the potential to isolate people but it can also promote sociability. Questions that rely on challenge and talk often deepen our understanding. How many times have you ever tried to work out how to use your new mobile phone and only got so far before having to ask someone else? By asking another person to be our expert and tutor we engage in the social talk dimension of using technology. With someone coaching us and by working together we gain confidence in using the technology.

- *Make memories* – positive (and sometimes negative) experiences of technology etch lasting impressions in our mind and affect our attitude towards how we use it. If, on the whole, your contact has been positive and rewarding then you are more likely to try out different technology more willingly. If these occurrences are experienced at the same time with family members, teachers and other people we enjoy spending time with then this deepens our attitudes.

Recognising the more able

So with all the above elements becoming more frequent in the modern-day lives of children, how do we recognise and identify the children who are more able in ICT? It is important to understand that children who are able will often have stronger strengths in certain particular areas. However, I believe that there are certain generic characteristics that these children will demonstrate:

- They will have good general skills in using the computer. They will navigate competently and are able to 'push the buttons' with confidence.

- They will make links between different applications. For example, they will recognise the B *(bold)*, I *(italics)* and U *(underline)* icons within a word processor but can also recognise these in other applications and understand what they mean.

- They will constantly push you within classroom ICT. They will want to know how things work and will often say, 'I know this; it looks like the program I've been using at home'.

- They demand excellence from the applications they use.

- They will spend time over and above what is asked of them, trying to refine their ideas or test new software.

- They will actively explore different alternatives for software they might use at school.

- They will often create and test things out at home.
- They may even try to hack into the school system or try to guess the administrator passwords, without really knowing the implications of their actions.
- They are keen to demonstrate their knowledge.

What are the different ways of stretching your more able children? You could look at a more differentiated curriculum by exploring the Secondary guidance on The Vital ICT website (www.vital.ac.uk) or talk to your Key Stage 3/4 colleagues or county inspector and advisers. Below are a few ways you might want to try to extend your more able primary pupils.

Enrichment tasks

Set some extra time aside to pull together your more able pupils so they can develop their skills on projects, applications and tasks outside the framework of usual ICT lessons:

- *School newsletter* – using digital cameras and video cameras, ask the children to design a school newsletter. This could either be produced as a paper copy or, if the correct permissions have been obtained, then it could be placed as an online version on the school website.
- *Media club* – the process of working on media can be long depending on the desired effect. Often the shooting and collection of footage is relatively short compared to the editing process. Teach the group how to edit video and then the children can practise making a short school news report. With Apple's iLife Suite (http://www.apple.com/uk/ilife/) which comes free with every Mac computer, there are predesigned templates, transitions, soundtracks and trailer creation templates which make the whole process a lot easier, while producing some stunning results.
- *Website design* – give the children responsibility for updating certain parts of the school website with current news.
- *Running an ICT club for children* – there are some children who enjoy taking on the role of teacher. Encourage these children to run their own ICT club in which they have to plan a four to six week module of work for children who are interested in joining.
- *Blogging* – with blogging websites like Wordpress (http://wordpress.org/) you can set the children to become contributors to your blog. All the posts still need to be moderated and approved but the privilege of becoming a guest writer for the blog is a great responsibility. They could write a blog about school events, internet safety, curriculum projects or simply collect and edit stories children have written.
- *Teach children to code* – for more advanced uses of ICT, you may want to look at programming or sequencing software. Scratch is an open-source piece of software you can use to create your own interactive stories, music, games and art (http://

scratch.mit.edu/). There are a number of guides on how to use the software online but it will require some research before implementation.

- *Games-based learning* – this is a great way to extend children's creative and programming skills. 2Simple, a software company which produces software for schools, has developed a program called 2Do It Yourself (http://www.2simple.com/2diy/). The software is designed to enable children to create their own content and in a do-it-yourself type way. One of the superb aspects is that it enables children to create their own games. There are different formats, from maze games to collecting games through to levelled-platform games. It allows children to enter the script/coding of their game and lets them add and manipulate settings so their character can jump higher, transport their character to a different location on the screen and so on. There are descriptions of what each code means and how to write it as well as some video help on their YouTube site (http://www.youtube.com/user/2SimpleTV) – just search for 2diy in the search bar.

Extra certificates or accreditation

For your children who are truly exceptional and gifted, you may want to consider working with them on industry-level certification. There are a few out there which would provide a challenge for most Key Stage 4 children. Although not for everyone, and very rarely do primary pupils reach these levels, it can provide a useful structured support to challenge these children while also helping them in a potential future career in ICT. Take a look at the following:

- The European Computer Driving Licence (CD) Foundation's certification programme (http://www.ecdl.org/index.jsp?p=93&n=100).
- E-kids (http://www.ecdl.org/programmes/index.jsp?p=771&n=774) – the Croatian Computer Society's Digital Literacy programme endorsed by the CD Foundation.
- Apple Certified Associate – iWork (http://training.apple.com/certification/associate). Providing training in different operating systems might also be a way of stretching more able children so they are able to work in different environments.
- Key Stage 3 modules – there are different materials on the web that have been written to support teachers in delivering the Key Stage 3 ICT programme. Teach-ICT is one example (http://www.teach-ict.com/ks3home.htm).

Developing digital leaders

Consider setting up a group to support the day-to-day problems or tasks the school has to tackle in terms of using ICT. Just as we have special children who sit on the school council or monitor the school environment, the same can be applied to ICT. Purchase some special badges for the children to wear and have a defined job description to make it official. Have some criteria, which the children have to reach in order to become a digital leader and encourage them to apply for the role. Necessary characteristics could include:

- an enthusiasm for ICT
- an ability to explain clearly how to use technology
- a commitment to attend lunchtime meetings for special projects
- to have support at home as it may require working on projects out of school
- to continue to aim for excellence when using ICT.

Some responsibilities for the digital leaders might include, to:

- Set up the computer equipment in the hall.
- Work the projector during singing practice or assemblies.
- Check to make sure the batteries in the programmable toys have not run down.
- Set up the interactive whiteboard welcome screen in the morning and choose the background and morning message. (You write the words on a sticky note and the child comes in early to set up the board.)
- Become an ICT tutor for other children. To provide guidance on how to support other children when they are having difficulty using the equipment so they do not take over but help the children to learn for themselves.
- Write blog posts for the whole-school blog.
- Manage a dedicated area for the children of the school on your Virtual Learning Environment.
- Take photographs of school events.
- Use the flip video recorder to record school events and produce a newsreel for each event.
- Select and replace the images to go on the reception screen for visitors to watch.
- Perform an ICT health check on equipment in the school. Are any cables torn or missing? Is there equipment which needs stock replacing (e.g. printers). Encourage the children to ask various members of staff.
- Test new software to be installed in the school. Provide the children with an evaluation checklist and see what they can create. When doing this, make sure the children repeat the task three times:
  - Firstly, ask them to have a general play and see what the software can do.
  - Secondly, ask them to spend a longer amount of time using it. Provide the children

with a *Can it/Can't it* list and *WOW it can do this* column. Ask the children to type up a list of all the things the software will allow them to do, all the things they had difficulty in doing and a *WOW it can do this* for those hidden extras which children would find great to use. This sheet can then be given to teachers to guide them after the software is installed to support them with their planning.

  - Finally, ask the children to create an excellent example of what the software will do so other children can see excellence when they have a go at using it.

- Be ICT tour guides for parents, inspectors and other visitors, demonstrating the great aspects of your school ICT.

- Count your vouchers from schemes to purchase any computer equipment for schools.

- Form part of your ICT review group. When looking forward and planning for next year, the children could be involved in what they would like to see in the school.

- Have input on the school website. What is our school website missing? What would make more people visit our site and more children use it?

- Convert video taken so teachers can use the footage in class. Or this could be converted for use on the school blog.

- Use a Twitter board to write messages of 140 characters about their learning which you can then edit or copy straight on to your school Twitter feed.

- Write ICT case studies about your school which they can then present to the school governors.

- Be involved in school training sessions for the staff. Invite them to a staff meeting or INSET day, put staff into small groups and then assign a child ICT tutor to each group so they can demonstrate how they have used new software. Staff are much less critical when children are demonstrating to them.

- Be part of the technical team at school productions, which includes monitoring the sound or working the projector, creating sound effects or putting together the production background.

- Train the new recruits of digital leaders. When selecting your first batch of digital leaders, try to select from a cross-section from the school; therefore, when Year 6 children leave you're not left with a training gap. This will also promote the concept, which is true, that able children at ICT can be recognised at any stage regardless of their age.

Developing the Digital Senate

Previously throughout the book, I have referred to schools using what I call the Digital Senate. A large majority of schools invest each year in building a school council, in which the children, along with members of staff, discuss issues and ideas which affect the personal, social, health and well-being of children throughout the school. Ideas are suggested by the children, which are then taken back and relayed to each class so that everyone receives the same message.

The Digital Senate takes a different perspective. ICT affects the whole school in all aspects of daily school life. Encourage people who are interested in driving ICT in your school to come together and work towards a vision for the school.

What tasks do the Digital Senate members undertake? They:

- Develop the vision for what ICT should look like in their school.
- Discuss ideas for how to get the most from the technology.
- Attend each of the half-termly meetings.
- Decide how the budget should be spent regarding technology.
- Discuss the rolling programme of replacing technology and what is not working so well from a user's perspective.
- Assign members to look after key tasks – the website, blogs, social media – and to feedback regularly to the Senate to report how things are going.
- Talk about the training that children and staff require and the best ways to achieve this, whether it is through staff meetings, organised Teach Meets (see below), the production of video help files/help sheets or attending ICT INSET days if necessary.
- Attend Teach Meets to share good practice. Teach Meets give teachers a chance to share classroom practice and ideas outside the immediate arena of their own personal schools. For more information on Teach Meets, take a look and the following YouTube video (www.youtube.com/watch?v=1A42kEELSSs).
- Help interview new digital leaders and work with them to induct them.
- Raise the profile of technology and its use across and around the school.
- Discuss whole-school incentives such as the introduction of mobile technology or what to do during World Internet Safety Day.
- Discuss ways to promote the safe and responsible use of technology and the internet around the school.

Who sits on the Digital Senate?

First and foremost, all digital leaders sit on the Digital Senate as part of their role. Adult members of the Digital Senate include: the ICT coordinator, technician, headteacher, finance officer and governor(s) responsible for ICT.

Why are those people needed?

Role	Why are they needed on the Digital Senate?
Digital leaders	The children's views are central to knowing how the ICT is working across the school. Digital leaders are already keen users of ICT and help to drive the school's vision for ICT forward.
ICT coordinator	They connect everyone together. They are the person who is leading the subject across the school and has the most contact with senior staff, students and governors.
Technician	It can be useful to have a technician present to add a different perspective, especially when it is time to replace the computers across the school.
Headteacher	Knows the overall vision and can feed back to the senior management team. They also know more about the budget (in conjuction with the finance officer). They will often lead initiatives in front of the whole school.
Finance officer	Knows the day-to-day state of the ICT budgets and can therefore advise the Senate on the price implications and whether the ideas discussed are realistic in terms of the school budget.
ICT governor(s)	The ICT coordinator will normally have a link ICT governor. By having the ICT governor on the Senate they are aware of what it happening in the school and can also feed this back personally during the appropriate curriculum and finance meetings.

The Digital Senate is important in a school because it helps to develop the following areas for the children:

- *Developing life skills* – children need to be able to work in teams and progress projects. They develop the skills of speaking and listening, teamwork, and problem-solving. They are able to develop their emotional literacy skills by understanding the ICT experience from other users. They also increase their self-esteem/self-confidence by being recognised as an expert or someone who has a keen interest.
- *Develop leadership qualities* – children can develop these skills as the focus is shifted away from teachers and towards child members of the Senate and their classes in the school community.
- *Improve communication and reduce frustrations* – ICT can be incredibly frustrating when the technology does not work. This is even more likely to be the case when the technology is old or breaks down for unforeseen long periods. By discussing these frustrations and asking the children to feed back the information to their classes, these children help to improve the understanding of the school community.

- *It builds the school community* – this is an issue that affects everyone. Everyone uses technology, from the interactive whiteboards in their classroom, to the devices in their hands. By actively involving the Digital Senate, then if led well, there is greater parity throughout the school. Digital Senates can demonstrate to children that they are a responsible part of the process, that they deal with technology issues that affect all school users and above all that the work they carry out through the Senate does one thing – it make a difference!

Celebrating ICT and pupil achievement

The Arts can in many ways be likened to ICT. Within the Arts, the hard work that goes into the process is partly so that the end result is communicated well to the audience, be that to an audience of parents, peers, teachers, extended family or the wider world. Many digital schools provide a platform for children to showcase their work. Below are some ideas and tips of how you can celebrate and promote the children's achievements and successes within ICT:

- *Website* – it used to be that, if you wanted to celebrate some of the achievements of pupils, then you either had to invite parents in, photocopy children's work and send it home or make an extra effort to show the rest of the school during a special assembly. The internet makes it much easier to share achievements with the school community and beyond. Your school website can connect with people on a local, national and even global scale. Why not use your school website to promote and celebrate the fantastic work your children have produced? In 2007, the Times Educational Supplement reported that Woodlands Junior School (http://resources.woodlands-junior.kent.sch.uk) was the most visited school website in the United Kingdom. Curated by Mandy Barrow, it is a true testament to how a school can use their website to support not only its pupils but children around the world.

- *Ask children to take on different roles in the school* – children relish the opportunity to take on responsibility within school and to be helpful. Create digital leaders within your school. We should never be afraid of letting children demonstrate their strengths in a subject even if they have more knowledge than we do. I visited one school recently that created the role of interactive whiteboard expert. When children are given responsibility they will often rise and exceed the expectations we have of them.

- *Learn from the children* – how many times do we ask the children in class for help? All children enjoy the feeling of being responsible and lending a hand to their teacher in some shape or form. Have you tried asking your children to become quasi-teachers? Often sitting in front of us are experts who have already found the pitfalls. Why not use them?

Involve parents and other adults – while children really enjoy showing their work to their peers there is nothing they enjoy more than displaying their work to their parents. There is something about the recognition we receive from our family and extended family that is very important and ICT can certainly make that easier to achieve now. Whether they are yours or not, the 'Grandparent effect' really makes a difference. If children create a podcast, web page or animated movie, at the click of a button they can display and show their work to the people who are important to them. Not only that, but if they embed their 'stuff' into the Virtual Learning Environment then parents and family members can see their work and make comments. The aunty who lives in Australia can see their latest painting and provide positive feedback or the proud mum can play the latest story podcast she has downloaded onto her iPod to her friends at the office. In other words, their content, their 'electronic stuff', can really become mobile for their family to see.

10 Protecting the digital child

The terms 'internet safety' and 'e-safety' have been used regularly since the internet got going in schools in the early 2000s. E-safety is used to describe how children should act within the online world, that is, staying safe while using computers and devices. Such terms can be restrictive, however, and can narrow the perception that safety is a matter that is just concerned with the internet. In reality, it is about allowing children to be themselves and develop their own online presence, personality, values and beliefs as much as they would in real life.

However, mentioning safety is very much just the tip of the iceberg. It is not simply about practical online usage but also:

- how they should behave ethically and morally
- the type of language they should be using
- the implications of anything they do while online.

Principles and aims

There is constant discussion concerning the teaching of and training in this area for everyone involved. So what should the basic principles and aims for our school be? I believe that we must:

- Teach children to be safe online.
- Teach children to be responsible for their own actions and work.
- Teach children to respond quickly and think smartly when faced with content or situations which make them uncomfortable, for example, 'I don't like what's just happened to me or what I've seen. It makes me feel uncomfortable – I will talk and tell so that an adult can support me and help me to understand.'
- Teach children about the digital footprint they leave and how it can affect them in the world of work.
- Teach children to make decisions quickly and go with what they believe.
- Celebrate the benefits and positives that can come from being online.

Within technology, schools can help children to do the following.

- *Find a healthy balance* – in developing the whole child, we want them to be balanced in their use of ICT. This not only means their amount of usage in terms of consoles, computers and mobile technology but also in terms of their ability to take daily rest from all of these and to find the 'off switch' so they can develop a healthy, balanced attitude towards technology. Technology is a great tool, however, we also want children to develop cognitively, socially and emotionally in other aspects of their learning.

- *Stay safe* – the 'draw' of ICT is like the bright lights of a city that never sleeps. It is exciting, fun, potentially dangerous, there's lots going on, plenty of people: friends, family and strangers to meet. Part of education is not saying that children can't go and play but educating them to play safely.

- *Recognise the web's value* – the web is a fun place to be a part of. The older children become, the more they use the internet and the other features of the web to research and communicate. Although there are dangers, if used for a purpose and a balance between focused work and social browsing is struck, then the web can be a valuable tool to use.

- *Make a positive contribution* – everyone can be a writer. Anyone can begin a blog and begin writing. Therefore, if you have something good to say and share, then it gives you a voice. Maybe you have a child who is an expert on the world of ancient artefacts, and through their blog they share this for all of their classmates to benefit from, or through their times-table podcast someone else now knows their multiplication tables.

- *Develop skills for the next generation workforce* – ICT is now a necessary prerequisite every child will need to have when applying for work in the future. Although the world of work continually changes, the more skilled our children become in using the technology flexibly, creatively, logically and resourcefully, the more efficient and productive they can be and will hopefully improve their own economic well-being in the future.

Safer children

The *Safer Children in a Digital World* (DCSF) document is essential reading for education professionals who want to find out more about young people's uses of the internet, video games and technology. Written by Professor Tanya Byron, it examines, 'the risks children face from the internet and video games' and the recommendations required to keep children safe.

The digital playground

Step out into any primary school in between lessons and notice the children's reaction when the words 'Break time' are announced by the adults. Relaxation time is just as important as the lessons participated in during the day. Within the hopefully relaxed confines of the playground, children learn a host of different skills through experiences that are important for their personal and social development:

- socialising and getting along with others
- making new friends
- playing games
- communicating
- working or talking about the lesson or learning they have just taken part in
- reinforcing learning
- learning resilience when excluded or becoming the target of unwanted behaviour from peers like bullying or unfriendliness.

Now, take all these skills and flip them from a physical into a digital space and you have a playground which:

1 Is real life.
2 Is entirely online.
3 Opens the flexibility to be able to connect with children from different schools, areas and even across the other side of the world.
4 Facilitates children playing, talking and learning from each other at the same time.
5 Provides access 24 hours of the day, seven days a week if they wish.
6 Develops communication.
7 Lets children create and consume content.
8 Lets children gain new experiences and socialise (in 2D).

What a playground! Security and knowing how to be safe is fundamental here. However, the caution we do not take is to *not* let the children out to play because of the dangers they might get into. We educate them and teach them to be responsible, caring and considerate when out in the real world. Many adults tend to shy away and step back when it comes to the digital world because of fears of what might well happen and/or how they deal with it when a child tests those vital barriers.

The truth is that the dangers or fears which you think may have happened, will have already happened. You won't be the first or the last. But with increased education, vigilance and knowledge, the digital playground can be one your children can enter into knowing exactly what the dangers are in front of them if they choose to make poor decisions. So don't succumb to letting your children not experience elements of this online environment. Let them explore and play out in this world but with greater skill and knowledge to be able to deal with whatever comes their way. Let us educate and **teach** them.

When you look at the list above, part of letting children play in the digital playground is letting them make mistakes in a *safe* environment. They are young and will test the boundaries that are presented to them and indeed go past them if they don't know what the appropriate sanctions would be.

There will always be incidents that arise, just like when you are cooking in school and chopping ingredients, someone is bound to cut their finger for some reason even though you gave them a health and safety warning at the start. Just like when you take your class on a school trip, you assess the dangers, and aim to reduce any risk down to its lowest form.

Minimising the dangers

Here are some of the dangers children might be faced with in the digital playground and how you could reduce the risk.

What's the danger?	What's the risk?	How can I help reduce that risk and tackle the issue in the classroom?
Electronic messaging	• Sending inappropriate messages. • The intention and meaning of the text is not fully understood or interpreted correctly by the receiver.	• Promote text writing within an English/PSHE lesson. Explore what the dangers are and then ask the children to rewrite a well-known fairy tale in text speak. Evaluate the differences between the original work and the text. What are the difficulties? • Talk about the different reactions a person gets from text messages. How do they differ when it is said face-to-face?
Stranger danger	• Children are contacted by strangers, groomed and asked to meet up.	• Promote stranger danger through PSHE lessons. What is a stranger? When is it appropriate to speak to strangers? Can a stranger be a stranger even if we've been messaging?

What's the danger?	What's the risk?	How can I help reduce that risk and tackle the issue in the classroom?
Personal details	• Children reveal too many personal details such as their name, address and phone numbers.	• Provide the children with a sorting activity. Ask the children to look at some personal information of a fictional character and decide what information they think would be suitable to use on an application form, a social website, in a Christmas card and so on. By the end of the lesson the children have to reflect on the personal information they already have out on the internet.
Seeing inappropriate web pages	• Children coming across material they are not ready to be exposed to or they don't want to see.	• Suggest to the child's parents or carers that they have the computer in a family space rather than a separate room. • Hold an e-safety evening for parents and tell them about the different computer and mobile settings that are available. Most devices and modern computers will have settings for disabling and blocking different sites as well as setting time restrictions for when the computer can be used. • Ensure the children know that they should tell a responsible adult if they are shown or come across inappropriate material that makes them feel uncomfortable. Discuss with the children the people they can trust to tell at home and at school. Some schools have a report button on their website for children to use.

Digital citizenship

With the development of the web and new technologies being introduced, a term that is often used instead of e-safety is 'digital citizenship'. Teacher and author, Mike Ribble, has been researching what digital citizenship involves. He identified nine areas to be aware of (http://www.digitalcitizenship.net/Nine_Elements.html). In summary, it is to do with children's *reputation*, their *online identity* and how they *develop into a person of good standing* in all their interactions in this digital world. Children can discover this world at any time and at any stage of their life. Any child can either enter the digital world by:

- *Conviction* – they can put themselves into this digital world with the understanding of what they are signing up for and what they will be doing while in that area.
- *Mistake* – these children fall into this world by mistake or a link they have clicked.
- *Peer Exposure* – while socialising, a friend shares this website usually listing all the exciting benefits it can offer while playing down or not knowing the negatives and implications of joining.
- *Parental/older sibling exposure* – parents might have different devices that are used for work but their children can also explore. For example, the iPad or other mobile technology which use apps may well have work apps but parents may also have a folder that their children can use. Some of these apps can also link to the internet, taking the children to different websites. Older siblings may also have their own device, computer or gaming equipment which younger sibling may access.

E-safety and communication

The main area where e-safety comes into play is when pupils are interacting and using different forms of the communication side of ICT. This includes the following areas:

- *Social networking* – the way by which we connect with people we know in our working life or in our social life.
- *Blogging* – an online journal/diary/way of recording our thoughts, ideas and opinions. Text, photos, video, sound clips and other web technologies can all be integrated to form a blog post.
- *Use of the mobile phone* – using a mobile phone to call, text message or record video footage.
- *Picture-sharing websites* – a website whereby the user can upload photographs they have taken.
- *Instant messaging* – communicating over a chat facility in real-time using the keyboard to type. Web links, photographs and video can also be sent while chatting. More than one person can take part in the 'chat' and the conversation can be saved as a record.
- *Online chatrooms* – a space where people can talk in real-time.

Real-life examples

This is not just a problem reserved for secondary schools. More and more primary schools are having to deal with issues. To provide a flavour, here are some examples from primary schools and the action taken.

Scenario 1 – a different identity

Year 6 child sets up a free internet account to send unkind messages to another child in the class.

Action taken

- *Parents of both children are informed so they can monitor the emails.*
- *Talked to Year 6 child to resolve issues with the other child and spoke about the friendly use of email.*
- *Children informed that school would be monitoring the situation. Date placed in school diary to check back with parents.*
- *Incident logged in the whole-school e-safety record.*

Scenario 2 – fake Facebook account

Older child in the school sets up a Facebook account under a similar name to male teacher. The child then locates different teachers who work at the school and request them to be friends with this 'fake' account. Child then sends malicious messages to a female teacher. Back in school, the female teacher is concerned that a colleague is sending her these messages and she and the headteacher confront their male colleague who knows nothing about it.

Action taken

- *The child's parents are informed and called to meet in school.*
- *Facebook is contacted and the account is reported and closed.*
- *The child is suspended.*
- *School policy is reviewed as a whole staff.*
- *Incident logged in the whole school e-safety record.*

Scenario 3 – young love

A boy in the lower school really likes a girl in his class and wants to ask her if she would go to the school disco with him. He writes a sweet and innocent message but not understanding how the internal message systems works, he sends the message to the rest of the year group as well! Major embarrassment for boy concerned and indeed the girl it was aimed at.

Action taken

- *Teacher speaks to both children separately. Teacher explains to the boy the appropriate uses of the school messaging service. The boy is informed that if it is used in this way again, then his email privileges will be removed. He's also reminded to always check who you are sending your message to before you click send.*
- *Incident logged in the whole school e-safety record.*

Scenario 4 – damaging lies

During a lesson, a teacher tells a child off for being silly. She follows the correct behaviour sanctions and nothing more is said. In a private message, between two pupils, a message is written saying that Mr _____ is evil and he hit her. She leaves the computer on and one of the parents reads the message and informs the teacher.

Action taken

- *Headteacher, parent, teacher and child meet together.*
- *Offending message is printed for the whole school e-safety record.*
- *Messaging is removed for that child for a fixed period of time and sanction given at home.*

Scenario 5 – parental disputes

Some parents became parent helpers when their children were in Reception and as a consequence became Facebook friends with the teacher. Six years later when their children are in Year 5, something happens in the playground which results in one child being pushed onto the ground. The child tells the teacher and the teacher says that she has been disruptive all day so she was not surprised. The parent hears about this and writes on her wall – 'Can't believe that they didn't believe [Child X's] side of the story. Just wait till tomorrow when I'm gonna march into that bloody school and tell Miss _____ where to … !!'

Another parent see this and informs the teacher. The angry parent is surprised that the teacher knew and to hear that intimidation and pre-meditated verbal abuse were actually a matter for the police.

Action taken

- *Headteacher proactively speaks to the parent first in the playground.*
- *Headteacher, parent and teacher then meet together to discuss the issue.*

- *Parent informed that if she had marched in and been abusive, because of the wall post then it would have been a matter for the police and that abuse towards staff will not be tolerated.*

- *Offending message is printed for the whole school e-safety record.*

Scenario 6 – a protected identity

A parent has written to her new school to explain that she and her partner have split up after alcoholic abuse issues and that she has had to move house to protect the children. She requests that no photographs be taken of the children. At the annual summer fair, the children take part and pictures are taken and put on a social networking site by another child. Some of the parents at the party are then tagged. The father, who knows one of the other parents, see the photographs and then knows exactly where his children are and which school they attend.

Action taken

- *Parent with legal responsibility is called in and informed.*
- *The parent who 'tagged' is phoned immediately and asked to remove the tag.*
- *A note is made in the whole-school e-safety record.*
- *School then monitors who collects the child at the end of the day.*
- *The issue is also mentioned at the annual e-safety talk to parents.*

Dealing with incidents as a school

The majority of issues that arise are as a result of social networking and other forms of communicating using technology. For schools, the policing and teaching of e-safety are really behaviour management issues wrapped up in a different way. There are many similarities between normal child protection and the online environment. Being safe online mirrors the practice we would follow in real-life, that is, being aware as a practitioner and protecting children under our care from any physical, mental, emotional or sexual harm. Although not physical abuse, we must be observant for signs of mental (cyberbullying), emotional (unkind remarks on social networking sites, exclusion due to not being able to afford the latest technology) or sexual harm ('sexting', inappropriate images taken).

All adults within schools must be vigilant and be part of the whole-school policy and practice ensuring that they maintain appropriate records. Here are some ideas for tackling e-safety as a school:

- *Make everyone responsible* – unwanted behaviour continues if the children believe it is going unnoticed and they can get away with it. If a child acts up in your classroom, that behaviour is noticed and dealt with. E-safety deals with *silent* behaviour. Anything goes behind the shield of secrecy. There are other ways you can be aware of how responsible children are being while on the internet. Listen out for the things they are saying. Because this type of behaviour is social, there will be other signs, such as children discussing what's happened in the playground or asking how to do further things on the computer without providing an explanation for why they want to know how to do it.

- *Ask the questions* – ask the children and parents how safe they believe they are online. E-safety is about dealing with facts and what is going on. The only way you find out what's going on is through asking those questions, being more open and informed.

- *Decide on your own school rules for dealing with incidents* – how your school responds to issues of safety depends on three crucial factors – the children in your school, the e-safety knowledge of parents and the knowledge and training of the school staff. Create a series of steps for everyone in the school that will help them to understand the procedure for reporting incidents. Display these in all classrooms and around the school.

- *Encourage openness* – one of the reasons some cases get bigger is through feelings of either embarrassment, shame 'it shouldn't be happening to me', excitement or 'no one can see what I am doing in school so it's OK to do it while the teacher is not looking'. Be vigilant, highly visual in shared school spaces and always act on information, even if it is an incident which has happened at home as the chances are that it will filter back into school.

- *Champion 'Make up your own mind'* – e-safety is not always clear-cut. Champion children to always make their mind up. Is it OK to write this in an email? Should I write this message/take this photograph? Give children hypothetical scenarios every so often *throughout the year* which they then need to think about and decide how they would deal with the situation.

- *Develop a reporting system* – e-safety is based on relationships. Have a way in which children and parents can report any incidents. This could either be by having a Report button on your website, through to having a report box in the classroom similar to a suggestion box.

- *Maintain a school record* – any incident a member of staff comes across or deals with should be recorded in the whole-school record. Place it in a staff-only area so that staff can record any incidents but can also read it to build their own awareness.

Advice for class teachers

As the class teacher, you are one of the main contacts for the children in your care. There are several things that you can do to make it easier for the children to report incidents to you. Below are some tips for you to use:

- *Model good practice* – provide examples of good practice you want the children to follow. During your teaching, if you are using mobile devices or the internet get the children to remind you how to use the devices safely.
- *Respect privacy without compromising the authority* – remember to respect a young person's right to personal privacy. They do not need to show you what is on their device but they do need to follow the school rules and policy and the rules you set for your classroom. At home, parents rule but at school the teacher does.
- *Be approachable* – make yourself accessible and approachable so that children can tell you if they have an e-safety concern.
- *Judge and jury* – do not jump to conclusions if something has happened without checking the facts first.
- *Be cautious and don't get complacent* – do not believe that incidents will not happen to you. It could.

How can my school promote the digital citizen?

There are a number of things schools can do to ensure they create a positive ethos around the school in terms of digital citizenship. Below are some suggestions:

- Establish a no blame culture. It is far better to tell and share than hide.
- When using the internet discuss strategies for being safe online. Explore the vast number of resources and links the organisation Childnet (www.childnet.com/resources) has collected together for schools to use.
- If incidents happen *talk* as a class about them. These things can happen to all of us at some time, whether deliberate or by accident. By talking about what has happened we are also building that culture of no blame and feeling supported.
- Make sure your Acceptable use policy (see the online resources that accompany this book) is written and clearly sets out the sanctions.
- Celebrate great uses of digital citizenship by children. They could create posters, guidelines or a podcast based on their experiences.
- Reward those children who use the system sensibly. They could be given level

certificates, extra privileges such as an email address or online access to different tools where they can create their own content.

- Make the children responsible for assessing the risk of different tools. Set up a small representative group from the school. Review ICT products and services the school intends to use and ask the children to identify the risks they see such as 'we need to keep passwords safe' or 'this site has an online forum therefore we must make sure that we check it and moderate this so no one can write things which are inappropriate'.

Cyberbullying

Cyberbullying is where a person is malicious or unkind to another person when online or through the use of mobile technology. This means bullying through:

- messaging/texting
- emailing
- social networking sites
- internet chat rooms
- other places on the internet.

Cyberbullying is quite different to normal bullying as no one can hear it taking place. Unless we are told then it is a form of bullying which can continue unnoticed. This is one of the many reasons why it is so important to encourage an atmosphere where this type of behaviour can be reported quickly. Cyberbullying is not limited to time or place. Unkind messages can sit waiting for their recipient and even the beep of the mobile can generate a response from a child which is out of character.

The sad reality is that we often only find out about the extent of severe cyberbullying when it is too late, and it has led to tragic events such as suicides. Because of the ease of being able to share information in a quick way and encourage others to take part, cyber-bullying is one form of bullying which builds and more often than not the bullying mounts as others become involved, thinking their part doesn't matter. The forwarding of a text to another person, snide comments indirectly made to friends in the playground or the spreading of texts further into their own different networks all play their part in progressing the bullying.

Dealing with cyberbullying incidents

There are many different reasons why incidents occur. Most cyberbullying problems occur through the social problems the children are experiencing and they use ICT as their outlet instead of other forms of conflict resolution. So how should incidents be handled? Below are some suggestions.

- *Make a record* – Set up a file, along with your child protection register and record any incidents, however small. Divide the sections of your file into Messaging/texting; Email; Social networking sites; Internet chat rooms and The internet.

- *Collect a hard copy* – if parents raise any cyberbullying concerns during the course of conversations make a record of these and file the record in the folder. If parents are reporting concerns about other children, encourage parents to print the screen of their concerns by using the snipping tool which is a tool that comes with Windows 7 or by taking a screenshot using CTRL and the printscreen option. Parents will sometimes become alerted to cyberbullying issues through their children.

- *Get the parents involved* – parents play an important part in e-safety education. Parents might not even be aware that their child is acting in this way. Parents will be necessary to support sanctions at home and also monitor their child's activities more closely.

- *Record the outcome* – even if the conclusion is that the child was given a warning about their behaviour, note down all the information. Ensure that it is dated and their class teacher is informed in order to monitor their behaviour within the classroom and the playground.

- *Talk, talk and talk* – whether a child is on the receiving end or the instigator of the cyberbullying, it is important to keep on talking and encouraging the children to understand how it makes them and others feel and how they can learn from the experience so it is not repeated. Good pupil relationships and the ability to speak openly and honestly are two required qualities.

- *Both sides of the story* – make sure the bully also hears the victim's side of how it has affected them emotionally, what it has done to their confidence and so on.

- *Enforce your Acceptable use policy* – if your policy has not been followed then ensure that you have sanctions depending on the severity of their action. Agree that if the incident happened at home then you will be monitoring the child's online behaviour at school as well. If children have abused the school email system then remove their privileges for a set period of time.

- *Use the police/community liaison officers to support* – these outside agencies can assist with explaining to the children the severity of actions in the grown-up world and how this relates to the law.

- *Ensure you have identified the relevant school personnel* – have a member of staff who is responsible for e-safety within the school. This could be the Child Protection Liaison Officer (CPLO) or someone who has also had appropriate e-safety training.

- *Share incidents confidentially with staff* – in the same way in which vulnerable children are discussed so all staff are vigilant, make sure you extend this vigilance to those children who have breached your e-safety guidelines. It will also heighten the awareness level for all staff.

E-safety advice for parents

For parents who are not familiar with the digital world, it is a rather daunting prospect to know how to keep their family safe while online. There are many help guides and websites to assist parents with what at times can be a tricky path to negotiate. It is a good idea to hold parent e-safety meetings in order to raise awareness. Below are some suggestions for some of the tips you can give to parents during that meeting to help them:

- Invest in good internet security. Know the controls and set a secure password consisting of letters, numbers and symbols so that young children cannot guess it. Partition (split the hard-drive) into different accounts. Have the children's accounts with no password so you can see what they have been browsing and have the accounts for adults password-protected, then you can adjust the settings.
- Have the computer in a family space so you can see what your child is doing.
- Set ground rules for how long they can be on the computer.
- Children's concentration skills are calculated roughly on their chronological age in minutes plus a little bit more (http://learnenglishkids.britishcouncil.org/en/parents/articles/how-children-learn). Using the computer is no different so break their time down into small chunks.
- If you are leaving them alone know how to access the history settings so you know what they have been looking at.
- Look at the range of technology your child has access to, which might include mobile phones, computers, netbooks, iPads, camera but can also include games consoles as many of the latest ones have access to the internet. If you confiscate the computer as a sanction, remember there are other ways to get online.
- Consider buying a digital camera for your child to use. This will also help to prepare your child to use the tools they will use in school and throughout their working life.
- Teach your child responsible use of technology, including how to look after it, how to use it, when to use it and when not to.
- More and more schools are using online learning services such as Virtual Learning Environments and other services that provide software which is accessed through an internet browser. Be aware that the children will be able to access this at any time with a password the school has set up and you might not know what it is.
- Be aware of how cyberbullying occurs. Use sites such as Childline (www.childline.org.

uk/explore/onlinesafety/pages/cyberbullying.aspx), Kidscape (www.kidscape.org.uk/cyberbullying) and Think U Know (www.thinkuknow.co.uk) to keep up-to-date.

- Know how to report inappropriate use or targeted cyberbullying to the mobile company.

- Know how to suspend or delete an email account, as some providers can take up to three months for an account to be suspended after it is left inactive.

- Instil in your child that although the technology is fun they have to respect that it is a tool for communication and can be misused and they have the responsibility to use it appropriately at home, at school and as they grow up in the workplace.

- Set firm family rules and boundaries for how it is used. Don't be afraid to reaffirm your control as a parent just because technology might not be an area that you are familiar with.

- Seek the advice of the school ICT coordinator if you are unsure how to deal with problems which may arise so they can guide you.

- Don't be afraid to set boundaries and rules, especially for younger children – their online reputation will follow them forever so it's never too young to start.

- Know the rating on computer games as they differ from the video classification system.

- Be aware of younger siblings and the exposure to the type of material that is meant for older children when older children are playing video games. Remind older siblings about responsible use around younger siblings.

- Be aware that technology is more than the computer, it includes mobiles, games consoles, iPads, the television and other devices.

- Know how to control the setting for web cam services like Skype so they cannot be easily accessed accidentally. Know how the parental controls for your television and digital satellite work so you can keep children safe.

- Talk, talk and talk about technology and the internet with your child so that they see the benefits but also the dangers of using it. Ensure that they know what to do if they come across material they are worried out. In the same way children might have an open dialogue about sex, the same openness needs to be encouraged about their use of technology. Learn from the children. Get them to teach you how it works as this can be a two-way street.

- Talk to other parents about how they use technology in their homes. What rules do they give to their children? Do they have any tricks when it comes to mobiles? Or for using the computer for homework and leisure?

Parenting guides

A great resource for parents is Vodafone's *Digital Parenting* guides and articles (www.vodafone.com/parents). Their magazine is very accessible, interesting and easy to read. If you are new to the area of e-safety and digital citizenship then this is a great way to learn more.

Website help

Take 20 minutes to explore the Childnet (www.childnet.com) and Common Sense Media (www.commonsensemedia.org) websites. These websites have a huge amount of information, resources and guidance for teachers to use.

There are also a number of classroom activities and lesson plans that you can weave into your planning or that will at least give you an idea of some things you could do with the children in your class.

Self-review tool

360°Safe (www.360safe.org.uk) is an online e-safety self-review tool that schools can use to assess where they are in terms of their e-safety provision. The structure map (www.360safe.org.uk/Files/Documents/360-degree-safe-Structure-Map) demonstrates how wide the field of e-safety is.

As a school, you can even apply for accreditation and earn the e-safety mark when you reach the required level in their assessment.

Useful resources for e-safety

There are many good resources and websites out there to support you in delivering safety awareness. Here are just a few links to get you started.

- www.thinkuknow.co.uk/

  This is a comprehensive website from the team at the Child Exploitation and Online Protection (CEOP) Centre. It aims to provide guidance on e-safety for teachers, parents and young people from the ages of 5–16.

- www.kent.gov.uk/childrens_social_services/protecting_children/e-safety.aspx

  Written by Kent County Council, this website provide links to various organisations as a starting point to finding out more about e-safety.

- www.nen.gov.uk/esafety

  A resource by the National Education Network which points towards some auditing tools for e-safety.

- www.stopcyberbullying.org/index2.html

  A useful start to finding out about what cyberbullying is and how to prevent it.

- http://yp.direct.gov.uk/cyberbullying/

  This is a governmental website with advice on different forms of bullying including cyberbullying.

- www.childline.org.uk/explore/onlinesafety/pages/cyberbullying.aspx

  Childline has long been associated with advising and guiding young people with issues they may have as they grow up. This website provides some advice on cyberbullying and is written specifically for young people.

- www.kidscape.org.uk/cyberbullying/

  This website page provides a start to finding out about cyberbullying. There are also some links to various organisations who also provide guidance on e-safety.

- http://archive.beatbullying.org/dox/what-we-do/cybermentors.html

  Cybermentors is a brilliant scheme aimed at young people supporting other young people. They are trained to offer advice on what to do if a person is being bullied. Because they are young people themselves, it can feel less scary for someone who is having difficulties. There are also trained counsellors for any serious problems.

- www.bebo.com/Safety.jsp

  Bebo was one of the first social networking websites for younger people. Tucked away under the safety link at the bottom of the page is a great set of videos about privacy, being safe in a social networking environment and what social networking is all about.

- www.bbc.co.uk/cbbc/help/web/staysafe

  Some advice from the BBC for children about staying safe online. There are some quizzes, hints and tips for children. The site is mostly aimed at primary school aged children.

- www.digitalme.co.uk or www.safesocialnetworking.org

  DigitalMe is a not-for-profit organisation passionate about using new technology to create amazing learning. They have produced some good resources as a starting point for using with primary school children.

How can teachers promote their own digital citizenship?

As well as looking out for and developing the digital citizenship of our children, it is really important that we also model good digital citizenship as practitioners. We have a professional responsibility to maintain the image of the teacher, however, we also have a personal life which is separate from our teaching and which may involve elements of social networking. Below are some ways teachers can promote their own digital citizenship:

- Model good practice to the children. When taking photographs for displays ask the children if it is okay to take their picture.
- Remember to ensure that your own personal devices and computers, if in school, are put away securely.
- Do not rely on your good name to protect you. It may not be enough. The insidious way sites such as Rate My Teacher (http://uk.ratemyteachers.com) operate can throw your name up in search engines even if what is written is fairly positive.
- Enjoy using technology. Experiment with using different apps and look for different ways they could be used in lessons and to support learning.
- Lead by example. Create blog posts with your class through shared writing opportunities. Use your 'thinking aloud' voice (the voice you use with your class when you want them to hear your thoughts). Talk about what an excellent post

looks like, whether you should include a photograph (and if so, should we just take one from Google or take the photograph ourselves), how we should respond to comments and so on. All these model the thoughts the children should be engaging in when they blog, whether it be in school or at home if they have their own personal blog.

Facebook and social media

There is no reason why you cannot have your own Facebook, Twitter and social media accounts. Here are some things to consider:

- Make it a policy not to add children you currently teach. My policy was, if past pupils I had taught wanted to add their old primary school teacher as a Facebook friend when they reached 18 then they could but, until then, the answer was always no.

- Get to know the 'Restricted' list on your Facebook account. Friends you add on this list can see posts and profile information you set to public. Use this list for any parent-helper/friend you add until their child has cleared the school and beyond.

- Go through your photographs and look for ones that may not reflect your true professional persona. Set the visibility on these albums so only 'Close friends' or 'Only you' can see these.

- Be careful and mindful that using social media can blur some of the professional boundaries.

- Consider altering your name on Facebook so only close friends can find you. Instead of using your full name, you could use your middle name or a nickname. For example, I could change my name from Jon Audain to 'Jon Bruno' or 'Jonofan Audain' so it provides some professional protection.

Keeping up to date

COORDINATOR

Ensure that you keep up to date with the ICT subject pages on the OfSTED website (www.ofsted.gov.uk/inspection-reports/our-expert-knowledge/information-and-communication-technology-ict). These provide useful guides on a range of issues connected with ICT and include e-safety. The report on *The Safe Use of New Technologies* (www.ofsted.gov.uk/resources/safe-use-of-new-technologies) is especially helpful in understanding the things inspectors looked for.

11 The ICT coordinator

So you've made the brave step of becoming an ICT coordinator. Feeling good? Nervous? Overwhelmed or just not sure what to expect? Well firstly, congratulations. You've signed up for one of the most exciting jobs to have in a primary school. I once worked with a deputy head who said that after the headteacher and deputy, the ICT coordinator is the person everyone wants to speak to. You are the keeper of the keys, the passwords, the cables and the interactive whiteboard pens! You have the ability to become an ICT whizz who can wave their wand and *abracadabra* the machine is working! (Or so everyone would like to believe.)

Some people fall into this role because of prior experience; others because they can turn on a computer and many because they really want to be an ICT coordinator. I hope for you it's the latter and that you will take real pride in joining the ranks.

I work with many ICT coordinators, so this chapter is for you and for aspiring teachers who will become coordinators. In this chapter we will look at the typical roles you need to fulfill and some of the common tasks. We will also look at how and where to get started if you're new to the role.

The role of the ICT coordinator

Coordinating any subject in a primary school is a demanding addition to your teaching commitments. Being an ICT coordinator means juggling a great deal at the same time. ICT can be divided into specific areas – hardware, curriculum, training, maintenance and vision. When you take on the job, it's very tricky keeping all the 'plates in the air'. Here are some of the common tasks ICT coordinators find themselves doing as part of their role:

- *Troubleshooting technology* – troubleshooting is a large part of the role and certainly one to get used to. Some staff need you to be reassuring and comforting and support them when they try to use technology. Some staff believe that all technology will fail at some point so why use it!
- *Auditing ICT* – you will be responsible for looking at how ICT is used across the school. Who uses what? What are the areas that need to be developed?
- *Keeping up to date with the latest kit* – you will need to keep an eye out for the latest hardware to hit the shops. Trends begin to develop and what starts out in the real world comes into businesses and then filters into the education markets. If a buzz is

generated around certain products like iPods, Gameboys and iPads then the likelihood is that parents will buy the products and let their children and family use them. The children will then look at other ways of using the technology, including in their own learning. The challenge as educationalists is to try to work out how new technology can be used in an educational context.

- *Trying out new technology with your class* – as an ICT coordinator you will probably be the type of person who can learn to use new software or hardware quickly, evaluate the children's responses and anticipate how easy it may be for other teachers to pick up. However, part of the excitement of being in the classroom comes from asking your class to explore how things might work. Your class will soon tell you the pitfalls as well as the best parts of the using a particular piece of software or hardware. They will also provide you with a unique way of testing it out and demonstrate how they would use it if you were to buy it. It can be fascinating to watch as they might demonstrate how they would use it in a way that differs completely from how you imagined. Also encourage other ICT enthusiasts among your staff to try out new technology. This will zap those cynics among your staff and provide back-up for you when demonstrating how to use it.

- *Seeing the wider school picture* – your subject affects how the school operates. A decision like the type of computers you will choose to have in school will affect every user who has access to them, so choose wisely.

- *Developing a thick skin when things go wrong* – although many staff don't want to admit it, everyone has an 'it's-fine-but-I'm-now-slightly-fizzing-because-the-technology-is-not-working!' type of face. This is a normal reaction when things break down. Anything electrical is prone to wobbles, so muster up your best smile, make two cups of tea (one for the other person as well) and tell them you will work as a team on this together and hopefully the angst and the resentment will dissipate.

- *Knowing why ICT makes a difference* – good ICT will only make a good teacher even better. It is your flexible tool that can support your lesson or move it on in a crucial way, as long as you think carefully about how to use it.

- *Using your spare time* – ICT can absorb much of your time. It is important to understand how it actually works, how easy it is to introduce and how it can be planned for within the classroom. The quicker children can understand the basics of how it works, the quicker they can work out how to really use the product in their learning.

- *Being informed in your choices* – it will take you anything between an hour-and-a-half to two hours and upwards to work out how a product works and its implications for the curriculum, but only 30 seconds for the children to tell you they don't like it or it's boring. So make your software/app choices wisely and know why you want to use them. Otherwise you could find your precious time and hard work goes down the plughole in under a minute. Research thoroughly, and speak to other ICT colleagues and ask for their opinions.

- *Being confident in your choices* – ICT is an expensive subject so be confident in your choices of software and hardware as this will provide you with a positive outlook and leave you more finely tuned when looking at how your choice is making an impact. Ask children, staff and parents to comment on how they think your new software/ hardware is making a difference.

- *Extending your ICT network* – with such a huge subject, it is essential that you build up support. Explore the different options in your local county. They may have established cluster groups allowing you to meet other coordinators so that you can pick their brains, present work you are really proud of to the rest of the group or just sit back and collect good ideas. There are also opportunities to replicate this type of learning at national events such as conferences and courses. However, although communicating in person is always great for building networks, there may be occasions when this might not be possible for whatever reason. If this is the case, explore several of the virtual networking arenas that will be full of like-minded people. Forums on Naace (www.naace.co.uk), MirandaNet (www.mirandanet.ac.uk) or Vital (www.vital.ac.uk) have other people ready and willing to offer advice.

Of course, one of the other ways of increasing your own ICT network is to become a member of Twitter (http://twitter.com/). Twitter is a great source of knowledge and people will be able help you answer a question you might be stuck on. Ensure that you follow people with similar interests and then you won't get swamped with rubbish. Follow teachers and people with a background in education, and always read the first page of their tweets to see what they are tweeting about and decide whether or not you would like to read more from them. Finally, follow people who have been recommended to you, people you have met in person or those who have a reputation within the ICT and education world. For more information on using Twitter, see page 67.

Troubleshooting technology

Everything from printers to projectors to blue screens with error messages will need to be dealt with. Before school, after school and even during lessons, be prepared to be told that a computer isn't working or the interactive whiteboard is on the blink. All this can leave staff feeling frustrated. Fix on your best smile and try saying 'Let's see if we can work this out together.' There are many requests to troubleshoot and they can be a little soul destroying to hear; but if you can encourage staff to work with you to fix their own difficulties then it can help you as well.

The most common complaints I have come across are:

- Cables that have come loose from the back of the computer. (Check that the computer has not been moved.)
- Loss of interactivity to the whiteboard (Check that the cable been put into the correct slot.)
- The printer is not printing. (Check the paper is loaded correctly or whether it has run out of ink. Are there any flashing lights that may provide a clue?)

Always keep a spare basket of cables and tools to replace stock or to swap when things do not work. Common items to have handy are:

- a kettle lead
- red and white audio cable connected to a headphone jack
- USB sticks
- a spare keyboard and mouse
- a SCART/HDMI lead for when the school television is wheeled out
- a monitor cable
- house cables – the ones that connect either the interactive whiteboard or the printer to the computer
- CAT5 network cables of different lengths (2m–5m) (You never know when you might need a longer cable and sometimes the 2m ones can be frustratingly short!)
- a spare extension cable
- a CD case to keep what I call 'vital CDs' all in one place – the printer, web cam and scanner drivers, the interactive whiteboard software, program suites and software which is commonly used in school. All of this usually comes with all the kit but it will get thrown away or lost over time.

Organising troubleshooting tasks

Remember to have a system in place for reporting problems. This could either be paper-based or stored electronically on your network. Ask staff to fill it in with more detail than they think is necessary and it should be a good record. Explain to staff that good trouble-shooting can be done more quickly when the problem can be traced back to what has happened before it went wrong. There is an example of a good record on the following page.

Date	Colour code (for ICT coordinator only)	Full description	Staff initial/ class	Additional comments from technician
12.03.11	RED	The scanner software is not working when I double click it. It comes up with an error message saying 'Missing system file .dll'.	JA – Class 16	Software has been reinstalled for you and now works on your profile – hope it helps!

Colour coding is useful for prioritising troubleshooting tasks for your technicians. If you ask staff to write down their issues, then as coordinator you can colour-code the log so your technician can see the more urgent requests. *Red* can indicate that the issue is server-related or needs to be resolved urgently, *yellow* can indicate software installations, and the box can be left white if a job can be done when there is a spare five minutes.

Take comfort from the fact that you can't always please everyone; but keep on top of things and make a note of how long different troubleshooting jobs take, especially when ordering replacement equipment as some items can take weeks to arrive.

Taking stock of where you are

When you start your role as an ICT coordinator, the first task of business is to assess where you stand in terms of the use of ICT across your school and your aspirations for the subject. Schools that demonstrate excellent curriculum practice in ICT have the following factors in common:

- They promote ICT and have a positive attitude towards its use.
- There is an ICT coordinator who has been able to take the subject and build on good practice that is developing in the school.
- The senior management team drives the change.
- There is a curriculum containing some ICT skills development and opportunities to put those skills into practice.
- The curriculum is refreshed and moves with developing technology.
- The whole-school community and beyond connects with the vision.
- There is a continual focus on staff development and training. The expectation is that you will know how to use the technology in your lessons.
- There is an approach to e-safety which all children and staff are aware of and are actively involved in its promotion.

- There are suitable amounts of working equipment to use.
- There are staff in school who know how to use the kit.

ICT in a primary school needs to be continually assessed. You have to keep looking at all the components and keep all the plates spinning. However, get your headteacher excited in the power of ICT and things will surely cascade from there.

Finances

Normally as a school you are provided with your ICT budget of 'X' money, which then has to be divided up accordingly. When you begin, ensure that you do the following:

- *Find out your budget* – have a handle on the finances and know how much standard equipment costs. How much does it cost to replace and install a new projector each time? How much do you pay for ICT technical support/website/broadband services to the county? Knowing the general numbers just helps you to spend more wisely.
- *Think in categories* – divide ICT into separate areas and think in these terms whilst you are a coordinator:
  - *hardware (for teaching and for admin/senior management team)*
  - *curriculum*
  - *maintenance*
  - *staff training and development.*
- *Talk to your headteacher* – where do they see the role of ICT within the school? Do they understand the impact that it can make? Are they prepared to fund it? Headteachers vary in their vision and liking for ICT in the same way as teachers do, so ensure you find out your headteacher's ICT views and values.
- *Talk to your finance/business manager* – you will probably have more contact in terms of ICT that the rest of your senior management team. From the ordering of equipment to 'how much do I have in my budget' through to how much money you plan to commit in the next five years, your finance manager should have this information at their fingertips.
- *Think in terms of three to five years* – create a long-term plan. ICT is an expensive subject, so plan for major replacements and initiatives. Make sure a certain amount of money is placed by each year so that it covers the yearly ICT running costs but also builds towards larger replacements such as computer suites or laptop trolleys.
- *Know your running costs* – look at the money spent in terms of hardware, curriculum, maintenance and staff training over the past two to three years. Work out what are the year costs you need so that all your basic ICT services run without disruption. Remember to include any annual subscriptions for website, curriculum software and home/school online platforms.

Assessing your ICT curriculum

There has been much discussion around the curriculum; whether it should change; how it should change and what a new ICT curriculum should look like. As technology makes the *doing* of tasks easier, the curriculum will rely less on the teaching of certain skills and more on drawing them all together to embed the final result somewhere, whether that be on a a learning environment or somewhere else like YouTube or a blog. Whichever form it takes, there are several core ICT attitudes and skills that will still need to be fostered regardless of how the technology invents itself. In Chapter 1, we explored the areas of ICT that should be included to give breadth of experience. Let's remind ourselves of them:

1   Creating and presenting ideas (use of Word, PowerPoint, Prezi, online tools, etc.)
2   Key computer skills (being able to save/open files, able to access the network folder, able to record a video evaluation)
3   Advanced technical skills (able to connect a computer/interactive whiteboard; connect devices using Wi-Fi/Bluetooth, HTML)
4   Mobile working (able to use a variety of apps, to store and retrieve work using cloud computing)
5   Evaluating information (use of web and search engines, validity and reliability of information)
6   Using data (use of spreadsheets, use of interactive teaching programs)
7   Verbal and written communication (blogging, use of video, podcasting, use of social media)
8   Computer programming (use of programmable toys, computational thinking, controlling devices)
9   Digital citizenship and e-safety (protecting children online, internet safety, protecting your digital footprint and reputation)
10   Working together across the web (able to send emails, use video conferencing such as Skype/Lync/Google Hangout).

Building an overview

Take a look at your planning. Look at the units of work you have already. If you don't have an ICT curriculum overview, then begin by creating one. An example can be found in the online resources that accompany this book.

Look at the coverage of subjects. The online example has a spread of coverage, however when looking carefully at the overview the following questions and more are raised:

• Are there areas of ICT missing?

- Have elements of digital citizenship been included?

- Can any subjects be combined? For example, the Year 5 topic of email has become much easier to teach and use and does it need a whole half-term dedicated to its use – the answer is no! So can it be combined with another topic to teach the skills but also to enrich another area of the curriculum?

- How will the ICT equipment I have in my school impact on this planning? Do I have the correct software? Do I have enough licenses?

- Are there any new areas of technology I need to integrate?

- How does this overview relate to the skills the children already have in my school? Does it challenge the children? Are there resource implications?

Tracking ICT coverage across other curriculum subjects

Now look at where ICT is being used across the whole curriculum. This is an important exercise for a number of reasons:

1 You discover where the gaps are in what is not being taught.

2 You discover if there is an overuse in one area, for example, too much Word, PowerPoint and digital literacy work.

3 It allows you to begin to look at progression of concepts and skills throughout the key stages.

An example of a grid to copy can be found in the online resources that accompany this book.

Auditing hardware

In the same way that the curriculum needs to be audited when you become an ICT coordinator, take a look at the hardware you have around your school. Look at the condition. Does it work? Will it need replacing? When will it need replacing? This year? Next? All this information will help you to formulate your development plan.

Setting your vision

Reflect on where you school currently is in terms of the ICT provision. Look for the positives as well as the areas to develop. Now flash forward and take me on a tour of your school. Imagine that I was a visitor looking at your ICT provision. What would I see?

- Children using mobile tablets during group reading?
- A laptop trolley in each classroom?
- A Digital Senate assembled and digital leaders supporting the ICT work?
- Increased technology in the classroom?
- An interactive whiteboard in every classroom?
- A visualiser in every classroom with children using it regularly throughout the day?
- A computer club?
- Foundation Stage and grandparent helpers working together on a digital photography project?
- Classroom ICT awards given to children during lessons for outstanding work?
- Children being assessed in different ways using video, written work and through photographs of their work?
- An annual Arts and ICT competition? Animation Challenge? Best photograph taken with a mobile device?
- Increased staff training/team-teaching or 1:1 support?
- A working website that sells the school?
- Class blogs and improved parent links?

List your top six and then prioritise these in order of importance for your school. Talk this through with your headteacher and finance manager. Ask the question, 'So what? It's a good dream but how will I get more children to…' On a piece of paper, write down Year 1 and then Year 2 and divide these up into half termly blocks. Place your top six 'visions' onto the timescale. Now you are ready to document the process to form your ICT subject development plan.

ICT subject development plan

An ICT subject development plan documents all the work you plan to cover over an academic year and beyond. Look at how your ICT objectives will support the whole-school picture. Remember to divide everything into hardware, curriculum, maintenance, staff training and development. The ICT subject development plan is where you set out your plan and look at how much things might cost, how long it may take and who is going to be responsible for the tasks. An example of some of the general elements to a development plan and some questions and examples to get you started can be found in the online resources that accompany this book.

Vision, policies and self-review

There are a variety of different ICT policies that you will need to write or review. Some have to be written separately while others can be combined if there is a common theme. A policy helps you to crystalise your thinking and ensure you have thought about all the necessary points. Some policies you might want to consider writing are listed below.

- *An ICT subject policy* – a general policy explaining the subject, aims, values, vision and organisation in the school.

- *An Acceptable use policy for staff* – a policy explaining what is acceptable in terms of adults using technology in the school workplace. This policy can also expand to include advice and protocols for using Twitter and Facebook in a professional capacity.

- *An Acceptable use policy for children* – a policy explaining the guidelines for how children should use technology safely and the appropriate sanctions which can be applied if there is misuse.

- *A digital citizenship/E-safety/internet policy* – a policy stating how children will be safeguarded in school with reference to using the internet, mobile devices and the learning environment. Included in this policy should be how matters of cyberbullying will be tackled as well as well as how e-safety incidents will be dealt with, recorded and actioned.

- *A Virtual Learning Environment/extended learning into the home policy* – a policy detailing how home/school learning happens throughout the school. This should cover how many times homework is set and guidelines to support parents at home.

- *A health and safety policy* – a policy explaining how staff can be safe in terms of using technology in their classrooms. How to move and lift laptops and sets of mobile devices.

- *A communications policy (email, website, messaging, school social media use)* – a policy explaining the etiquette for how staff should communicate with parents and children. It should cover the responsibility of the school website and how the school will use social media tools. If the school has a Facebook page, what content will go onto the site, who will maintain this and what will happen with any unwelcome comments or communications to members of staff.

- *A video conferencing policy (if relevant)* – a policy that explains how the video-conferencing equipment will be used in the school as well as useful information, usernames and phone numbers to contact when using the equipment.

- *A data protection and freedom of information policy* – a policy that covers what will happen to sensitive data on the school system. How passwords will be managed and what will happen to the back-up tapes that are either taken offsite or stored in a fireproof safe.

- *A disaster recovery policy* – a policy that looks at what will happen if you need to restore data after power cuts or if you have to rebuild your server. What is the plan for how the data will be recovered so there is minimal 'downtime' of the network.

- *Use of digital media with children policy* – a policy that explains what will happen to photographs and video taken of the children. It should differentiate between how images will be used on class blogs to the website and to the use in the press. This policy should also include the permission forms parents sign when their child begins at the school.

So what should actually go into these policies? There are many examples on the internet that different schools and authorities have put on their websites which provide a useful place to begin. I have also provided a selection of policy templates in the online resources that accompany this book, which are only a start, but should hopefully help when writing your policies.

Using ICT in administration

Technology should make it easier for staff to collaborate, share, communicate and join up systems and infrastructures. It should reduce the paperwork which floats around the school if tackled in a proactive way. The paperless school is the ICT-heaven we all strive for. Here are some ways you could help staff in your school to use ICT to support their administration loads as teachers:

- *Place your planning on the network* – in Chapter 2, we looked at a few tips for getting the most out of your network. By placing your planning on the network in school it allows all staff to add to topics, re-use ideas from planning as well as store useful website addresses and worksheets.

- *Use the cloud to help* – access to learning and information from outside school is becoming more used and acceptable. There are various 'cloud' services where information can sit on secure servers and can be accessed from anywhere through the internet. Services such as Dropbox (www.dropbox.com); box.net (www.box.com) and Google docs (http://docs.google.com/) all provide this. Devices like Pogoplug (http://www.pogoplug.com/) also help to create your own personal cloud from which you can then access files from anywhere.

- *Collect data in a spreadsheet* – spreadsheets have picked up a poor reputation over the years as being dull, boring and complicated. The truth is that they don't need to be. Why not use them to collect test data so that trends can be seen? Along the bottom of the page you can create different workbooks enabling you to have all your data in one place.

- *Use your network* – on your network, create a Meetings folder. Label one Staff and the other one Governors. Ensure that you make it a policy (even for your headteacher) that any handouts for meetings must be in electronic form – no paper copies. This way people can find the information instead of searching for paper on their desk. It also enables you to upload different files so staff can access all the documentation they need to. Having an INSET day? Why not video the inputs from the speaker, so that people who were away can watch them. Different methods need to be explored so that training can include all the staff. At the very least it ensures that all staff have access to the training.

Making technology choices

One of the exciting things about ICT is that we get shiny flashing technology to play with and buy. However, if you visit the BETT Show exhibition (www.bettshow.com) every January the reality is that there are so many suppliers of ICT equipment and services to schools it's difficult to know how to choose which ones are right for your school. Evaluation is key. Here are some ideas that may help:

Evaluating hardware

- *Speak to others* – some pieces of hardware, such as netbooks or specific laptops or tablets, might seem like a brilliant idea, but there may be hidden downsides which are not immediately apparent. Ask other ICT colleagues in your county or on Twitter for their opinions as it could save you a lot of heartache and money. Most companies will also have worked with schools before. Ask to hear how such schools have used the product and why they have liked it. Also ask about schools that were not happy and see if you can find out why. This will reveal how they deal with schools and how they resolve matters when things don't work out so well.

- *Ask for a trial* – or at least a demonstration of the product at your school. Most companies will have a demonstration version. You might need to wait a couple of weeks but at least you will find out about any annoying habits or quirky things it does before committing money.

- *Total cost of ownership* – remember to consider this carefully. Ask yourself: After I have bought the product, will I have to spend any more money maintaining or replacing it? Also consider the time you or your technical support might have to spend looking after it. These 'hidden' costs can mount up, particularly when thinking about printers, toner cartridges and batteries for different products. Here are some questions to ask:
  - Will it need servicing?

- Are the spare parts expensive?
- Are there similar products being sold? What have the reviews been like?
- What are the costs? Don't be tempted to go for a low-quality product because the price is good. Nine times out of ten there will be performance or driver issues and you will probably end up replacing it for something a little more robust and a little more expensive.
- Will it need replacing after a certain amount of time?
- Who will benefit from using it?
- How many different curriculum uses can I think of? This will also help you to sell it to the staff.

Evaluating software

- *Use the children* – you might spend a couple of hours reviewing new software, only to find out that within three minutes of using it the children remark, 'This is rubbish!' or 'What're we using this for?' So give it to them to play with. It will also show you how intuitive the software is. For the majority of work at primary level, we want children to use ICT to demonstrate their understanding instead of getting tied up in the complexities of software.

- *Subject-specific or cross-curricular* – how many different uses will it have across the curriculum? Can it only be used for a particular area of ICT? A healthy balance between the two is needed.

- *Consider how much research time you invested* – could you pick up the software quickly? Was it easy to use? If the answer is yes to both of these questions then it will give you more time to think about the curriculum uses.

- *Cost* – do you need to buy a site or network licence for it? How much access do you want people to have to it? Is there an online version? Are there annual costs for these?

Assessing ICT

The assessment of ICT is an interesting process compared to other curriculum areas. This is due to the fact that as a teacher you have to assess the children's capability to produce work as well as the level of skill they have. Assessing ICT raises questions when you look at a child's piece of work. Below are some ideas for assessing ICT:

- *Develop a baseline* – collect a team of interested colleagues together from each year group. Take a look at the following areas:

- Creating and presenting ideas (use of Word, PowerPoint, Prezi, online tools, etc.)
- Key computer skills (being able to save/open files, able to access the network folder, able to record a video evaluation)
- Advanced technical skills (able to connect a computer/interactive whiteboard; connect devices using Wi-Fi/Bluetooth, HTML)
- Mobile working (able to use a variety of apps, to store and retrieve work using cloud computing)
- Evaluating information (use of web and search engines, validity and reliability of information)
- Using data (use of spreadsheets, use of interactive teaching programs)
- Verbal and written communication (blogging, use of video, podcasting, use of social media)
- Computer programming (use of programmable toys, computational thinking, controlling devices)
- Digital citizenship and e-safety (protecting children online, internet safety, protecting your digital footprint and reputation)

Take each element and then consider as a team what you would expect from each year group. In terms of creating and presenting ideas, what would you expect a middle Year 1 child to produce? Or a Year 3 child, or a Year 6 child? Now look at the progression between each of these stages.

- *Create assessment grids* – after you have worked out what you expect from each child, create an assessment grid for each year group.
- *Variety is the spice of life!* – use as many different methods for assessing the children's ICT work as you can. Use video or screen capturing software to record the children's computer movements and work out whether they are doing things by accident or whether they know the buttons they need to press. Consider having skills booklets that the children fill out or set mini-challenges that one child completes while another child assesses their skills and then the pair swap over.
- *Be creative* – try to put assessment tasks into real-life contexts for the children so you assess their ICT capability in the meaningful way.

Are you on the technology train?

Unlike any other subject, the development of ICT depends on the infrastructure in place which in turn helps to inform your hardware choices which then allows the curriculum to shine more and more. The use of technology in society continues to move at such a ast rate which does have implications for schools. Do we go for the latest technology? Is our kit working well? Do our staff use it effectively? All these questions set the school on a journey very much like being on a train. The continual development on this journey is crucial. Some schools will be leading from the front of the train and will be using ICT highly effectively, constantly pushing the train forward while other schools will have just begun. It is important that all schools do get on and make that journey otherwise the opportunity for children to use ICT and engage in their learning is greatly reduced.

And if ICT is to move forward it is essential that everyone in the school gets onboard the train with this vision and not just the people who can turn a computer on.

Exploring the self-review assessment frameworks

So where do you begin with your journey? The first step is with an audit. The ICT self-review framework (www.naacesrf.com) provides a structure for schools to assess their ICT as they build towards the ICT Mark (www.naace.co.uk/ictmark/srf).

When the self-review framework first began, this used to take many hours to complete, section by section, and was quite a massive project for new ICT coordinators and their senior management teams. As with all of these marks and assessment grids which schools can apply for, serious dedication to the subject (and to seeing less of life) is required when collating evidence.

The self-review framework has been reduced considerably making this an essential tool for schools looking to assess their progress. The framework provides a comprehensive review for your school across all areas and is something all schools should be using to help the development of ICT.

The framework is divided into six elements, which are:

1 Leadership and management
2 Curriculum planning
3 Teaching and learning
4 Assessment of ICT capability
5 Professional development
6 Resources

The framework provides a great start for any ICT coordinator wanting to assess the school and certainly provides a structure so you can identify where any gaps may be. Combine this with the 360° Safe – e-safety review tool (www.360safe.org.uk) and you will have a comprehensive assessment of where your school is.

Index